WE CANNOT CONTINUE LIKE THIS

Facing modernity in Africa and the West

WE CANNOT CONTINUE LIKE THIS
Facing Modernity in Africa and the West

Copyright © 2022 Wipf and Stock Publishers. All rights reserved. Except for brief quotations in critical publications or reviews, no part of this book may be reproduced in any manner without prior written permission from the publisher. Write: Permissions, Wipf and Stock Publishers, 199 W. 8th Ave., Suite 3, Eugene, OR 97401.

Wipf & Stock
An Imprint of Wipf and Stock Publishers
199 W. 8th Ave., Suite 3
Eugene, OR 97401

www.wipfandstock.com

PAPERBACK ISBN: 978-1-6667-5303-5
HARDCOVER ISBN: 978-1-6667-5304-2

Cover image: Original design created with the use of provided images. The images are (globe) https://www.freepik.com/vectors/map'>Map vector created by freepik, (praying hands) https://www.freepik.com/free-photo/african-american-male-hands-resting-open-bible_2999287.htm#page=1&query=spiritual%20 guidance&position=0&from_view=search, released under Freepik License, and (hillside town) https://www. pexels.com/photo/old-town-with-colorful-buildings-on-hill-slope-3883320, (cheering crowd) https://pixabay. com/photos/cheering-black-people-hands-crowd-1031743/, and (factory) https://www.pexels.com/photo/photography-of-factory-929385, released under Pexels License.

WE CANNOT CONTINUE LIKE THIS

Facing modernity in Africa and the West

EDITORS
Attie S. van Niekerk
Sytse Strijbos

WIPF & STOCK · Eugene, Oregon

Social Sciences, Humanities, Education & Business Management domain editorial board at AOSIS

Commissioning Editor: Scholarly Books
Andries G. van Aarde, MA, DD, PhD, D Litt, South Africa

Board Members
Jan Botha, Professor, Centre for Research on Evaluation, Science and Technology, Stellenbosch University, Stellenbosch, South Africa
Joan Hambidge, Deputy Dean, Faculty of Humanities, University of Cape Town, Cape Town; Professor, School of Languages and Literatures, University of Cape Town, Cape Town, South Africa
Sakari Häkkinen, Dean, Diocese of Kuopio, Finland
Glenna Jackson, Associate Editor, Professor Chair, Department of Religion and Philosophy, Otterbein University, Westerville, OH, United States of America
Gregory C. Jenkins, Dean-elect, St George's College, Jerusalem, Israel
Reina-Marie Loader, Director and Filmmaker, CinémaHumain, Vienna, Austria
Babita Marthur-Helm, Senior Lecturer, Organisational Transformation & Development, Managing Diversity Gender Empowerment, University of Stellenbosch Business School, Stellenbosch, South Africa
Christopher Mbazira, Professor of Law & Coordinator of the Public Interest Law Clinic, Makerere University, Kampala, Uganda
Piet Naudé, Professor, Ethics Related to Politics, Economics and Business & Director, University of Stellenbosch Business School, Stellenbosch, South Africa
Charles Neill, Professor, Department of Business Administration, The British University in Egypt, El Sherouk, Cairo Governorate, Egypt
Cornelia Pop, Full Professor, Department of Business, Faculty of Business, Babes-Bolyai University, Cluj-Napoca, Romania
Michael Schratz, Professor, Institut für LehrerInnenbildung und Schulforschung, Dekan der School of Education, Leopold-Franzens-Universität Innsbruck, Innsbruck, Austria
Johann Tempelhoff, Professor, Research Niche for Cultural Dynamics of Water (CuDyWat), School of Basic Sciences, Vaal Triangle Campus of North-West University, Vanderbijlpark, South Africa
Anthony Turton, Professor, Centre for Environmental Management & Director, TouchStone Resources, University of the Free State, Bloemfontein, South Africa
Willie L. van der Merwe, Professor & Chair, Philosophy of Religion, Apologetics and Encyclopaedia of Theology & Professor Extraordinary, Stellenbosch University, Stellenbosch, South Africa; Vrije Universiteit Amsterdam, Amsterdam, the Netherlands
Christi van der Westhuizen, Associate Professor, Department of Sociology, Faculty of Humanities, University of Pretoria, Pretoria, South Africa
Joke van Saane, Professor, Amsterdam Center for the Study of Lived Religion, Vrije Universiteit Amsterdam, Amsterdam, the Netherlands
Paul van Tongeren, Professor, Department Philosophy, Radboud University Nijmegen, Nijmegen, the Netherlands
Robert G. Varady, Deputy Director and Research Professor of Environmental Policy, Udall Center for Studies in Public Policy, The University of Arizona, Tucson, AZ, United States of America
Xiao Yun Zheng, Professor & Assistant President, Yunnan Academy of Social Sciences (YASS), Kunming City; Director, International Center for Ecological Culture Studies (ICECS-YASS), Yunnan Academy of Social Sciences, Kunming City, China

Peer Review Declaration
The publisher (AOSIS) endorses the South African 'National Scholarly Book Publishers Forum Best Practice for Peer Review of Scholarly Books.' The manuscript was subjected to rigorous two-step peer review prior to publication, with the identities of the reviewers not revealed to the author(s). The reviewers were independent of the publisher and/or authors in question. The reviewers commented positively on the scholarly merits of the manuscript and recommended that the manuscript be published. Where the reviewers recommended revision and/or improvements to the manuscript, the authors responded adequately to such recommendations.

Research Justification

This scholarly book is strongly focused on the context of Africa, with two chapters that are written by authors from the Netherlands for the purpose of a North–South dialogue. The main thesis of the book is based on the insight that the trajectory of modern development ought not to continue as it is. It is ecologically unsustainable and continues to enlarge the gap between rich and poor. The present-day decolonialisation movement has pointed out, among other things, the specific role of religion, culture and values in human affairs and the need for a robust element of indigenisation and contextualisation. The research results prevalent in the book are original. The book centres on an academic analysis of current development practices, mostly in Africa, that have not often been studied before. It addresses four topics that are often neglected in studies on development and sustainability, as summarised by one of the peer reviewers:

- The divide between the Global North and the Global South, by listening to voices from both in order to counter the hegemony of the Global North.
- The split between issues of a spiritual and secular nature, a fundamental mistake of modernity that disregards the importance of spiritual issues in the secular affairs of society.
- The separation between theory and practice, which often goes hand in hand with an assumed supremacy of the first.
- The importance of households rather than just governments or businesses or academic institutions.

The manuscript seeks to integrate academic reflection and insights gained from practical involvement with sustainability issues in local communities and low-income households, with contributions from Theology, and Natural and Social Sciences. The authors respond to the question: How can modern science and technology help to solve dilemmas such as unsustainable development? With regard to methodology, grounded theory was mostly employed in the sense that theory was derived from data that were obtained and analysed in a systematic way and was compared with existing theories. In a few cases, the focus was on a philosophic analysis of theories and the development of new theories. The authors declare that they did not plagiarise any material in the book and that the book represents a scholarly discourse. It is written by academics and people who work at development institutions and churches, and it is meant to contribute to and enrich academic debates.

Attie S. van Niekerk, Sustainable Communities Research Cluster, Centre for Faith and Community, Faculty of Theology and Religion, University of Pretoria, Pretoria, South Africa; and NOVA Institute, Pretoria, South Africa.

Sytse Strijbos, IIDE-Europe, Maarssen, Netherlands; and Centre for Faith and Community, Faculty of Theology and Religion, University of Pretoria, Pretoria, South Africa.

Contents

Abbreviations, Figures and Tables Appearing in the Text and Notes	xiii
List of Abbreviations	xiii
List of Figures	xiv
List of Tables	xv
Notes on Contributors	xvii
Preface	xxv

Introductory Part   1

Introduction: We cannot continue like this   3
Attie S. van Niekerk & Sytse Strijbos

Scope and delimitation of the research	4
To conclude	6
Conceptual framework of the book	6
Outline and overview of the book	8
Introductory Part	8
Part 1: Issues	9
Part 2: Approaches	11

Chapter 1: Where do you feel Africa's heartbeat? The World Bank, Africa and the Christian mission   13
Attie S. van Niekerk

Introduction	13
Africa's Pulse Volume 22	15
How much buy in did *Africa's Pulse* get from a key role player in sub-Saharan Africa?	20
Case study of the way of thinking of a former World Bank official about the gap with African leaders	23
Reflection on the discourse about development among a number of African writers	25
Exceptionalism	26
Local government	28
Reflection on the way forward and the role of Christianity	30
Conclusion	33

Contents

Chapter 2: Re-integrating technology and economy in human life: On the disclosure of society — 35
Sytse Strijbos

Introduction — 35
For a turn toward the local (Helena Norberg-Hodge and others) — 37
From the bottom up or from the inside out (Stuart L. Hart and others) — 40
From profit-maximising business to social business (Muhammad Yunus and others) — 44
On the disclosure of society — 46
Conclusion — 48

Part 1: Issues — 49

Chapter 3: Energy transition challenges in South Africa: A study of residential coal use practices — 51
Kristy Langerman, Farina Lindeque, Montagu Murray & Christiaan Pauw

Introduction — 52
Status quo of residential coal use in South Africa — 54
    Geographical pattern of coal use — 54
    National trends in residential coal use — 56
    Local trends in residential coal use — 56
Coal use practices — 58
    Qualitative insights into coal use — 62
Housing conditions in coal-using areas — 65
    Qualitative insights into perceptions of housing — 65
Personal, geographical and societal context of coal use — 66
    Being a person in a coal-using community — 67
    Being in the place of a coal-using community — 68
    Being a coal-user in a larger local, national and global society — 69
Conclusion — 70
Acknowledgements — 72

Chapter 4: Towards a complementary approach in sustainable food production — 73
Betsie le Roux, Mike Howard

Introduction — 73
Characteristics of sustainable production — 75

Perspectives on sustainable food production	75
Upscaling production versus sustainability	76
Establishing feedback mechanisms	76
Analysing the current food production system	77
Drivers	78
Food production alternatives	79
Regenerative versus industrial agriculture	79
Small-scale/subsistence versus large-scale	80
Consequences resulting from various food production alternatives	81
Socio-economic states that result from food production systems	82
Carbon footprint	83
Water quality impacts	84
Quality of ecosystems	86
Pathways into sustainable food production	86
Creating circular economies, for example, by reusing sewage effluent for crop production	86
Addressing consumer behaviour and household cultures	88
Diversifying food production responses	89
Conclusion	90
Acknowledgements	91

Chapter 5: Partnerships that flourish or fail: A case study of social entrepreneurship in the Eastern Free State, South Africa — 93
Deidré van Rooyen & Willem F. Ellis

Introduction	93
Partnerships in the social entrepreneurship space	95
Location of the Moahisane Development Fund	99
The partners in the Moahisane Development Fund	99
The Moahisane Development Fund in action and the role of the Committee for Ethical Development	106
The demise of the Moahisane Development Fund	108
Environmental factors	109
Partnership-related factors	110
The position of Institute for Development and Ethics	110
The position of the Dutch donor consortium	112
The position of the University of the Free State	112
Learnings from the Moahisane Development Fund	113
Conclusion	117

Chapter 6: Stones, bricks and windows: Searching for a sacred place — 119
Willem Jan de Hek

Introduction	119
Sacred place	122
Holy place	126
Ratzinger: Sacrament	127
Inge: Pilgrimage	128
Bartholomew: Placemaking	129
Sheldrake: Connection	130
Storied place	131
Searching for sacred place	133
Conclusion	134
Acknowledgements	136

Part 2: Approaches — 137

Chapter 7: From isolation to relation: A trans-disciplinary analysis of an improved cookstove project in Molati, South Africa — 139
Pierre Reyneke

Introduction	139
Approaches to sustainable communities	141
Multi-disciplinary	141
Interdisciplinary	141
Trans-disciplinary	141
Innovative departures	142
Theory and history	143
Assemblage and relational comparison in conversation	144
Ingold	144
Hart	144
NOVA Institute: A brief history	147
The formation of NOVA and the Molati community relationship	149
Brickstar stove project: Case study	151
The rocket stove concept as innovative technology	152
The Green Economy Machine	153
Conclusion	154

Chapter 8: Decolonising the engineering curriculum at the university — 155
Willem van Niekerk & Attie S. van Niekerk

Introduction	155
The engineering curriculum	158
Mathematics and natural sciences	158
Engineering sciences	159
Design	160
Attitudes	162
Decolonising the curriculum	165
Conclusion	166

Chapter 9: Mobilising people to emerge as transformation agents for society building: A reflection on a missional team practice — 167
Luc Kabongo

Introduction	167
The knowledge of local history	169
Inferiority complex	170
Self-hatred	171
Naivety	172
Learning about the history of a local context	173
Learning from doing	175
Active listening	176
Intentionality in contextual observation and analysis	178
Attention to arising issues	180
Networking	181
Engaging the body of Christ in its diversity	181
Engaging like-minded organisations	182
Engage potential partners located outside a local community	182
Engaging governors	182
Learning to engage disempowering structures	183
Hierarchical nature of the culture	183
Patriarchy	183
Violence as an expression of grievances	184
Conclusion	184

Chapter 10: The quest of sustainability in this present 'wicked world': How to overcome Enlightenment modernity? — **187**
Sytse Strijbos

Introduction	187
Rittel and Churchman on the scientific method in design and social system problems	190
Technology, society and our natural environment	195
An interim assessment	200
The problem of evil in our 'wicked world'	201
Conclusion	206

References — **209**

Index — **229**

Abbreviations, Figures and Tables Appearing in the Text and Notes

List of Abbreviations

APS	Australian Public Service
CDM	Clean Development Mechanism
CDS	Centre for Development Support
CED	Committee for Ethical Development
CFC	Centre for Faith and Community
CPTS	Centre for Philosophy Technology and Social Systems
CSR	Corporate Social Responsibility
CURE	Culture in City Reconstruction and Recovery
DRC	Dutch Reformed Church
ECSA	Engineering Council of South Africa
EMS	Economic and Management Sciences
ESEM	Earth Systems Engineering and Management
EWB	Engineers Without Borders
IIDE	International Institute for Development and Ethics
IPCC	Intergovernmental Panel on Climate Change
MDF	Moahisane Development Fund
MDG	Millennium Development Goals
MTBA	More Than Brides Alliance
NGO	Non-governmental Organisation
NPO	Non-profit Organisation
NWU	North-West University
PPE	Personal Protective Equipment
RDP	Reconstruction and Development Programme
SADC	Southern African Development Community
SDG	Sustainable Development Goal
UE	Unit for Entrepreneurship
UFS	University of the Free State
UNESCO	United Nations Educational, Scientific and Cultural Organization
UNFCCC	United Nations Framework Convention on Climate Change
UNICEF	United Nations Children's Fund

URCSA	Uniting Reformed Church in Southern Africa
USA	United States of America
VER	Verified Emission Reduction
WF	Water footprint
WFDD	World Faiths Development Dialogue
WRC	Water Research Commission
WWTW	Waste Water Treatment Works

List of Figures

Figure I.1:	Schematic representation of society.	7
Figure 3.1:	Map of regions in South Africa where more than 5% of households use coal as an energy source (from Census 2011) and active coal mines.	55
Figure 3.2:	Percentage of households connected to electricity mains per province (2002–2018) and households using coal for cooking (a) and heating (b).	57
Figure 3.3:	The frequency of fire making episodes in (a) winter and (b) summer measured in 19 households in eMbalenhle and Zamdela between July 2016 and February 2018.	61
Figure 3.4:	Simultaneous use of energy carriers by households in (a) eMbalenhle, (b) Lebohang and (c) Zamdela.	62
Figure 4.1:	Analyses of the current food production system.	77
Figure 5.1:	Region where case study plays an important role – Eastern Free State.	100
Figure 5.2:	Moahisane Development Fund organisational structure.	105
Figure 5.3:	Some of the products delivered by the 2009/2010 batch of entrepreneurs, (a) Palesa collections – Event cards and printing, (b) Thaba blinds – Grass woven window blinds and room dividers, (c) Simon's cars – Toy cars, (d) Ilholomelo's – Copper jewellery, (e) Nteffeleng Sibeko's shoes – Shoes from recycled materials, (f) Modise's steel and Window Frames – Steel products for the home.	106
Figure 5.4:	The capacity building undergone by Moahisane Development Fund entrepreneurs.	107
Figure 6.1:	Areal view Park Frankendael in Amsterdam-East.	123
Figure 6.2:	Areal view Hofkerk and its surroundings.	126

Abbreviations, Figures and Tables Appearing in the Text and Notes

Figure 6.3:	Aerial view De Nieuwe Ooster cemetery entrance area.	132
Figure 6.4:	Areal view Oude Kerk and its surroundings.	135
Figure 8.1:	A comparison between the flagships of Zheng He and Columbus.	163

List of Tables

Table 3.1:	Residential coal use trends in six district municipalities in coal-using areas of South Africa between 2009 and 2018, based on data collected in 630 household surveys.	58
Table 3.2:	The population, location and number of households that participated in the General Household Surveys for the five low-income, coal-using communities on the South African Highveld.	59
Table 3.3:	Proportion of coal users, coal buying formats, device types and ignition method in eMalahleni, Lebohang and eMzinoni in Mpumalanga and Zamdela in the northern Free State.	60
Table 3.4:	Seasonal differences in residential coal consumption (kg) in eMbalenhle, Lebohang and Zamdela in 2016.	61
Table 3.5:	Characteristics of coal sold by five coal merchants in KwaZamokuhle, Mpumalanga, in winter 2015.	62
Table 3.6:	Housing conditions and satisfaction with housing in coal-using communities: eMalahleni, eMzinoni, Lebohang, Kwadela and Zamdela.	65
Table 5.1:	Partners in the Moahisane Development Fund.	104
Table 5.2:	Summary of entrepreneurs assisted by the Moahisane Development Fund.	105

Notes on Contributors

Attie S. van Niekerk
The NOVA Institute,
Pretoria, South Africa;
Sustainable Communities Research Cluster, Centre for Faith and Community,
Faculty of Religion and Theology, University of Pretoria,
Pretoria, South Africa
Email: attievanniekerk@nova.org.za
ORCID: https://orcid.org/0000-0003-0663-6969

Attie S. van Niekerk studied Theology at the University of Pretoria. He was a minister of the (black) Dutch Reformed Church in Africa in Venda from 1978 to 1984 and professor for the church's theological training at the University of the North from 1984 to 1993 and rector of the Theological School Stofberg from 1988 to February 1993. His book on four poets from Soweto and Alexandra in the seventies, *Dominee, are you listening to the drums?*, was co-winner of the Sunday Times Literary Award for Political Writing in 1984. He has published several books and more than 50 academic articles. In 1994, he became a founding member of the NOVA Institute, a not-for-profit organisation that aims to enable poverty-stricken communities to improve their quality of life. NOVA makes use of scientific methods, including surveys, academic debates and trans-disciplinary research, in which researchers from a diversity of backgrounds, together with a number of low-income families, are engaged in a process to design, and evaluate in practice, household products and processes that are effective, sustainable, affordable for low-income households, desirable, replicable and socially beneficial.

Sytse Strijbos
IIDE-Europe,
Maarssen, Netherlands;
Centre for Faith and Community, Faculty of Theology and Religion,
University of Pretoria, Pretoria, South Africa
Email: strijboss@iide-online.org
ORCID: https://orcid.org/0000-0002-5607-7352

Sytse Strijbos is a founder of the International Institute for Development and Ethics that has been established in 2004 as an independent legal entity with a branch in South Africa and Europe. Currently, he is the chairperson of the International Institute for Development and Ethics (IIDE) in Europe. Previously, he taught at the Philosophy Faculty of Vrije Universiteit, Amsterdam, and as a special professor at North-West University (Potchefstroom Campus), South Africa.

Notes on Contributors

Kristy Langerman
Department of Geography, Environmental Management and Energy Studies,
Faculty of Science, University of Johannesburg,
Johannesburg, South Africa
Email: klangerman@uj.ac.za
ORCID: https://orcid.org/0000-0003-0936-2051

Kristy Langerman is based at the Department of Geography, Environmental Management and Energy Studies at the University of Johannesburg, where she coordinates the Energy Studies Honours programme. She is the director of the University of Johannesburg's Joint Research Centre for Smart Mobility and Climate Change. She is an editor-in-chief of the *Clean Air Journal* and a past president of the National Association for Clean Air. Kristy received a PhD from Wits University in 2003. She conducted brief postdoctoral studies at the National Center for Atmospheric Research in Colorado and worked at the Climatology Research Group at Wits University until 2005. Thereafter, she worked in the Research and Environmental Management departments at Eskom until 2017. She is interested in minimising the environmental impact of all forms of energy use, from large coal-fired power stations to individual household fires.

Farina Lindeque
Department of Geography and Environmental Studies,
Faculty of Science and Agriculture, University of Limpopo,
Mankweng, South Africa
Email: farina.lindeque@ul.ac.za
ORCID: https://orcid.org/0000-0002-2221-8225

Farina Lindeque received an MSc in Geography and Environmental Management (*cum laude*) at the North-West University (NWU) in 2018. She is a PhD candidate at the Climatology Research Group at the NWU, with a research focus on the drivers and health impacts of urban air quality in South Africa. She has been a lecturer at the Department of Geography and Environmental Studies at the University of Limpopo since 2019. Farina is interested in developing a better understanding of environmental health inequities and risks in both the urban and rural contexts, through risk and vulnerability assessments and mapping.

Montagu Murray
The NOVA Institute,
Pretoria, South Africa;
Department of Religion Studies, Faculty of Theology and Religion,
University of Pretoria, Pretoria, South Africa
Email: montagumurray@nova.org.za
ORCID: https://orcid.org/0000-0001-5296-9209

Montagu Murray attained a DD degree in Systematic Theology from the University of Pretoria, South Africa. His academic studies included pregraduate studies in Minnesota, United States, and postgraduate research at the Universities of Utrecht and Leiden in the Netherlands. He is a research associate of the Faculty of Theology of the University of Pretoria. Montagu is particularly interested in trans-disciplinary approaches to poverty alleviation, quality of life improvement and sustainable lifestyles. He is a director of the NOVA Institute, a not-for-profit organisation that endeavours to co-create, with household and networks, ways to improve the quality of life of low-income households in Southern Africa. He is married to Carien Murray. They have two daughters, Renée and Marita.

Christiaan Pauw
The NOVA Institute,
Pretoria, South Africa;
Centre for Faith and Community, Faculty of Religion and Theology,
University of Pretoria, Pretoria, South Africa
Email: christiaan.pauw@nova.org.za
ORCID: https://orcid.org/0000-0002-1546-1024

Christiaan Pauw is the managing director of the NOVA Institute. He studied theology at the University of Pretoria and received his doctorate in 2006 with a dissertation on the significance of the concept of human needs in systematic theology in the protestant tradition. Through his involvement with the NOVA Institute since 1998, he has worked on research and implementation of projects aimed at improving the quality of life of low-income households in Southern Africa. This includes quantitative and qualitative research and participative design, as well as participation in project planning, management and implementation. He specialises in development, implementation, monitoring and evaluation of interventions aimed at improving air quality in low-income communities in South Africa. He is also a key contributor to a number of ongoing projects in the field of climate change mitigation, food security, water benefit credits and air pollution offsets.

Betsie le Roux
Food and Water Research (Pty) Ltd,
Pretoria, South Africa;
Centre for Faith and Community, Faculty of Religion and Theology,
University of Pretoria, Pretoria, South Africa
Email: betsie.leroux@fawr.co.za
ORCID: https://orcid.org/0000-0002-2079-5539

Betsie le Roux became an ecologist, receiving an M.Sc. Botany in 2007. She started working at BKS (Pty) Ltd as an environmental scientist from 2008 to 2013, with specialisation in ecology. During this time, she also got experience in water quantity and quality management, wetland delineations and wastewater treatment. Water management became her passion. In 2017, she received her PhD in Agronomy at the University of Pretoria on the water footprints of vegetable crops. She developed a simplified framework to determine the volume of water used by agriculture in a catchment, by using crop water footprints together with production data. In 2018, she started research on water use management in South African Agri-parks, aiming to uplift previously disadvantaged, small-scale farmers. Betsie is one of the founders of the company, Food and Water Research, in the year 2020 aiming to conduct research on finding locally appropriate solutions to achieve sustainability in the Water–Energy–Food nexus in Southern Africa and to uplift and empower rural poor communities

Mike Howard
Food and Water Research (Pty) Ltd,
Pretoria, South Africa;
Centre for Faith and Community, Faculty of Religion and Theology,
University of Pretoria, Pretoria, South Africa
Email: mike.howard@fawr.co.za
ORCID: https://orcid.org/0000-0001-5182-7946

Mike Howard graduated from the University of North London in 1980 with an Honours degree in Biology and Geography. After graduation, Mike was employed by the Department of Water Affairs in Pretoria, South Africa. Mike's research focus was on limnological processes focusing on nutrient loading, algal succession, operating rules for impoundments and development of technology. After 10 years, Mike started his own company with two other scientists. The focus of research moved to mine water management, and he undertook a number of research projects for the Water Research Commission in Pretoria. The focus of the research was on water quality impacts from mines, information management, water quality modelling and acid mine drainage. After 10 years, Mike moved to a global consulting company. Mike's research and consulting projects focused on developing water management systems (such as artificial wetlands), catchment water quality studies, predictive modelling for new impoundments and managing impacts from wastewater treatment works. Over the last five years, Mike has been undertaking research on aquaponics and the use of effluent from wastewater treatment works in hydroponics.

Deidré van Rooyen
Centre for Development Support,
Faculty of Economic and Management Sciences, University of the Free State,
Bloemfontein, South Africa
Email: griesd@ufs.ac.za
ORCID: https://orcid.org/0000-0002-2325-5087

Deidré van Rooyen currently works as a senior researcher (and Programme Director: Development Studies Programme) for the Centre for Development Support, within Economic and Management Sciences, at the University of the

Free State (www.ufs.ac.za/cds). She completed her master's degree in Gender Studies (2003) and her PhD in Development Studies (Civic culture and local economic development in a small town) (2012) (University of the Free State). She further completed a certificate course in Social Entrepreneurship at the Gordon's Institute of Business Studies (University of Pretoria) in 2014. She has also supervised several masters and PhD students with diverse topics. She has authored, co-authored and compiled numerous research reports and published widely in peer-reviewed conference papers (15), journals (15) or chapters (13) in books. In 2018, Dr van Rooyen co-edited her first book through Routledge publishers – Mining and community in South Africa. From small town to iron town. By 2021, there were two more edited books – Coal and energy in South Africa. Considering a just transition, published by Edinburgh University press, and Mining and community in the South African platinum belt: A decade after Marikana, published by NOVA Publishers. Her specialisation fields of research are Social Entrepreneurship (SE) and Local Economic Development in small towns.

Willem F. Ellis
Centre for Gender and Africa Studies,
Faculty of Humanities, University of the Free State,
Bloemfontein, South Africa
Email: elliswf@ufs.ac.za
ORCID: https://orcid.org/0000-0003-3848-746X

Willem F. Ellis obtained a B.Proc degree from the University of the Free State (UFS) in 1989. After being involved in conflict transformation work during South Africa's political transition, he joined the Free State Centre for Citizenship Education and Conflict Resolution as programme director of the conflict resolution unit in 1998. In 2004, he received a master's degree in Governance and Political Transformation from the UFS. Since 2004, he has been involved with the International Institute for Development and Ethics (IIDE) (based at the UFS) researching issues of development ethics and social entrepreneurship in Southern Africa. As an academic, he is involved with the Department of Political Studies and Governance at the UFS, the Centre for Development Support and the Centre for Gender and Africa Studies – lecturing on a variety of topics relating to conflict, security, governance and development. He lectures Alternative Dispute Resolution at the Law Faculty of the UFS and is involved in compiling short courses related to conflict resolution for the Centre for Gender and Africa Studies. He further delivers lectures in Political Dynamics and management courses at the UFS Business School. He is involved with Non-Government Organisations (NGOs) in issues of social entrepreneurship and NGO governance and obtained a postgraduate certificate in Social Entrepreneurship from the University of Pretoria's GIBS Business School in

2014. His current research interests lie in the fields of Infrastructures for Peace (I4P) and conflict sensitive development.

Willem Jan de Hek
Department of Practical Theology,
Faculty of Theology, Protestant Theological University,
Amsterdam, the Netherlands
Email: wdehek@gmail.com
ORCID: https://orcid.org/0000-0002-0595-4095

Willem Jan de Hek currently works as a Minister in the Protestant Church in the Netherlands. Besides, he runs his own architectural design studio and is involved in PhD research at the Protestant Theological University in Amsterdam. Willem Jan holds a bachelor's degree in Building Technology (BSc, HU University of Applied Science Utrecht, 2001), a master's degree in Architecture (MSc, Technical University Delft, 2004) and a master's degree in Theology (MA, Protestant Theological University Amsterdam, 2018, cum laude). In his ongoing PhD research project in the field of Practical Theology, he combines research in urbanism and theology. Results have been presented at UIA Seoul World Architects Congress on 'Soul of City' (2017) and at JCP Jerusalem Conference on 'Holy Places' (2018).

Pierre Reyneke
The NOVA Institute,
Pretoria, South Africa;
School of Geography, Archaeology and Environmental Sciences, Faculty of Humanities,
University of the Witwatersrand, Johannesburg, South Africa
Email: 2289293@students.wits.ac.za
ORCID: https://orcid.org/0000-0001-9329-1684

Pierre Reyneke is a researcher with a background in Anthropology. As a researcher and project manager at NOVA Institute (NPO), his current work entails developing and implementing sustainable solutions with low-income communities in South Africa. His research to date has focused on the contribution of the informal sector to waste management. He has a personal interest in the way that materiality shapes relations between people, specifically how people relate to each other regarding their own relation to waste materials. Pierre Reyneke joined the NOVA Institute in the year 2013 after completing his Social Science (Honours) degree in Anthropology. He took up the role of Project Manager of the Brickstar improved cooking stove project. He has fulfilled this role ever since. Parallel to his employment at the NOVA Institute, he completed a master's degree in Social Anthropology at the University of Pretoria. This research project entailed an ethnographic study of the waste management system at the Garstkloof and Hatherley landfills, situated in the City of Tshwane. This approach involved identifying changes brought about by the City of Tshwane Metropolitan Municipality within the waste management system and offered a detailed account of how individuals making a living from waste have responded to these changes. He is currently enrolled in a doctorate programme at The University of Witwatersrand in the School of Geography, Archaeology and Environmental Sciences. His study investigates the form and role of 'reuse and remake' practices in the production of space and the urban waste economy of The City of Tshwane.

Willem van Niekerk
Department of Mechanical Engineering,
Faculty of Engineering, North-West University,
Potchefstroom, South Africa
Email: willem.vanniekerk@nwu.ac.za
ORCID: https://orcid.org/0000-0001-9947-6612

Willem van Niekerk qualified as a chemical engineer and worked in the coal-to-liquid petrochemical industry before becoming a lecturer at the Department of Chemical Engineering at the University of Pretoria where he obtained his M. Eng. (Chem). He is currently an undergraduate programme manager at the Department of Mechanical Engineering at the North-West University at Potchefstroom, lecturing Thermodynamics and Philosophy of Science. He obtained a PhD in Education Science on cooperative learning. He has published in the fields of solar energy, community development and engineering education. He is a registered professional engineer with the Engineering Council of South Africa (ECSA) and has been an accreditation team member for the accreditation of engineering qualifications at universities and technical universities.

Luc Kabongo
InnerCHANGE,
Pretoria, South Africa;
Department of Religion Studies, Faculty of Theology and Religion,
University of Pretoria, Pretoria, South Africa
Email: kablut@yahoo.fr
ORCID: https://orcid.org/0000-0001-8343-1794

Luc Kabongo is a naturalised South African citizen who was born in the town of Bukavu in the Democratic Republic of Congo. He obtained an honours degree in Philosophy and Administration in 1998. He moved to South Africa in 2002. He is a mission worker with InnerCHANGE, an incarnational order among the poor. He and his family live and serve in an urban poor community, the township of Soshanguve. His major focus is on community development and discipleship. He completed all his postgraduate theological studies at the University of Pretoria: first an MPhil in Applied Theology in 2009, then an MA in Missiology in 2015 and finally a PhD in missiology in 2019. His academic interest is in the area of Urban Theology, Community Development, Trans-disciplinary Research, Grassroots Christian Education and African Theology.

Preface

Attie S. van Niekerk[a,b]
[a]The NOVA Institute,
Pretoria, South Africa
[b]Sustainable Communities Research Cluster, Centre for Faith and Community,
Faculty of Religion and Theology, University of Pretoria,
Pretoria, South Africa

Sytse Strijbos[a,b]
[a]IIDE-Europe,
Maarssen, Netherlands
[b]Centre for Faith and Community, Faculty of Theology and Religion,
University of Pretoria, Pretoria, South Africa

This book is the first result of a quite unique and emerging research collaboration between three organisations, NOVA, the International Institute for Development and Ethics (IIDE) and the Centre for Faith and Community (CFC) that is housed at the Faculty of Theology, University of Pretoria. The central aim is to chart an innovative course in the debate on 'sustainability and development'. NOVA and IIDE are independent entities that both want to operate as an intermediate between the university and broader society.

■ The organisations at a glance

About NOVA

NOVA Institute NPC[1] is a not-for-profit company that was established in 1994. Our vision is *a healthy household culture in Southern Africa.* NOVA's overarching strategic goal is to be the professional partner of choice for households and other stakeholders working towards improving the quality of life of low-income communities. NOVA has more than 20 years of experience in co-creating solutions for everyday problems with low-income households in a trans-disciplinary research and development process, and in implementing such solutions on a large scale in a phased approach, as well as in monitoring and evaluating the impact of these solutions against a defendable project baseline.

---

1. See www.nova.org.za.

> **How to cite:** Van Niekerk, A.S. & Strijbos, S., 2021, 'Preface', in A.S. Van Niekerk & S. Strijbos (eds.), *We cannot continue like this: Facing modernity in Africa and the West*, pp. xxv–xxvii, AOSIS, Cape Town. https://doi.org/10.4102/aosis.2021.BK283.0p

Preface

About the IIDE

The early roots of the IIDE go back to 1995 when an international group of about 15 scholars, junior and senior researchers from different disciplines (philosophy, technology and engineering science, management and systems science) came together in Amsterdam. This meeting became the start of a formal cooperation between scholars affiliated with several universities and institutions in different countries and various cultural spheres of the world. During its first phase, this cooperation has been active as a network under the name CPTS (Centre for Philosophy Technology and Social Systems). After a decade of operations, the CPTS was transformed in 2004 into the IIDE, registered in the Netherlands as a Public Benefit Organisation, in Dutch an *Algemeen Nut Beogende Instelling*. With the aim of stimulating North–South exchange, an independent IIDE partner organisation has been established in South Africa and is housed at the University of the Free State, Bloemfontein.

About the Centre for Faith and Community

The CFC is based in the Faculty of Theology and Religion at the University of Pretoria. Its vision is healthy communities through the formation of community and faith-based leaders. It works towards this through a bouquet of basic courses and specialised programmes, aimed at grassroot practitioners and understanding theology as change-making. It also hosts various engaged research programmes, working in and with communities, in support of their emancipatory and transformational processes. Our research themes include faith in the city, pathways out of homelessness, social justice and reconciliation, doing theology with children, spirituality and healthcare and sustainable communities. We host the Urban Studio, using the city as classroom and focusing on six geographical sites in the City of Tshwane. We also manage the Unit for Street Homelessness, doing research on street homelessness locally and nationally, contributing to policy-making processes and facilitating the Pathways Operational Centre, supporting the city and NGOs in their evidence-based homeless interventions.

Charting the course

The collaboration between NOVA, IIDE and CFC deliberately did not start with a sharply defined and detailed programme. To initiate the research process, it was decided to carry out an exploratory project, linking up to fieldwork of NOVA, IIDE and other partners in building sustainable communities. It is expected that by working together in a process of academic reflection as well as learning by doing, a programme will evolve, paving the way for the longer term. An important goal of the research is to enable local churches and other entities to get involved in their local communities in a meaningful way. This includes developing resources such as skills, knowledge, funds and networks.

Acknowledgements

First of all, we gladly acknowledge Prof. Jerry Pillay, the Dean of the Faculty of Theology and Religion, University of Pretoria, for his financial contribution that has made the publication of this book possible.

We also thank the Publisher, Prof. Andries van Aarde, Dr Anna Azarch and Mrs Trudie Retief and Mr Michael Maart of AOSIS for their friendly and professional assistance, as well as the professional language practitioner, Corrie Geldenhuys.

Finally, we wish to thank the anonymous reviewers for their constructive engagement with our work.

Introductory Part

Introduction

We cannot continue like this

Attie S. van Niekerk[a,b]
[a]The NOVA Institute,
Pretoria, South Africa
[b]Sustainable Communities Research Cluster, Centre for Faith and Community,
Faculty of Religion and Theology, University of Pretoria,
Pretoria, South Africa

Sytse Strijbos[a,b]
[a]IIDE-Europe, Maarssen, Netherlands
[b]Centre for Faith and Community, Faculty of Theology and Religion,
University of Pretoria, Pretoria, South Africa

The collaboration for writing this book began in November 2019 at a two-day working conference in Pretoria, South Africa, with the aim of better understanding how we can find ways to build sustainable communities. Some of the participants are affiliated with universities and some are affiliated with NGOs and churches, mostly in South Africa but also in Europe. Together they represent a wide range of backgrounds and academic disciplines.

The basic idea in the composition of the team was that the book should make a contribution to a dialogue between and integration of views from a diversity of approaches, such as practitioners and scholars in the humanities, philosophy, theology, the natural sciences, agriculture, architecture and engineering. They all have a vital contribution to make to the broad field of sustainability studies.

How to cite: Van Niekerk, A.S. & Strijbos, S., 2021, 'We cannot continue like this', in A.S. Van Niekerk & S. Strijbos (eds.), *We cannot continue like this: Facing modernity in Africa and the West*, pp. 3–12, AOSIS, Cape Town. https://doi.org/10.4102/aosis.2021.BK283.00

In this way, an effort has been made to bridge divides that often become apparent in discussions about sustainability:

- The divide between the Global North and the Global South, by listening to voices from both in order to counter the hegemony of the Global North.
- The split between issues of a spiritual and secular nature, a fundamental mistake of modernity that disregards the importance of spiritual issues in the secular affairs of society.
- The separation between theory and practice, which often goes hand in hand with an assumed supremacy of the first.
- The importance of households rather than just governments or businesses or academic institutions.

The chapters in the book deal with a wide variety of topics, but each one does so from at least one of these angles – in some chapters all four are dealt with. The chapters are small incidents spread across the whole picture, rather than being the whole picture even when taken together.

■ Scope and delimitation of the research

During the above-mentioned event in November, there was a lively exchange of views about ideas and proposals for separate chapters and also about the book as a whole and its internal coherence. With regard to the latter, an important question arose: what is the central message we want to convey to the reader? One thing became clear in the discussions. All agreed that the present trajectory of modern development cannot continue as it is now. The various contributions to this book have, therefore, been brought together under a title that reflects this sentiment of all authors and their concern about the future of our societies.

Members of the group argued from different points of view that we cannot go on like this. There are practical reasons, such as the global economy's use of resources beyond the capacity of the earth to provide (e.g. phosphorus) and to process the waste (nitrates, or increase of toxins and residues of medicines in the water, etc.). Development programmes on the macro- and micro-levels often fail to achieve their aims, even if there are successes that could help to find alternative approaches. Closely related to this, there are important ethical and philosophical–theological considerations for seeking alternative solutions to the problems people grapple with.

The anti-colonial movement in South Africa, Africa and the rest of the world has drawn our attention again to the specific role of religion, culture and values in human affairs. Some of the proponents of this movement argue that modern development fails to solve many of Africa's problems and often have unforeseen, negative results for human societies and the environment. There is enough truth in this view to say that the present approach to develop Africa according to the models of modernised communities cannot go on like this. A robust process of indigenisation and contextualisation is needed. It is not only in Africa, however, that modernity has run into difficulties. It also happens in its birthplace, Europe and in all other parts of the world. Modernity seems to have become a problem in itself. In our view, this confronts us with the key struggle of our age on a local and global level.

Taking a stand in this book against the dominance of modernity as it has emerged in the West does not mean that we distrust or even reject science and technology and their ongoing development. Such a Luddite view is not only unrealistic, even more important is that it is based on a serious mistake. It is true that modern science and technology can be a part of the problems of our contemporary world but it is also true that they can become a part of their solution. It is all about our basic values and beliefs that drive these powers in our societies: they can make a destructive global arms industry possible or an economic development that destroys cultures and ecological systems, but they can also make a good and sustainable quality of life possible for all on earth. Crucial is how the powers of science and technology combine with human values and our view on the ultimate meaning of human life. That combination of faith and science is one of the central problems that our societies grapple with and that we are looking for in this book.

Science and technology are not the exclusive property of any tradition or culture, but can be accepted with gratitude as a good and liberating gift from heaven to humanity and the world as a whole. Just think for a moment of the Corona pandemic we are still in the middle of. It has made us aware again of the risks of our hyper-connected world, because a virus does not require a passport or visa. The pandemic has made us aware how much we depend on the scientific-technical ingenuity of humanity for shaping a sustainable future. At the same time, it has made us aware how unpredictable human behaviour is. Countless well-researched papers and reports warn us continuously that the stress of modern development on the environment poses a danger to the future of our children, through climate change, pollution and the exhaustion of natural resources, but this scientific information has little effect, compared to the way in which, all over the world, economies were shut down in haste because of fears for the virus. As real as the threat of the virus is, the fact that there is no comparable response to the threat of an ecological breakdown shows that science alone does not give direction to human behaviour, we also need good faith, good values and good convictions to be responsible.

As the Encyclical Letter Laudato Si' (Pope Francis 2015) has clearly pointed out, the problem we face is that many of the present combinations and interactions between these factors are destructive and unsustainable. The modern age has not used science and technology to shape a common home for humanity that cherishes the wonderful diversity of cultures and of the ecology, and many traditional cultures struggle to find a constructive role to play in the present world. Our challenge for the field of sustainability studies is, therefore, to find pathways beyond our present dilemmas and to rethink our understanding of sustainability and development. We must rethink the norms, values and guiding beliefs that influence our understanding, emotions and behaviour, both in the North and the South. At stake is finding normative directional perspectives on humanity-and-world to guide our lives in different contexts.

Acknowledging this diversity does not imply that we adopt here a viewpoint of cultural relativism using basic distinctions that have been proposed by Mouw and Griffioen (1993:17–19) for classifying different types of pluralisms in public life. One could speak here of 'normative contextual pluralism', advocating contextual plurality as a good state of affairs. This implies that the growing integration and uniformity of our global world through technology and science is not wiping out all cultural diversity in the world (Strijbos 1997). It is precisely this question that is central to the search for ways to build sustainable communities that concern the authors of this book. What we find, and need, is rather a large number of unlikely combinations in different contexts, as is illustrated by several authors of this book.

■ To conclude

Addressing the issues of 'sustainability and development' requires what can be called a 'wide' and 'deep' interdisciplinary research approach in a North–South collaboration (Frodeman & Mitcham 2007). 'Wide' means that an attempt is made to bridge the gap between natural science and humanities, while 'deep' refers to the effort to bridge the gap between theory and practice. The latter is sometimes defined as a trans-disciplinary approach, primarily aimed at solving a practical problem involving other social actors, such as churches, industries, businesses, households and communities in close cooperation with scientists of different disciplines, all depending on the context and the problem at hand.

■ Conceptual framework of the book

NOVA and IIDE share common ground in their quest to go beyond the different mindsets of our diverse contexts in the Global North and the Global South and to take up the task of rethinking sustainability and development agendas. Taking up this task in this book does not have to start from scratch, however. A valuable run-up has already been made on several earlier occasions in which NOVA and the IIDE have collaborated (cf. Rathbone, Von Schéele & Strijbos 2014; Van der Stoep & Strijbos 2011). The insights gained so far are helpful in placing the contributions of this book within a conceptual framework, as shown schematically in Figure I.1. We will first give a very brief explanation of this framework, followed by an outline and overview of the book.

Introduction

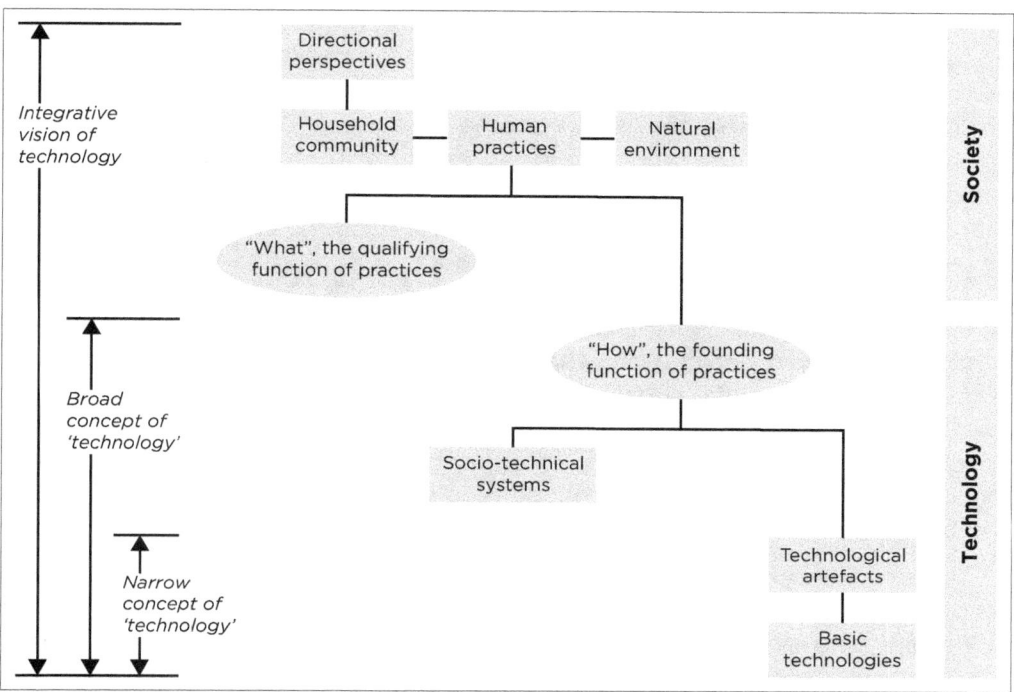

FIGURE I.1: Schematic representation of society.

Through the centuries, the household and extended family have been the fundamental building stone of human society. That is to say, in all cultures, daily human life has enfolded itself in a variety of practices that centred on the household and extended family. In the household and family, the exchange between the generations, the transmission of traditions and culture and the care for each other traditionally take place. However, this has fundamentally changed in our modern technology-based world. While the household still persists in its central role, a broad range of human and social practices has differentiated itself, at least partly, from the household, such as education and training of the young, the care for the sick and elderly people. The challenge for sustainable social change can now be understood as the dual task to preserve the household as the normative core of the local culture but at the same time to open up the household and the potential of the various human practices for the benefit of the local community and broader society within the constraints of the natural environment.

Referring to Figure I.1, this implies that the technical-organisational part of society (the lower part of the scheme) should enable a rich variety of life in local sustainable communities (the upper part of the scheme). Technology should, however, not be regarded as the determining factor in development.

The failure of modernism is a consequence of a culture in which the possibilities of science and technology have free passage and thus take the lead. Modernism is turning the world upside down: technology that makes life for society possible tends to become its cultural basis, often leading to an erosion of traditions and a spiritual vacuum in local communities (Van Niekerk 2014).

■ Outline and overview of the book

Against the background of this understanding of social change in a technology-based world, the contributions that follow the Introductory Part have been brought together in two subsequent parts of each four chapters. While Part 1 discusses some important technological–organisational issues of a sustainable society, Part 2 shifts attention to the upper level of the scheme in Figure I.1, discussing various approaches that seek to overcome a modernist mindset in the building up of a sustainable world.

The chapters of the book are bound together by their search for ways to recognise the importance of households, Global South perspectives and spirituality and everyday life. It searches to move beyond an approach based on governments, businesses and academia, Global North perspectives, the marginalisation of spirituality and theory irrespective of context. It is driven by the search for sustainable and flourishing communities in Africa and also in Europe. In our South–North dialogue, unlikely connections between diverse elements are made.

▪ Introductory Part

As has been pointed out in the Preface, this book is meant as a first step towards longer-term research cooperation between NOVA, IIDE and CFC at the University of Pretoria. The introductory part written by the editors, may clarify the way of thinking that underlies and drives the activities of both organisations.

In Chapter 1, Attie S. van Niekerk gives an overview of the way the World Bank approaches development in Africa, mostly with reference to the annual publication *Africa's Pulse*, and shows that many African leaders do not identify with that approach. The views of the African leaders are made more understandable by the views of African writers. It is argued that the World Bank has followed the same approach for four decades, to little avail. It cannot continue like this, and all role players need to listen to Africa's voices. Some Christian missionaries from the West have learned over the years to take African cultures and traditions seriously and to engage with them in a process of enculturing the Christian faith in the contemporary African context. NOVA has taken this a step further and engages with low-income households in search of ways to improve their quality of life, which involves ways to enculturate technology within the practices of households. We believe that the World Bank can learn from the churches' experience in enculturation and that the Christian faith has something to say to both the modern world, represented here by the World Bank, and the African world, about the way forward in our context.

In Chapter 2, Sytse Strijbos reflects with his discussion partner, Darek Haftor, on the IIDE research that seeks to focus on the role of 'technology' and 'economy' in today's world. They conclude that the modern world cannot continue like it does. The central question now and for future research is: how can we attain a humane and sustainable development amidst all the pressures and structures of our modern globalising world? After a short discussion of three (in some regards) overlapping streams of thought that aim for the reintegration of technology and economy in human life and society, the chapter concludes with briefly elaborating the normative idea of 'disclosure of society' as a paradigm for future research. The chapter argues against the hegemony of modernist theories and presents an approach that is open towards the future, towards other cultures and towards religion.

Part 1: Issues

In all times, the availability of energy in any form and providing food for every mouth has been necessary prerequisites for building a society. Modern science and technology have created many new possibilities for this, but at the same time pose new problems with regard to sustainability, as discussed in the next two chapters for the current situation in South Africa.

Kristy Langerman, Farina Lindeque, Montagu Murray and Christiaan Pauw deal in Chapter 3 with current energy-transition challenges. The authors provide a thorough overview of residential coal use in South Africa. Numerous initiatives to phase out residential coal use have been implemented, usually motivated by the harmful health effects of air pollutants released when coal is burnt. However, households that use coal usually have a choice of several energy carriers and choose to continue to use coal. This chapter analyses the external conditions and the household needs that influence the continued use of coal. It argues that a solution to the problem of coal use cannot be implemented by a technology-driven approach from outside, and we cannot achieve success if we continue on that route. The human needs theory of Manfred Max-Neef facilitates an understanding of practical coal usage as a satisfier of fundamental human needs in our specific context, so that alternative behaviours that are more beneficial to general well-being and quality of life can be designed together with households.

Betsie Le Roux and Mike Howard look in Chapter 4 at the problem of sustainable food production and the role of South African households in the future. Previous advances in food production, though they have solved many problems over the short term, have most likely led us up to the pinnacle of a pyramid. We cannot go forward on the same route, and because of population growth, we cannot go back down along the same route. We need new approaches. The concept of sustainable food production is discussed, and different agricultural approaches are compared, for example, regenerative versus industrial agriculture and small-scale versus large-scale agriculture, followed by a discussion of the impacts of different food production systems. It makes a case for enabling households and smallholder farmers in Africa to produce more food and to do so through organic farming methods and circular agricultural practices. As an example of a circular economy that should be developed, it is proposed that the current linear supply chain of nutrients in food production be converted into a lifecycle where waste products become resources. The problem of nutrient accumulation in the South African water system in relation to the increasing demand for agricultural products is discussed. It is concluded that a complementary approach in sustainable food production offers a strategy for the future.

The transition to a technology-based world also strongly affects other aspects that are foundational for human existence. In Chapter 5, Deidré van Rooyen and Willem F. Ellis compare development theories to their practical experience with a project in social entrepreneurship in the Eastern Free State of South Africa. While Chapter 1 deals with the macro-economy in Africa, this chapter deals with the micro-economy. Research on social entrepreneurship is rife with examples of 'success stories'. Yet, the study of entrepreneurial failure is just as crucial to understanding the potential sustainability of social enterprises. The authors argue that social entrepreneurship is essential for human development in South Africa and then highlight the main causes why the Moahisane Development Fund (MDF), in the Eastern Free State, South Africa, was not successful as a social entrepreneurial venture. The aim of the MDF was to create a revolving fund in terms of which identified budding entrepreneurs could be assisted through the provision of financial means and ongoing business support. Various challenges had an impact on the success of the MDF but the most important lesson that can be conveyed is that the format of the involved partnerships and relationship between the parties had been critical as far as the lack of success of the fund was concerned.

The last chapter of Part 1 draws attention to the expression of 'religiosity' in society. While the previous three chapters focus specifically on situations in the South, in Chapter 6 Willem Jan de Hek deals with the need for sacred places in the built environment of secularised high-tech societies in the North. He also bridges the gap between theory and practice.

Introduction

Part 2: Approaches

Central to this book is to find a sustainable future and to develop approaches that overcome the problems of modernity, considering the different context of the societies in the North and South. The next three chapters deal with different approaches aimed at the specific context of South Africa, while the final chapter of this book extends to the discussion of the Enlightenment tradition of the modern era.

Global domestic wood use has become unsustainable, and efforts to find solutions for that have not been very successful, mostly because of a technology-driven approach. In Chapter 7, Pierre Reyneke describes Nova's search for a different approach. He analyses Nova's trans-disciplinary method, which emphasises the importance of co-creating solutions with households and community members for their everyday problems, that presents an alternative to the general pattern of technology-driven solutions. He describes the project to develop a stove with reduced wood consumption and which households can build themselves, which is led by households rather than developed by experts and given to households. The project is then discussed through the lens of two current theoretical frameworks that incorporate trans-disciplinary methodologies, namely, Tim Ingold's (2000) relational–ecological–developmental approach and Gillian Hart's (2016) 'relational comparison' method. Where the chapter on coal use discusses the issue of domestic coal use from a perspective of fundamental human needs, this chapter develops a method from the perspective of the changing networks of relationships in which things and humans exist.

Chapter 8 is born out of a process of reflection by Willem van Niekerk, the lead author of this chapter, together with Attie S. van Niekerk, on the issue of decolonisation at the Engineering Faculty of the North-West University in South Africa. Engineering studies started off as a response to find solutions to specific needs, such as building a bridge. During the course of the 20th century, the emphasis on the curriculum for the training of engineers has shifted to the basic knowledge of the sciences and mathematics, and achieving basic skills, with the assumption that the engineer would then be able to adjust to different contexts. However, this was the period of technology-driven industries and economies. Towards the end of the 20th century, the emphasis shifted again: things became more and more complex, and it became increasingly clear that the engineer cannot continue to rely on technology without understanding how technology is interwoven in social and ecological systems, so that design in interaction with other role players became paramount. Postcolonial Africa has its own social and ecological systems, and the decolonisation of the engineering curriculum needs lecturers and students to understand these systems and interact with them in a constructive way, rather than merely accepting the hegemony of theories from the Global North.

In Chapter 9, Luc Kabongo reflects on his work as a transformation agent from inside a community of poverty in a township in South Africa, as part of a Christian ministry called InnerCHANGE. This ministry seeks to deconstruct a colonised mindset that leads African communities into a cul-de-sac, through practical ministry initiatives in the area. An improved quality of life for African households and communities of poverty requires inside out efforts. However, communities of poverty are often passive recipients of top-down plans from powerful institutions such as the government, international non-profit organisations or the church. Although these plans may be put together with the best intentions possible, they can be disempowering because they disarm ordinary people from an opportunity to be part of the solution to the problems they face. Attention is given to specific aspects of a colonial mindset such as feelings of inferiority, self-hatred and naivety. To be a change agent, one needs to know local history, learn by doing, practice active listening, form networks and so on. The chapter makes good use of theories that are developed by African writers and Christian theology in his search for practical solutions.

The book closes in Chapter 10 with some reflections by Sytse Strijbos in which he links the discussion about sustainability to another contemporary discussion, the discussion about what are called 'wicked problems' in policy and management sciences. While in the flood of scientific literature the term 'wicked' emphatically does not want to be associated with something like 'evil', Strijbos hears ancient religious questions resounding here. The quest for sustainability in our modern technological world is thus seen as, in the deepest sense, a religious issue that invites us to a critical reflection on the foundations of Enlightenment modernity on which we cannot continue as before. The central purpose of this chapter is to explore how biblical–theological notions can help to overcome the crisis of the modernity of our age. As an alternative to the now widely criticised dream of progress, the author refers to Chapter 2 and the earlier proposed idea of 'disclosure' of society, which he connects in his argument with the biblical view of the unity of God's 'commands' and 'promises' as guiding factors for human life.

Chapter 1

Where do you feel Africa's heartbeat? The World Bank, Africa and the Christian mission

Attie S. van Niekerk[a,b]
[a]The Nova Institute,
Pretoria, South Africa
[b]Sustainable Communities Research Cluster, Centre for Faith and Community,
Faculty of Religion and Theology, University of Pretoria,
Pretoria, South Africa

■ Introduction

There was a time when both modern development and the Christian mission in Africa were seen in fairly simple and clear-cut ways: not only did many see them almost as one thing, but both the Christian message and modern development were seen as a given that merely had to be transferred to Africa. An example of the close association between modern development and the Christian mission in Africa can be seen in the life of David Livingstone, a well-known missionary and explorer in Africa.

Livingstone arrived in Africa in 1841. He supported the militant 'Clapham' group of evangelicals, of whom William Wilberforce was the best known,

---

How to cite: Van Niekerk, A.S., 2021, 'Where do you feel Africa's heartbeat? The World Bank, Africa and the Christian mission', in A.S. Van Niekerk & S. Strijbos (eds.), *We cannot continue like this: Facing modernity in Africa and the West*, pp. 13-33, AOSIS, Cape Town. https://doi.org/10.4102/aosis.2021.BK283.01

in their drive to abolish the slave trade – this group also persuaded the British government to do the same. This group argued for the relevance of economic arguments to moral issues (Walls 1994):

> [*T*]he real remedy, the real ransom for Africa, will be found in her fertile soil'. African agricultural development would undercut the slave trade at its source, by providing much more profitable access to the Western manufactured goods that Africans clearly wanted. The slave trade, demonstrably the enemy of a Christian enterprise in Africa, could be extinguished by calling forth Africa's own resources; and by this means agricultural development and enhanced trade would help to produce conditions in which Christianity would spread. Such development would in turn lead to literacy and thus to printing, to new technologies in Africa, to roads and transport, to new forms of civil organization – in fact to 'civilization'. Christianity, commerce and civilization had interests in common and could unashamedly support one another. Their united effect would be to improve the life and prosperity of Africans, stem the loss of population, and shrivel up the more violent institutions of African society. (pp. 141–143)

There are many who still think along these lines, that is to say, that the Christian message and modern development not only belong together, but that they are a given that must be taken over as such by Africa. However, missiologists and Africa church leaders have realised more than a century ago that the biblical message must be contextualised in non-Western contexts. It is an insight that has not been taken over by most agents of the development industry, not even by many church people themselves when they engage in development activities. Modern development is still, by and large, seen as a given that must be transferred to Africa, in spite of talk in some circles about things like community participation and stakeholder engagement.

In August 1944, the World Bank and its sister institution, the International Monetary Fund, were founded at an international conference at Bretton Woods, New Hampshire, by Western powers who believed that raising the living standards of the poorest countries would help everyone across the world (Calderisi 2006:17). In 1949, the 'development industry' of the 20th century received a major boost when US President Harry S Truman announced a programme to develop the 'less fortunate nations'. Before that time, there was relatively little serious discussion related to the causes of mass poverty and likewise very little of its remedy. Subsequent to Truman's announcement, there was a flood of conferences, workshops and publications on the development of poor countries (Galbraith 1980:36, 37, 40). The 'development industry' has spent huge amounts in programmes to develop Africa and have prescribed stringent measures to promote economic development and eradicate poverty, but with little positive result. Various authors have sought an explanation for the disappointing results, such as Patrick Marnham (1980), Robert Calderisi (2006), Dambisa Moyo (2009) and Volker Seitz (2018). A strong theme that emerged is that development aid feeds corruption, as well as competition for resources and passivity. In my view, these authors have missed the main point, namely, that a Western version of modern development that is not contextualised is not the ideal solution for Africa.

This chapter will argue that well-known problems of the development industry in Africa have something to do with the gap between the underlying worldviews, values and cultural patterns of the development industry on the one hand and Africa on the other hand – something that some Christian missions and African churches *have* grappled with.

This argument links up with the *CURE Framework,* an initiative of the United Nations Educational, Scientific and Cultural Organization (UNESCO) (2018) which is part of the World Bank Group. The CURE Framework is (UNESCO 2018):

> [*A*] culture-based approach to the process of city reconstruction and recovery in post conflict, post disaster and urban distress situations that accounts for the needs, values and priorities of people. In the CURE Framework, culture is mainstreamed into all sectors and areas of intervention and across all phases of the reconstruction and recovery process, including needs assessments, scoping, planning, financing, and implementation. While current place-based strategies prioritize the reconstruction of physical assets, integrating culture strengthens a community's sense of belonging, as well as the livability of the built environment. (p. 8)

The next section presents a few remarks on the discourse on economic development in the World Bank's publication *Africa's Pulse*, followed by an illustration of the (lack of) buy-in of the Southern African Development Community (SADC). After focusing attention on a case study of the thinking of a former World Bank official about the gap between the Bank and African leaders, we listen to a few insights from African writers. Against this background, the section titled 'Reflection on the way forward and the role of Christianity' will reflect on the way forward and the role of Missiology. In the 'Conclusion' of this chapter, we conclude by summarising the main message of this chapter.

■ *Africa's Pulse Volume 22*

Africa's Pulse Volume 22 forms part of a series of editions that started with *Africa's Pulse Volume 14* (World Bank 2016). The series focuses on various aspects of the taxonomy of growth resilience in Africa. Each of the subsequent editions of *Africa's Pulse* deals with different growth performers in the region.

In 2006 a former World Bank official wrote (Calderisi 2006):

> Some of the best economists in the world worked hard on Africa's problems, to little avail. In 2000, the World Bank published its third major study in 20 years on the continent's economic prospects ('Can Africa Claim the 21st Century?'). Its prescriptions were essentially the same as those of 1989 – and 1981. (p. 184)

It seems that the prescriptions of *Africa's Pulse* are still essentially the same as in 2000 and 1981. The following remarks are meant to show that *Africa's Pulse* presents the modern economy as the solution to Africa's problems.

This discourse will be compared to some of the discourses that took place between numerous other African leaders and writers.

In October 2020, during the spread of COVID-19, the World Bank Group published the *Advance Copy* of *Africa's Pulse Volume 22. An analysis of issues shaping Africa's economic future. Charting the road to recovery* (World Bank 2020). On the front page is a silhouette of the continent of Africa in light blue, against a darker blue background, with dark patches on the periphery. There is a mesh of small squares formed by parallel thin lines, and seven arrows in different colours that are all going upwards and forward, like the lines of a graph. Different versions of the same basic picture appear on several former editions of *Africa's Pulse.* The *look and feel* is one of optimism, of progress, of having everything neatly in place.

In spite of the severe impact of COVID-19, the general tone of the advance copy of 2020 remains optimistic. On page one, there is reference to the severe impact of COVID-19 on the continent and the fear that it may erase years of progress in fighting poverty and may result in a set back to the progress in building human capital, as school closures will affect nearly 253 million students. But the optimistic tone soon returns: the crisis creates opportunities for policy reforms and several countries in the region are seizing the opportunity of the crisis to accelerate the necessary reforms.

Volume 22 emphasises policy actions and investments that can be described as wide-ranging structural reforms, with the aim to create more, better and inclusive jobs, rebuild the economy's fiscal buffers, generate a steady flow of revenues and to enlarge a country's capacity to repay its debt obligations and hence support to build up the fiscal space. 'These transformations will put countries on a high and inclusive path of economic growth' (World Bank 2020:45, 65).

The general macro-economic thought-patterns in World Bank circles are demonstrated by the detailed guidelines for three transformations that are deemed necessary to put the countries on the high road of economic growth): *Sectoral transformation, technological transformation* and s*patial integration* (World Bank 2020:65–129).

Modernising the economy is mentioned repeatedly in these documents, for example, sectoral transformation is meant to diversify the economy away from agriculture and other traditional sectors, like mining, to modern economic activities such as services and, to a lesser extent, manufacturing (World Bank 2020:70). Agriculture itself must be modernised (World Bank 2020:70). Digital technologies in agriculture are discussed several times, for example, in *Africa's Pulse Volume 19* (World Bank 2019a:115–119), the importance of harvesting the digital revolution is dealt with, including its role in modernising agriculture; and in *Africa's Pulse volume 14,* there is a substantial discussion of agriculture that considers various strategies to encourage a greater adoption of modern technologies (World Bank 2016:55ff.).

The macro-economical policies are presented as a given, a basic fact to be accepted as being true, as the only possibility, with hardly any attention to the need for synergy with local cultures – or with the ecology.

The sustainable development goals (SDGs) are highly interdependent. The World Bank played a leading role in the formulation of the United Nations' SDGs, but the SDGs did not result in a paradigm shift in the World Bank's approach towards Africa, as described in *Africa's Pulse*. In practice these publications mostly ignore a key aspect of the SDGs, namely, that they are highly interdependent. It seems that the World Bank (2019b) regards the work that it is doing, as it is, as being completely in line with the SDGs:

> The World Bank Group has set two goals that we are helping the world achieve by 2030: Ending extreme poverty and Promoting shared prosperity. These goals, which are fully consistent with the SDGs, need to be pursued within a socially, economically and environmentally sustainable framework. (p. 15)

How does the World Bank plan to pursue the two goals 'within a socially, economically and environmentally sustainable framework', if the rest of the discourse in these publications practically ignores the social and environmental elements? There is no indication that these publications resonate with the CURE Framework's approach of 'using culture as driver and enabler of post-crisis city reconstruction and recovery' (World Bank 2018:21). *Africa's Pulse* seems to assume that any form of international cooperation to end inequality and poverty upliftment would suffice. That is questionable. The trade-offs between the economic development measures that the World Bank promotes and their impact on social and cultural life and the natural environment in different local contexts have to be considered. The Intergovernmental Panel on Climate Change (IPCC) Special Report on Global Warming of 1.5 °C (Roy 2018) gives numerous examples of the way in which various elements of the 17 SDGs can interact and combine. The content of the *Africa's Pulse* series would look very different if this type of thinking is used.

The SDGs hardly appear in any of the editions of *Africa's Pulse* since 2016. Sustainability throughout refers to sustainable *economic* growth, for example: 'sustain the growth of productivity' (World Bank 2019a:39, 2020:125) or 'debt sustainability' (repeatedly mentioned in vols. 20–21).

Environment refers almost exclusively to the context in which the economy functions, such as 'business environment'.

A few examples of the way in which the ecology is considered: In *Africa's Pulse volume 14* the word renewable is mentioned once, where it is stated that

Africa's renewable water resources are substantially underused (World Bank 2016:57). The word renewable is not used in connection with water resources that are overused or used in an unsustainable manner – it is used only where growth is still possible.

Another example: In *Africa's Pulse Volume 17* and other volumes there are frequent references to the improvement of renewable energy technology, that becomes more and more affordable – but always from the perspective of economic considerations such as affordability, not from the perspective of the way in which economic growth will impact on the natural environment.

Lastly: one may find a remark that irrigation sometimes has a negative social and ecological cost, but that this does not have to be a problem anymore: 'But recent advances in planning and design techniques have provided the ability to minimize the adverse environmental and social consequences of large irrigation infrastructure' (World Bank 2016:70).

It seems that ecological sustainability is mentioned in those cases where it is not a problem, but that there is little emphasis on the cases where it is a problem.

Cultural clumsiness. Over the decades there have been those who complained about the World Bank's 'cultural clumsiness' while others felt that the Bank does not need to engage in culture (Alkire 2004:186). I would align myself with those who emphasise on the fact that local cultures cannot be ignored and that the Bank must find intelligent ways to work with them if it wants to achieve anything worthwhile.

The word *culture* is not, as far as I could see, used in the *Africa's Pulse* publications to describe traditional contexts in which modern development is meant to take place, or where traditional African cultures may play a role in solving some or other pressing problem – it is used to describe something within the context of a modern economy, for example, the need to create a culture of trust between the state and citizens (World Bank 2019a:72, 98).

Traditional cultural patterns are seen as restrictive factors that must be addressed: traditional social norms such as community- or inheritancebased, non-market mechanisms for land allocation that result in lower productivity because it disincentivises firms or farmers from undertaking productivity-enhancing investments. This contributes to the low productivity of sub-Saharan African countries because of low levels of human capital (World Bank 2018:88, 93, 2020:68). That these traditions are deeply imbedded in the social structures of communities and that there are constructive and destructive ways to engage with them are hardly considered.

There are only a few references to values and norms (i.e. apart from economic value), for example, cases where state and civil society actors have used narratives to strengthen the norms of social cohesion and tolerance (World Bank 2019a:60–61).

There are a few references to religion, for example (World Bank 2019a):

> Companies have also managed risk through practices related to good corporate citizenship. For example, money transfer firms in Somalia, which aligned themselves with religious principles and local values, provide widely used services. (p. 60)

The way in which girls' education and child marriage are approached in the Sahel is a case in point. The Sahel Women Empowerment and Demographic Dividend project brought together influential Muslim scholars and religious and traditional leaders from the participating countries to get their support on issues related to a wide range of gender rights, including child marriage, family planning and girls' education. These issues have negatively affected the development and health of girls and young women and their ability to prosper and formally contribute to the economy. The World Bank engaged the regional network of religious leaders to support the project goals (World Bank 2019a:65).

Such a top-down approach is seldom effective when it comes to deep-seated popular practices.

In Mali the rate of child marriages is particularly high. In this country, the World Bank (2019a:65) focuses on measures to curb the school dropout phenomenon. About 900 young girls received bikes to enable them to get to school, more than 3000 girls received school kits, their parents or host families received food supplies and extra classes in certain subjects were arranged. These measures were intended to enable girls to escape the marriages that their parents arrange when they stay at home.

Africa's Pulse does not provide an in-depth analysis of the reasons why this practice persists and gives no indication of an informed search, with the people who are in the situation, for meaningful efforts to deal with its root causes. There is no indication how they have concluded that the above-mentioned measures would have the desired effect, or how they have monitored the outputs of the efforts.

The More Than Brides Alliance (MTBA), that is related to Oxfam, also deals with child marriages in Mali. They do more, it seems, than the World Bank, to understand the phenomenon and to find a viable solution to deal with it. According to research conducted by the United Nations Children's Fund (UNICEF) in 2017, more than half of women in Mali were married off in their childhood. This phenomenon is attributed to a lack of quality education for girls as a viable alternative, as well as traditional practices such as polygamy. The Population Council, the research partner of the MTBA, is conducting an analysis and providing a description of the context of child marriages and reviews collected data and other data, including secondary data, to determine what measures to curb the practice work and what do not.[2]

---

2. See https://morethanbrides.org/where/mali/.

That is a good beginning, but one would have to go further than that. What is needed are viable practices that could replace the existing practices. Such new practices have to be effective, sustainable and desirable to the people themselves and that would require a long-term process of working closely with a small number of households who are in the situation, in order to come to a common understanding of the problem and of the available solutions, followed by reaching consensus on what solutions have the greatest potential, implementing the most promising ones on a small scale, evaluating them together, adjusting them, iterating, until all agree that a certain solution complies with their requirements. Only when that stage is reached can ways be found to take it to scale.

To conclude: it seems that the World Bank discourse has, through the years, remained focused on the macro-economy and on promoting modern economic development. Ecological sustainability, and cultures and religions, when mentioned, remain very much on the periphery and are mostly seen as a problem. A bottom-up process is required, where development agents and local households and communities put their heads together, find common ground and experiment with possible solutions until they develop practices that both parties find to be good, or at least *good enough*.

The question is: how can development initiatives succeed without synergy between these initiatives and its stake holders' ways of thinking and doing, with what *they* regard as meaningful and rational, with their habits and patterns of living, with their views of life and the world?

■ How much buy in did *Africa's Pulse* get from a key role player in sub-Saharan Africa?

The SADC, with its 14 member states, is the regional economic community that should promote economic development in the area. The SADC and the political leaders of the area that meet at the SADC's Summit are key role players if modern economic development is to succeed. The World Bank needs them to succeed.

The formal objectives of the SADC include phrases such as achieving economic development, peace, security, growth, alleviating poverty, enhancing the standard and quality of life of the peoples of Southern Africa, supporting the socially disadvantaged through Regional Integration, democratic principles and equitable and sustainable development.[3]

These sentiments seem to be well-aligned with the World Bank's thinking, as expressed in *Africa's Pulse*. However, it is not as simple as it seems to be.

---

3. See https://www.sadc.int/.

Africa's Pulse recognises that there is a lack of 'strong champions for democratic norms' in regional economic communities such as the SADC: Regional institutions lack sufficient funds, common identities and shared values, things that hinder the fulfilment of their core mandates (World Bank 2019a:70).

Nathan (2006:605–606, 622), likewise, found that the SADC lacked shared values. He wrote that the SADC Organ on Politics, Defence and Security, a common security regime whose functions include the prevention and resolution of inter- and intra-state conflict, was itself bedevilled by acrimonious conflict. It was split between the pacific and militarist camps, but the variations are greater within the camps than between them.

However, there are, at least on certain occasions, strongly felt values shared by a majority in the SADC. The problem is that these values are not aligned with the World Bank's values, as can be seen in the following report in a Rwandan daily newspaper, *The New Times* (Quartz 2013):

> Zimbabwean President Robert Mugabe received a standing ovation at Saturday's opening of the SADC Summit held in Malawi's capital Lilongwe.
>
> At the same meeting, Mr Mugabe also apologised to a member of South African President Jacob Zuma's facilitation team whom he once labelled a 'street woman'.
>
> Mr Mugabe's applause came during introductions of the heads of state and government and other delegates at the summit over the weekend.
>
> When SADC director of communications Charles Mubita introduced the Zimbabwean president to the jam-packed Bingu International Conference Centre Hall at the opening of the summit, delegates and the entire audience gave him a standing ovation, clapping and ululating.
>
> An excited Mugabe stood up and waved to the delegates and sat down. But when the clapping continued, the Zimbabwean leader had to stand again and he made his famous 'fist up' gesture, driving the audience's excitement to the brim.
>
> Mr Mugabe, who recently got elected with over 60 per cent of the vote, told journalists on Saturday upon arrival at the Kamuzu International Airport that he is an African and that he had nothing to do with the West. 'I have nothing to do with the British, I have nothing to do with the Americans', said the 89-year-old Zimbabwean leader. 'We make our decisions as African people, and those are the decisions we go by'.
>
> Mr Mugabe further accused the West of wanting to think for Africans, and tell them which direction to take. But he said what Africans decide to take as the right direction is always the right direction for them and not for the West. 'I am Robert Mugabe, a Zimbabwean, and African', said the adamant African leader, whose country the West continues to put on sanctions.
>
> While apologising to Ms Lindiwe Zulu, the 89-year-old leader had to kiss her, in front of fellow bemused Heads of States and governments. (n.p.)

One asks yourself: is this not where Africa's pulse is to be taken?

It was not the first time that Mugabe was honoured with a standing ovation. In 2003, he received standing ovations at the Summit of the SADC in Dar es Salaam, although the 2002 Summit replaced Mugabe as the Deputy Chair of SADC, preventing him from assuming the Chair the following year (Nathan 2006:612; Sirota 2004:243). There was a lot of conflict around Mugabe, not least his dislike of Nelson Mandela who was becoming a prominent leader and played a reconciling role. The views of those who opposed Mugabe are expressed well by Tanonoka Joseph Whande (2007):

> Robert 'Pol Pot' Mugabe got another standing ovation for capably pulling in the opposite direction of where the SADC is trying to go. The ovation came, not from those rent-a-crowd mobs we see at airports whenever an African president leaves or arrives home, but from the African Heads of State themselves.
>
> In the last 15 years and more, Mugabe has done nothing but ruin a country, murdering a nation and its economy. It's sad that we are losing count of those citizens whose deaths he is responsible for. (n.p.)

In similar vein, Sirota (2004:243–244) wrote that Mugabe, while receiving the standing ovation in Dar es Salaam in 2003, faced 'massive poverty, inflation, unemployment, and political opposition in his own country, as well as widespread condemnation from the West'. SADC leaders sided with Mugabe and 'urged Western nations to lift sanctions on Zimbabwe while declining to address Mugabe's numerous human rights abuses'. Tanzanian Foreign Minister Jakaya Mrisho Kikwete boldly stated, 'We are 14 countries in SADC. The EU can either fund us as a group or keep its financial aid'. Sirota (2004) concludes:

> These initial declarations signaled that the SADC, a body founded primarily to achieve economic integration in Southern Africa, was expanding its role in the international political arena [...]. By the end of the summit, the SADC had gone one step further, casting its power in explicitly military terms. (p. 344)

Chebvute (n.d.) argues that the SADC, like other regional organisations in Africa, has its roots in the Pan Africanist drive for solidarity or 'brotherhood' of Africans against forces of colonialism, imperialism and neo-colonialism. The ideals of solidarity and unity made it difficult for the SADC to acknowledge acts of violence by a government within their fold. The result was that they failed to end the violence of the state of Zimbabwe against its own population and to cooperate with Western entities to promote economic development.

This divergence from the economic-focused policies of the SADC should have a significant impact on the World Bank's strategy in Africa. We now look at the way a former World Bank official responded to the dilemmas that the Bank faces in Africa.

■ Case study of the way of thinking of a former World Bank official about the gap with African leaders

World Bank officials are obviously very aware of the divergence between their own way of thinking and that of African leaders and officials.

In 2006 Robert Calderisi, who had worked for the World Bank for more than 20 years as a high-ranking official, published a book *The trouble with Africa: Why foreign aid isn't working,* in which he argues that foreign aid leads to corruption, to competition to gain control of the funds and oppression.

Calderisi argues that the trouble in Africa is caused by its own leaders' mismanagement and indifference to public opinion and key issues like AIDS, while they play intentionally on Western guilt; by their widespread animosity towards business; by African family loyalty and fatalism that have been even more destructive than tribalism. He is of the opinion that Africans have probably been crueller to each other than anyone else has been: 'If character keeps Africans fatalistic and corruption binds their elites together, political correctness in the West adds a final touch to Africa's misery' (Calderisi 2006:7, 91).

Calderisi argues that the clash of values between Westerners and African governments prevents large development projects from benefitting Africa (2006:195). He devotes a whole chapter to the clash of values. The chapter consists of a whole number of anecdotes about the writer's experiences in Africa which clearly illustrate that these African officials and politicians do not share his views of what is required in Africa and what he feels every reasonable person would agree with (2006:195–204).

However, he does not sufficiently address the clash of values and the existence of 'an African world' that operates according to its own values and views. This can be illustrated by his understanding of Wole Soyinka's view of negritude. Calderisi (2006:78) states that contemporary Africans, unlike an earlier generation, are uncomfortable with subjects such as the *African Personality*. He refers to Léopold Senghor, the first president of Senegal, as an example of the 'earlier generation'. Senghor coined the word *negritude*; he regarded the European and African worldviews as being fundamentally different. Senghor's concepts seem simplistic today, said Calderisi, referring to the Nigerian writer Wole Soyinka who had 'poked fun' at the concept by stating that a tiger does not have to proclaim its tigritude.

On the next page Calderisi (2006:79) quotes Nadine Gordimer, a 'white South African' who rejected Senghor's views. Calderisi (2006:79) then concludes that if Senghor's view is true, development planners were knocking at the wrong door.

Calderisi, who clearly represents the World Bank's belief in modern economic development, came close to a valuable insight: the possibility, which he promptly rejects, that development planners so misunderstood Africa that they were knocking at the wrong door. But was Calderisi right when he regarded the idea of an African world that is different from the modern (Western) world as outdated?

The idea of an African world is not only propagated by an 'earlier generation'. After 2006, ideals of African identity have continued to be pronounced forcefully, as can be seen in the decolonisation movement. On a grassroots level African thought-patterns remain resilient – Calderisi (2006) himself refers to the tenacity of 'family loyalty'. This loyalty has deep cultural roots.

Secondly, Calderisi invokes Soyinka's comment on the word *negritude:* 'A tiger doesn't have to proclaim its tigritude', as proof that such concepts are out of date. However, Soyinka (1976) strongly objected against the way his statement was used:

> From a well-publicised position as an Anti-Negritudinist (if only one knew in advance what would make one statement more memorable than the next!) it has been with an increasing sense of alarm and even betrayal that we have watched our position distorted and exploited to embrace a 'sophisticated' school of thought which (for ideological reasons) actually repudiates the existence of an African world! [...] Could this be why of late we Africans have been encountering a concerted assault, decked in ideological respectability, on every attempt to re-state the authentic world of the African peoples and ensure its contemporary apprehension through appropriate structures? In vain we conjure with the names of Mbiti, Bolaji Idowu, Ogotommeli, Kagame, Willie Abrahams, Cheik Anta Diop, and foreign triers like Father Tempels, Pierre Verger, Herskovits etc. (pp. ix, x)

Soyinka (1976:viii) pleaded for an academic approach that would express Africans' 'true self-apprehension, [...] the apprehension of a culture whose reference points are taken from within the culture itself' rather than from 'the reference points of colonial cultures'.

This is exactly where Calderisi's blind spot is: when he discusses cultural patterns in Africa, and African values that clash with the values of the World Bank, he uses reference points that come from Western or modern culture. He does not seek for an understanding of 'the self-apprehension of the African world' (Soyinka 1976:ix).

The logic of Calderisi's statement is, however, correct. We can apply it as follows: if Soyinka's idea that there is an 'African world' is true, development planners have been knocking at the wrong door.

A consequent key question would be: If we can indeed make such a conclusion, or at least accept it as a possibility, what would the implications be? What would happen if the World Bank took 'the self-apprehension of the African world' seriously?

It seems that the CURE Framework, that UNESCO is developing, is knocking at the right door. It is vital that the cases that the CURE Framework presents as examples of how their approach works, be studied diligently, that lessons are learnt from their experience and that those lessons are applied and developed further.

Thirdly, Calderisi (2006) seeks the fault with the Africans rather than with the Bank, for example:

> Much of Africa's potential, and the causes of its current difficulties, are hidden in the shade of major misconceptions – about the slave trade, colonialism, the World Bank, and so on – which simply need to be whittled away. Individual Africans have risen to the challenges confronting them for decades, but their governments have not; even worse, most leaders have stood in the way of individual initiative and innovative solutions, fearing some loss of control. African talents – at home and abroad – need to be given a chance to prosper. They need fresh air and light. (pp. 223–224)

Calderisi may be right in pointing out that African leaders have misconceptions about what the West has done and what the World Bank is doing. Different views can always be debated. My point is that there have been mutual misconceptions from both sides.

Calderisi tends to place his hope on individuals while he tends to see the cultural and political structures, from the family to the state, as obstacles in the way of individuals. His solution is to whittle away at all these obstacles to modern development. Is that the only, and the best, strategy?

■ Reflection on the discourse about development among a number of African writers

The anchor text for this section is: *Journal of Public Administration* Volume 49 Number 1, March 2014, published by the South African Association of Public Administration and Management, hereafter called the *Journal*. It was selected because it looks back at 20 years of democracy in South Africa, and it contains 30 articles written mostly by black South Africans at traditionally black universities. Maybe Africa's pulse can be felt here too.

In this text there are a number of viewpoints that are very compatible to what we find in *Africa's Pulse,* such as (Ijeoma & Okafor 2014):

> Access to quality and affordable electricity is therefore, vital in achieving the United Nation's Millennium Development Goals especially in the crucial areas of service provision and empowerment. (p. 34)

Also (Mbeki & Phago 2014):

> [T]here has been a serious lack of skilled staff in water services and sanitation (such as plumbers, engineering technicians, planning technicians, plant managers, artisans, water treatment specialists, engineers and assistant managers) [...] local government protests can therefore be a manifestation of frustrations and unhappiness with, among others, local government service delivery efficiencies and effectiveness. (p. 212)

The modern world, and specifically Western countries, is mentioned as an ideal destination in a matter of fact manner, for example, when it is said that some refugees from other African countries see South Africa as a passage to better opportunities somewhere in 'the developed countries like the United Kingdom, the United States of America, Australia, etc.' (Mpehle 2014:248).

It seems that the World Bank has decided to proceed with those in Africa who do agree with their views and who cooperate with it.

However, a significant part of the journal contains a discourse that rather resonates with the SADC than with the discourse in *Africa's Pulse*. Their views should be considered seriously, even where one does not agree with them, to understand the context in which solutions to existing problems have to be found.

Attention will be given to the following: the question of 'exceptionalism' (is South Africa different from the rest of Africa?) and the importance of local government, with specific reference to the functioning of the Western legal system in Africa.

Exceptionalism

An issue that surfaces repeatedly in the Journal, but that is largely absent in *Africa's Pulse*, is the question of identity. A few examples are given (Tsheola & Lukhele 2014):

> South Africa's conduct of international relations invoked a longstanding question of whether it was an African state or European outpost in Africa, set to modernize, if not civilize, the rest of the continent. (p. 389)

This country's hope, as expressed by former President Mbeki, was to counter the legacy of Afro-pessimism and mobilise Foreign Direct Investment. Consequently, the Western 'civilizing missions' are codified in the New Partnership for Africa's Development, which is the pan-African strategic framework for the socio-economic development of the continent. Its overriding objective was 'to consolidate democracy and sound economic management on the continent'. The article is not positive about this: Mbeki's notion of an African Renaissance is 'treading a well-known, dusty path: a postcolonial, neoliberal cul-de-sac of predictable direction and duration [...] globalist modernization has become an empty policy vessel, fading with time'. It states that Mbeki's globalist modernisation mission has exposed Africa to an externally driven consumerist movement in which Africa would continue to be 'valued' only for its ability to absorb and popularise foreign ideas, trinkets and junk – it was not emancipatory (Tsheola & Lukhele 2014:384, 386, 387).

For Tsheola and Lukhele nothing is exactly what it seems, for example, the African Renaissance is postcolonial, neoliberal, globalist modernisation, and the notion of 'Diplomacy of Ubuntu' of the Department of International Relations and Cooperation was merely a spirited reinvention of the 'human-rights-based' foreign policy (Tsheola & Lukhele 2014:385).

They state that South Africa's foreign policy over the 20 years until 2014 consisted of a mission of securing 'liberal democracy, human rights, good governance, civility, peace-building and market reforms, among other imperial objectives and policies'. This mission originated in 'a concoction of issues of nationalist pride, glory, morality and religious zeal, which is puerile and boastful'. South Africa's puerile geopolitical self-imaginary (Tsheola & Lukhele 2014):

> [/]s evident in former President Mbeki's comment to the International Marketing Council [*IMC*] in 2002 that 'The rest of the world wants us to succeed because success in South Africa is an investment in success in their own countries'. (pp. 376–378)

South Africa's self-selection as a leader of the African Renaissance illustrates its notion of exceptionalism (Tsheola & Lukhele 2014:387).

This discussion of identity forms part of a much wider discourse in a number of academic disciplines. In recent years, it has led to the decolonisation movement, which is also debated in various disciplines. Two publications are mentioned here.

The importance of identity is illustrated by the detailed analysis in which Sabelo Ndlovu-Gatsheni traces the various intricacies of the resurgence of Afro-radicalism and nativism in post-settler and post-apartheid societies (Ndlovu-Gatsheni 2009:61). He draws a complicated picture.

In another lengthy article, *The De-Africanisation of the African National Congress, Afrophobia in South Africa and the Limpopo River fever,* Masemola John Lamola (2018) gives a passionate analysis of the various layers, tensions and gaps in African identities in South Africa (Lamola 2018):

> The manner in which South Africans, especially 'black' South Africans, relate to their identification with the African continent and its populace, which empirically and

discursively, is part of them, can at best be described as an identitarian dysfunctionality. This equivocal Africanity, I suggest, has assumed a psychopathological form. As such, it manifests itself [...] in a range of social and political deviances that inter alia, have earned post-apartheid South Africa the status of one of the unacceptably violent societies on earth. A person not reconciled to her Self, cannot be at peace with others (other 'Selves'). One obvious cause of this un-embraced Africanness, and its consequent psychosocial expressions, is decades of the apartheid education system that had deliberately sought to inculcate into South Africans that they are 'better off' than their fellow Africans 'up north'. (pp. 72–73)

Pan-Africanism takes a clear stand regarding exceptionalism. In December 1957, Robert Sobukwe declared (Lamola 2018):

I wish to state that the Africanists do not at all subscribe to the fashionable doctrine of South African exceptionalism. Our contention is that South Africa is an integral part of the indivisible whole that is Afrika. (p. 85)

The hotly debated question of identity forms part of the complex phenomenon that we can call *Africa's pulse* – a beat that is not noticed in the World Bank' *Africa's Pulse* discourses.

Local government

Several articles in the *Journal of Public Administration* 49:1 deal with local government.

In an article, *The community policing philosophy and the right to public protest in South Africa*, M.P. Sebola links local government to the justice system.

In South Africa, there are numerous public protests. Some are about macro-economic issues such as salary pay hikes and improvement of working conditions, others are related to local issues such as cultural taboos, including *muti* murders. 'The police services failure to solve *muti* murder cases will lead to political violence at the end when communities take the law into their own hands' (Sebola 2014:307, 309).[4]

In an article, *Crime rate in Africa: time for African criminological theory*, A.A. Olutola (2014) takes the connection between the justice system and the local community a step further. Olutola argues that most criminological theories originate from scholars outside the African continent and that those scholars naturally assume that a general criminological theory will work for all. Olutola advocates for an Afrocentric criminological theory. He sees no basis for the expectation that 'Eurocentric or Americancentric criminological theory(ies)' (Olutola 2014:313) will produce the desired results in Africa's struggle against the menace of crime, to both combating crime and preventing it.

---
4. *Muti* murders are committed to obtain human body parts for use in traditional African medicines.

Olutola (2014) emphasises that knowledge in the African context is local and tribal. Crime is dealt with at a local level by taking all factors into account and by integrating all experiences, feelings and reasoning (Olutola 2014):

> [/]n the traditional African setting knowledge is not attained through labour but given by the ancestors. In other words, knowledge is not universal but local and tribal. This confirms further the argument in this paper that generic criminological theory cannot work for all [...] knowledge is passed from one generation to the next. In the conventional African setting no knowledge of reality exists if the individual is not connected to the mainstream [...] African epistemology postulates that knowledge is the integration and cooperation of all human experiences, feelings, reasoning [...] care must be taken not to present the African view as if it were a Western view, as the two are worlds apart [...] a proposed idea or legislation (criminal justice legislation inclusive) will be passed into law after it has been meticulously discussed at the village square on the principle of equal participation by the members of the community. However in today's world, the criminal justice legislations in Nigeria and South Africa do not take cognisance of the traditional methods [...]. Constitutions of Nigeria and South Africa respectively recognise traditional institutions, but not to the extent of involving locals in the prosecution, adjudication and rehabilitation of offenders in the way and manner it was done in the traditional African society. (p. 321)

Secondly, there are two basic theories of cause of events (Olutola 2014):

> [/]n the traditional African thought, there are two basic theories of cause of events, namely mechanistic and nonmechanistic [...] when a person is attacked by malaria as a result of a mosquito bite, a Westerner would attribute the malaria to the mosquito bite and sees a nexus between the bite and the malaria; in other words it would be seen as the mechanistic cause of event. Conversely, in the African nonmechanistic way of life, a person inflicted by malaria will dwell on thoughts such as: 'Why should such a malaria attack be on me or my family, why not on another person or family?' (pp. 321–322)

Olutola (2014:323) argues that the criminal justice systems and generic criminological theories of the indigenous people of African countries are still important because of the inefficiency of the English law and its judicial system in the African context. This English-based common law and social control that are imposed in Africa lack the foundation they enjoy in their native England and or Europe. African people take great pride in their culture.

There is also a practical side to this. African people desire swift, inexpensive justice that is provided by the traditional system but not by the adversarial justice systems in Nigeria and South Africa that were imposed by the colonialists and are based on the English common law system, which is expensive, time consuming and insensitive to the indigenous African. It is adversarial in the sense that both parties want to win, and the outcome is that there is one who wins and one who loses (Olutola 2014:323).

Both the economic growth approach of *Africa's Pulse* and the culture-driven approach of the *CURE Framework* will have to consider the implications of evidence, both in academic publications and in everyday life, of the significant influence of cultural patterns that are clearly presented as alternatives to Western ones. In this they may get some help from the experience of Christianity in Africa.

■ Reflection on the way forward and the role of Christianity

Publications of the World Bank do give evidence of an awareness of the key role of religion in Africa from time to time.

In 1998 James D. Wolfensohn, then President of the World Bank, and Lord George Carey, then Archbishop of Canterbury, took the initiative to establish the World Faiths Development Dialogue (WFDD). It is claimed that the WFDD 'bridges between the worlds of faith and secular development'. Wolfensohn and Carey brought together a small group of senior leaders from nine major world faiths at Lambeth Palace, London, in February 1998. There was 'a total meeting of the minds', and the initiative was expanded. The WFDD was established in 2000 (WFDD n.d.):

> At the heart of WFDD's vision is an effort to bring voices and experience from poor communities more forcefully into development thinking at all levels, by facilitating a more active participation by faith communities in the strategic reflection processes on which development programs are based.[5] (n.p.)

The WFDD is active with research, conferences, workshops and so on. It is 'a not-for-profit organization working at the intersection of religion and global development'. The WFDD is housed at the Berkley Center for Religion, Peace and World Affairs and collaborates with them in their Religion and Global Development program.[6]

The World Banks' awareness that it has to engage with communities can also be seen in some of their own publications. Reflecting on the previous 50 years, the World Bank itself declared in 2001 that they had learned four critical lessons (World Bank 1999:1). These lessons include the insight that growth does not trickle down but that development must address human needs directly; that no one policy will trigger development; that a comprehensive approach is needed and that sustained development should be rooted in processes that are socially inclusive and responsive to changing circumstances.

A few comments are presented in response to these critical lessons.

---

5. See https://berkleycenter.georgetown.edu/wfdd/about.

6. See https://berkleycenter.georgetown.edu/wfdd/programs.

The first lesson is that 'development must [...] address human needs directly'. It is a difficult task. The *CURE Framework* has made good progress in developing this approach. But here too, many questions need to be sorted out, such as the clash of values. The CURE Framework (2018) gives the following guideline:

> In designing the engagement process, the team must first identify the relevant stakeholders. The engagement process should include the stakeholders who are directly affected by the rebuilding process and decisions, such as community leaders and organizations, religious and ethnic groups, private sector, owners, renters, informal community, youth, and women. (p. 41)

Let us say, for argument's sake, that the values underlying this guideline are those of fairness to and equality of all human individuals: all must have a say. Such values resonate with those of a liberal Western democracy, but one must be aware that there are often inherent tensions present.

Klitgaard had long before the *CURE Framework* appeared, quoted Jonathan Rigg who pointed out that, in many rural development projects in Thailand, in ostensibly participatory programs, 'projects are very rarely assessed in a democratic fashion, and the opinions and desires of individuals and cliques are extremely influential'. Klitgaard (1992:96–97) comments that, if Rigg is right, the question that arises is how local cultures should be considered. It may happen that a local group does not take all factors into account by integrating all experiences, feelings and reasoning, as Olutola claims does happen in the African tradition, but is hierarchical, dictatorial, sexist and unjust. Klitgaard points out the dilemma, and the different possible ways to respond: one could, nonetheless, rely on its 'culturally appropriate' mechanisms for decision. Or one could try to introduce change. Or only support or aid the local cultures and institutions that are deemed appropriate. Ways must be found to deal with such dilemmas.

We should not be surprised if we find, anywhere in the world, that the 'opinions and desires of individuals and cliques are extremely influential'. For this reason, the NOVA Institute takes special care to communicate directly with households too, in order to be able to 'address human needs directly' – the first lesson mentioned by the World Bank earlier.

Klitgaard's statement, as quoted earlier, is relevant for the fourth lesson mentioned above by the World Bank, namely, that 'sustained development should be rooted in processes that are socially inclusive and responsive to changing circumstances'. What Klitgaard had found by 1992, that there is little in the literature that can help us to face up to the dilemmas we face in socially inclusive processes, is to a large extent still true. When *Africa's Pulse* (World Bank 2019c:39) reflects on the highly risky environments in which households and firms in Africa operate, often with limited capacity to cope, and the risk management strategies that are needed, it notes: 'To date, few interventions exist to tackle directly the "psychology" of poverty'.

The second lesson that the World Bank mentioned in 2000, namely, that no one policy will trigger development and that a *comprehensive approach* is needed, is also quite complicated.

The meaning of the term *comprehensive approach* must be reconsidered in light of developments that have taken place since 2000, such as the SDG discourse and the models for an integrated approach that have been developed by the IPCC (e.g. Roy 2018). The urgency to reduce our impact on climate change and on the ecology in general cannot remain on the periphery.

The World Bank may perhaps learn something from the Christian missionaries and churches, especially their experience with their own 'comprehensive approach', which includes economic and community development, since the first half of the previous century. This approach is based on the insight that human life in all its diversity forms a totality and that interventions in one aspect could influence all other aspects. For economic development, this means that a person or a community cannot take ownership of modern economic practices with only one part of their being – it requires corresponding thinking and acting in all other aspects of life. For faith it means that one cannot be a believer in only one aspect of your life, namely, Sunday in the church – your whole life is relevant and must receive attention.

Initially, the missionaries and the indigenous people tended to regard modern Western culture and the Christian message as identical: if you become a Christian, you must learn to read and write, and to attend a Christian school you had to become a member of the church (Kritzinger 1994:119). Gradually, efforts have developed to communicate at a more fundamental level: *indigenisation* largely replaced the traditional *comprehensive approach.* Indigenisation is an effort to understand the core or soul (heartbeat) of a given group of people and to discover the relevance of the Christian message for that – which often did not require modernisation. *Contextualisation* wants to do the same, but includes attention to other aspects of the context, such as socio-economic conditions, political injustices, etc. as part of the scope that the church has to attend to.

These approaches give an indication of the variety of ways in which some missionaries and African church leaders have experimented with the question as to how the Christian message can function in a meaningful way in African contexts. Insights from experiences that these missionaries and leaders have had, in close encounters over time with people with a non-Western background in joint efforts to improve the quality of life of those people, could be of value for economic development agents who have not had such experiences.

In his book *Afrika wird arm regiert oder Wie man Afrika wirklich helfen kann* [Africa is ruled into poverty or How one can really help Africa] the former German diplomat Volker Seitz (2018), who has worked in embassies all over Africa for 17 years, is highly critical of the development industry. He says that churches and especially religious Non-Government Organisations (NGOs) are very often much more efficient in their sustainable development projects and better connected with other global players than public government institutions. In contrast to the government, these NGOs operate at the grassroots level and therefore have personal contact with the people who are perceived as the ones in need. And they have a better understanding of the religious and cultural dynamics of communities.

The missionaries and churches asked themselves how the biblical message could function in the African context. Olutalo asked himself how a Western judicial system could work in Africa, and it may require more than a few superficial adjustments. The same question must be asked about education, agriculture, democracy and economic development: how do these systems work in Africa? To merely transfer what has worked in the West to the African context seldom works.

■ Conclusion

It would be easy to blame the major role players mentioned in this chapter for the situation in Africa.

We can blame the World Bank - or the West as a whole. We can blame the SADC and Africa itself – Chebvute (n.d.) argues that the 'SADC worked to protect sitting regimes more than the interests of the people'. We can also blame the churches.

Instead of destructive blaming, this chapter suggests that development beyond modernity would have to go through a similar process as the Christian mission and churches, a process of inculturation in the African context, and that all would have to search for ways to help communities to become sustainable and equitable.

All these entities have a role to play:

- *Modern science and technology* provide the means to a good and sustainable future, but they need to connect in a constructive way to local values and ultimate ends to direct them, before they could play an optimum constructive role.
- *African traditions and social structures* provide a certain strength and resilience that provide some of the values that are needed, but they also present obstacles, as Calderisi has pointed out, such as fatalism and when the family requires loyalty that leads to corruption.
- *The biblical message* provides key values and can help us find the direction that is needed, but the churches need to find ways to present their message in relevant ways, that is, ways that are based on a good understanding of the structures and dynamics that shape Africa today, in countless local contexts.

The question is if we, all together, can find a way to a future Africa that would be sustainable and equitable, a vision that can unify enough role players to generate a critical mass.

To quote the CURE Framework again: It has become clear that culture can no longer be a dividend of development, but is rather a prerequisite to its achievement.

Chapter 2

Re-integrating technology and economy in human life: On the disclosure of society

Sytse Strijbos[a,b]
[a]IIDE-Europe,
Maarssen, Netherlands
[b]Centre for Faith and Community, Faculty of Theology and Religion,
University of Pretoria, Pretoria, South Africa

■ Introduction[7]

While writing this chapter, I was thinking about a visit I had made in the past to QwaQwa, one of the poorest rural areas in South Africa near the border of Lesotho. In the running up to the launch of a fund for 'small enterprise development', the Moahisane Development Fund (the MDF), I drove around with the other initiators of the fund to visit some small entrepreneurs who had been selected for support of their businesses.[8] The executive manager

---

7. This chapter is an abridged and revised version of Strijbos in conversation with Haftor (2011a), and has been reworked by more than 50% from the original text.

8. The Moahisane Development Fund was established in 2008 and operated till 2012 in cooperation with the University of the Free State (Bloemfontein, South Africa). The MDF aimed to develop strong links with the local communities of Qwaqwa and to provide a support structure for small enterprise development that includes the consideration of normative and cultural issues.

How to cite: Strijbos, S., 2021, 'Re-integrating technology and economy in human life: On the disclosure of society', in A.S. Van Niekerk & S. Strijbos (eds.), *We cannot continue like this: Facing modernity in Africa and the West*, pp. 35–48, AOSIS, Cape Town. https://doi.org/10.4102/aosis.2021.BK283.02

of the fund introduced us, among others, to David, a local entrepreneur whom we met at a crowded and messy informal settlement with bumpy roads. When we arrived at the shack where he lived with his family, David was awaiting our arrival, very eager to demonstrate his technical skills in making toy cars out of a tin plate with just some simple tools. He told us that at a petrol station not too far from where he lives he succeeds in selling a couple of these cars in a week, providing him with just enough income for him and his family to survive. In Chapter 5 of this book that provides a case study on the MDF, the small business of David is referred to as 'Simon's Cars'.

Although David impressed me as a person, especially because of the passion that he showed, it is true that this story can easily be replicated with many other similar stories about small entrepreneurs and their families in the developing world who live in poverty and have to struggle to make a living each day. The following text does not provide a detailed case study of David as a small entrepreneur in QwaQwa, but his story may serve as a typical example of what the economist Schumacher in his famous *Small is Beautiful* ([1973] 1993) refers to as the unsolved 'problem of production' and the underlying dominant belief that merely by expanding our industrial techno-economic system we can create universal prosperity. It is an illusion (thus Schumacher) that by allowing a free passage to the progress of modern science-based technology and economy as the main powers that drive modern society, we pave the road to peace and plenty for all humankind (Schumacher 1993):

> The message to the poor [...] is that they must not impatiently upset or kill the goose that will assuredly, in due course, lay golden eggs also for them. And the message to the rich is that they must be intelligent enough from time to time to help the poor, because this is the way they will become richer still. (p. 11)

David's case illustrates the fact that the 'problem of production' entails two closely related aspects of 'technology' and 'economy'. On the one hand there is the working power of people and the ability to make something. Human labour is a technical process of production with its own rules. Closely related to that is the economic process of the entrepreneur, who is in search of those who are interested in his product. These two sides, the role of the craftsman or manual worker and that of the entrepreneur, usually go together, as in David, in one and the same person. However, in the turn to a modern industrial society – a complex set of phenomena that started in Western history around the middle of the 19th century in England – these roles separated, a separation that came with the growth of the mechanical and technical production process as well as the size of the enterprise in economic terms. Even more important is the fact that in this change we meet two fundamentally different expressions of culture, the change from the manors and guilds to the modern industrial age, from typical household production, as in the case of David, to that of the profit-driven enterprise.⁹ While the guideline for household production is the (Goudzwaard 1997):

> [/]nternal provision for the sustenance of its inhabitants [...], the decisive guideline for [*industrial*] production is maximum financial yield by means of the most profitable expansion of an external market for its products. (p. 62)

The IIDE seeks to focus its research on the role of 'technology' and 'economy' as the two major drivers of today's world. The key question is: how can we attain a humane and sustainable development amidst the pressures and structures of our modern globalising world, respecting the diversity of peoples and cultures as well husbanding the natural environment on which humankind depends, and build a common house for humankind? In addressing this central normative question, the focus of the following is specifically on the enterprise and the innovating role of entrepreneurship, including the development of new technologies. After a short discussion of three (in some regards) overlapping streams of thought that aim for the reintegration of technology and economy in human life and society, some notes will be made in the following section about a paradigm for future research.

■ For a turn toward the local (Helena Norberg-Hodge and others)

In September 1996, I took the opportunity to have a quick look at the latest books in the nice bookshop at Stockholm airport, while waiting for my connecting flight to Luleå, which is located in the north of Sweden. There I found, hot off the press, a book edited by Mander and Goldsmith with the telling title, *The Case Against the Global Economy: And for A Turn Toward the Local*. It was a bit ironic to find such a title on the bookshelves of an airport bookshop, probably the most globalised spot in our societies, urging the reader to make a turn towards the local. Before having read a syllable, it dawned on me that a book with such an argument is dependent on a global framework to find its readers. The title triggered in my mind; therefore, the question of whether a plea for a *turn* to the local is the same as a plea for a *return* to the local, that is, a return to a world with separate cultures and with scarcely any interaction and exchange.

Indeed, we live in a technologically integrated and interconnected world where distance no longer determines who your 'neighbour' is. This is an irreversible situation, whether we regret that or not. A plea for re-localisation, a turn to the local, therefore cannot be simply a return to the world of the past. But it surely

---

9. It is therefore no surprise that in the operation of the MDF it has been observed that in the case of some small entrepreneurs in Qwaqwa, the economic concept of profit does not easily fit in with their cultural frame of mind (Cf. Strijbos 2011c:160-161). A seemingly value-neutral economic concept such as profit is in fact a clear-cut cultural expression of a certain view of human life that we are usually not aware of any more.

makes sense to think through the new relationship in today's society between the local and the global, and the implications both for our personal lives and the shaping of our societies. Notwithstanding the fact that we can easily connect with everybody else in any remote corner of the planet, we still remain rooted in a concrete living community and dependent on local contacts and provisions. The authors of the book, well-known scholars and/or activists such as Wolfgang Sachs, Herman Daly, Helena Norberg-Hodge, Wendell Berry and David Korten, share serious concerns about the global economy. What is their view on the local–global relationship in our contemporary world? What is their main message?

Acknowledging the fact that there are significant differences among them, one can say that all the authors are very critical of the idea of the unrestricted 'free market', an idea that goes along with the advocacy for a uniform worldwide development model that does not acknowledge the value and importance of the different cultural spheres in our world. Let me comment here more specifically on the linguist-philosopher, teacher and activist, Helena Norberg-Hodge, who was born in New York and grew up in Sweden. As she is a pioneer in the localisation movement, her ideas are particularly interesting, because they are not just academic dreams born in a study but flow from her practical engagement with the people of Ladakh and the Kingdom of Bhutan in the 1970s and 1980s.[10] Since that time she has been in continuous contact with Buddhist communities in both traditional cultures and the industrialised West. Being keenly aware of the spiritual roots of our modern world, Norberg-Hodge believes that the Buddha's teachings can help us to find a way out of the problems of the global economy and society.

In the Buddha's days, human life and society were deeply rooted, according to Norberg-Hodge (2002), in the local natural world that is characterised by its constantly changing cycles of day and night, summer and winter, birth and death and so on. In those days. the relation between people in society and between culture and nature were relatively unmediated by technology. In fact, in modern society we made a shift from a biotope to a technotope as our human habitat. Modern society is based on the belief that we are separate from and able to bring under control the natural world, including our own human bodies and our social lives. The structures and systems of today's society are in Norberg-Hodge's view the reifications of our denial of interdependence with our local environment: a denial of direct connections to the local community and to the living world around us. Globalisation means the creation of a disconnected society, that is, the destroying of smaller-scale social and economic structures and the undermining of the livelihoods and cultural identities of the majority of the world's people. So the way out is a

---

10. This is documented in her book, *Ancient Futures: Learning from Ladakh* (1991), which is available electronically at http://gyanpedia.in/tft/Resources/books/ancientfutures.pdf. See Norberg-Hodge (1996a) for a short presentation of the Ladakh story.

fundamental change in the direction of our societies, a moving away from global dependence to local interdependence.

During my career as a university teacher at the Vrije Universiteit, Amsterdam, I had to teach an introductory course on ethics and philosophy of technology for students in information technology. In the Reader that I prepared I included some articles of Norberg-Hodge. I remember very well how the students felt embarrassed or even shocked by her story about the effects of modern life on the people of Ladakh; they started thinking about the possible negative impact that can be caused by their own field of study on people and communities. Some of them openly wondered whether it would not be better to take a step back and leave those communities as they are. Why should we intervene in a seemingly harmonious way of life? Would it not be better to protect those still unspoiled parts of our globe against the continued expansion of an urbanised Western lifestyle? Norberg-Hodge would probably answer something like, yes indeed, this is a step in the right direction but it is not enough; we also need a shift of direction in our own culture and to learn from traditional communities like that of Ladakh how to move towards rebuilding smaller-scale social and economic structures, structures that are in tune with Buddhist notions of interdependence and impermanence.

I will describe my own position in more detail further. For now it will suffice to say that I wholeheartedly agree with Norberg-Hodge's critique of the dominant modernisation paradigm in development and her insight that the real problem of development and globalisation, therefore, lies in so-called developed countries, not in underdeveloped countries. Indeed, the encounter of the West with other cultures has often been ruinous, and the problem of poverty in the developing world is chiefly the result of our own technocratic aid programmes, which arrogantly ignore the ethical and spiritual dimension of human life and destroy original indigenous social structures (cf. Strijbos 2011b, 2011c). The story of Ladakh is a shameful and sad illustration of what happened in many other places in the world. However, for me, although this is a valid criticism of the modernisation paradigm, it is not the same as saying that our current global system built on technology and corporate institutions is totally corrupt, or as thinking of places such as Ladakh as the last endangered small spots of heaven on earth. Such a romantic appraisal of traditional cultures leads to an extreme localism.[11] The reality of good and bad in human life and also in our contemporary globalising world is more arbitrary and mixed in my opinion. A shift to extreme localism, if this were at all possible, would, therefore, not be a helpful remedy for the problems of today and might

---

11. In view of their shared inspiration by Buddhism one can intuit that Norberg-Hodge's 'localism' shows a close resemblance to Schumacher's idea that 'small is beautiful'. Emphasising the embeddedness of man in nature, both authors fear that the larger man-made systems of modern society are detrimental to the quality of human life.

even make the situation worse. As Nelson (2011) has correctly noticed, Norberg-Hodge overlooks the damage that a one-sided emphasis on localism could do to some of the economically marginal areas of the world:

> In some places, where trade and tourism now support a larger population than a country could otherwise support. Too much emphasis on localism could, in some cases, cause harm. [...] Issues of scale and structure need to be addressed as we deal with economic life and global pain as it presents itself. But simply reacting to dogmatic neoliberal globalisation, marketization, and dreams of technological progress with an equally dogmatic localism, communalism, and idolization of 'the natural' causes us to miss opportunities. (p. 30)

To conclude: the solution to the problems of today is in my view not a radical shift to localism. What is needed is a fundamental rethinking of the relationship between the local and the global, and a search for practical strategies to interconnect the local and the global – which means that we need to move towards a global interdependency parallel to a process of fostering local interdependency. We do not need a return to traditional local interdependence, as Norberg-Hodge (1996b) suggests, but a shift from local dependence upon an apparently autonomous global system to a global interdependency of local societies and economies. At this point we can learn from a second stream of contemporary thinking that has emerged from the business world.

■ From the bottom up or from the inside out (Stuart L. Hart and others)

About a decade ago a discussion came up in the corporate sector about opportunities for business people to make a contribution in the global struggle against poverty. A new school of thought emerged under the leadership of C.K. Prahalad – who passed away in 2010 at a relatively young age of 68 – and his younger colleague Stuart L. Hart from Cornell University. These authors became widely known for their ground-breaking article 'The Fortune at the Bottom of the Pyramid' (2002) in which they articulated for the first time how the business world could be turned in the direction of serving the needs of the more than 4 billion poor at the bottom of the pyramid instead of just serving the interests of the privileged rich at the top. Further elaborating this idea, both business scholars published books that have become bestsellers: *The Fortune at the Bottom of the Pyramid: Eradicating Poverty Through Profits* by Prahalad ([2006] 2010) and *Capitalism at the Crossroads: Next Generation Business Strategies for a Post-Crisis World* by Hart ([2007] 2010). In the Preface of his book Prahalad (2006) raises the penetrating ethical question:

> Why is it that with all our technology, managerial know-how, and investment capacity, we are unable to make even a minor contribution to the problem of pervasive global poverty and disenfranchisement? *Why can't we create inclusive capitalism?* (p. xv; [author's added emphasis])

His answer is that we should commence by respecting the potential of the poor as allies in joint problem-solving and no longer regarding them as a burden. Such a shift in mentality among the stakeholders involved, such as firms, civil society organisations and local governments will open up new avenues for cooperation (Prahalad 2006):

> If we stop thinking of the poor as victims or as a burden and start recognising them as resilient and creative entrepreneurs and value-conscious consumers, a whole new world of opportunity will open up. (p. 1)

Both from an ethical and practical point of view there is indeed a need for more humility towards the poor – ethically because we have to accept other people in their own dignity, human creativity and responsibility, practically because such an acceptance will strengthen the cooperation and mobilise the involvement of the other people from their own perspective and motivation. In this respect, I, therefore, fully agree with Prahalad. Yet, I must confess that I am a bit allergic to the optimistic message that after all the development failures in the past decades, the business sector will now save the world and will provide us with the golden key to make poverty history. Hart (2010:19) sounds too optimistic in his conviction 'that business – more than either government or civil society – is uniquely equipped at this point in history to lead us towards a sustainable world in the years ahead'.

I do appreciate the practical directness of a business approach very much and I also accept the claim that business is not our enemy, but has the potential to play a unique role. However, is there not more? Do we really fathom the depth of the problems in our societies if we just operate on the practical level of business? We should not forget that 'technology' and 'economy', as noted above, are expressions of human culture, which means that they are concretisations of how people understand the world and themselves. Business and economy are, therefore, not just value-neutral and culture-free matters. In this respect, we can learn, as we saw, from Norberg-Hodge. Although I differ from her when she argues for a turn to the local as the key to a humane future for our endangered planet, I welcome her sharp eye for the crucial role of 'culture and religion' in development, urging us to take this into account. One does not have to agree with her Buddhist engagement, but one should at least admit that she makes a valuable contribution when she frankly elaborates on the dimensions of 'culture and religion' in her argument. The question now arises: in what way do Prahalad and Hart handle this dimension in their thesis about the 'bottom of the pyramid' and in the practical strategies they propose to involve the people of the communities?

Of these two authors Hart is more explicit regarding the role of culture, especially in the final part (of three) of his book *Capitalism at the Crossroads*. Part One is 'mapping the terrain' for a transformation to global sustainability as a catalyst for new business development. In this process of transformation we are faced with the challenge of bringing together three worlds that seem to be in collision; three interdependent economic spheres: the money economy of the modern world, the traditional economy of most developing countries and nature's economy of our natural environment.[12] 'In fact, the money and traditional economies are actually *embedded* in nature's economy because the former could not exist without the latter' (Hart 2010:58). Part Two develops strategies for business to take into account nature's economy and to move 'beyond greening', while Part Three, about 'becoming more indigenous', is in search of business strategies wishing to take account of traditional economies and society. For the purpose of this paper I shall focus on the last part.

Being aware that the dominant concepts of 'development' and 'modernisation' reflect a Western cultural bias, Hart opens Part Three by giving a short and sympathetic account of Norberg-Hodge's story of Ladakh. He concludes that although Old Ladakh was far from ideal, on balance, with all its flaws and limitations, it was probably more sustainable than the New Ladakh, both socially and environmentally. In the current situation of our societies, according to Hart, we should not make a choice regarding either one of them: neither are viable any more. The challenge for businesspeople today is to create a third way; to find a middle road between full-scale modernisation strategies on the one hand and returning to the old days on the other hand – that means to identify strategies that serve the real needs of those who have been bypassed and damaged by the modernisation policies of the past because they had no voice. Such a third way should, in Hart's view, break free from the planner's mentality and develop an approach that is based upon local knowledge, integrate the views of those on the periphery and engage stakeholders at the 'fringe' – 'the poor, the weak, the isolated, the disinterested and even the voices of other species with which we share the planet (through a human interpreter of course)' (Hart 2010:211).

The challenge for the business world, as Hart sees it, is thus to create a more inclusive form of economy, an enterprise that is built from the bottom up and combines the best of the two worlds that meet each other – 'the resources and technological capability of the formal economy and the indigenous knowledge, human face, and cultural understanding of the informal sector and love economy' (Hart 2010:223). Driving innovation from the bottom up or from the inside out is not an easy thing and Hart recognises that most recent corporate efforts continue to rely on a 'disembedded' way of thinking (Polanyi 2001; Sachs 2015) and still grapple with the issue of how to integrate

---

12. These three economies relate to the subtitle, 'Aligning business, earth and humanity', of the second edition of his book, and together they constitute also the contemporary triple P-creed in business: Profit (the money economy), People (the traditional economy) and Planet (nature's economy).

'economy' and 'society', thus how to re-embed innovation strategy into society and the community.[13] For Hart (2010), 'embeddedness' means:

> [C]o-creating a new business from the ground up, with the company as the key part of its foundation. Achieving this level of integration and trust requires an entirely new business process – one based on dialogue and joint action, not just market research data and sales targets. (p. 256)

Although he focuses on the bigger corporation, the multinationals, he believes that his thesis applies equally to Small and medium-sized enterprises and new ventures as well as large, established corporations.[14]

I found the reading of Hart extremely stimulating for my own thinking about the fundamental problems in business and the question of how we should shape economic support to the poor in developing countries. As I have said, he is aware of the cultural bias in the planner's mentality that ignores a good knowledge or understanding of the history, complexity or resources that exist in the Third World. Aiming to move beyond that mentality, Hart proposes a new approach that he labels as 'radical transactiveness' and regards as crucial to the development of a more indigenous form of enterprise.[15] The approach is 'radical' because it (Hart 2010):

> [F]ocuses on gaining access to stakeholders previously considered extreme or fringe [...] 'transactive' because it seeks to engage the firm in a two-way dialogue with stakeholders so that each influences and is influenced by the other. (p. 211)

I shall not go into the technical details of the third way as elaborated by Hart. The fundamental question can be raised whether 'radical transactiveness' is radical enough. Indeed, in my view it is of vital importance that we start listening to all stakeholders in business and are really open to learn from them. It is necessary to be aware of the cultural bias in the mentality of the scientific planner that presumes that (s)he knows best, but one should also become aware of the underlying human and cultural self-understanding in the idea of planning as such. It is a great idea, I believe, to go to the bottom of the pyramid for the renewal of entrepreneurship. But I should like to ask, slightly provocatively, what is the fortune that one hopes to find at the bottom of the pyramid, and whom will the discovery benefit? There is nothing wrong with it when Prahalad and Hart suggest that a material fortune can be explored at the bottom by expanding the market. However, I believe that something more is needed that we easily overlook in business strategies for a post-crisis world, namely, the spiritual side of life and business. I should like to suggest that, together with finding access to the market at the 'bottom of the pyramid',

---

13. A first articulation of Hart's ideas about the notion of re-embedding and innovation strategy was presented in a co-authored article on the topic: Simanis and Hart (2009).

14. Personal communication, 02 February 2011.

15. The idea of 'radical transactiveness' is borrowed from Friedmann (1973).

we should try to reconnect with the spiritual roots at the 'bottom of life' that determine our basic choices. I do not want to romanticise the situation of poverty and human misery – it can be and it is usually ugly – but the poor often have something to offer that the rich have lost and that they desperately need: a renewed self-understanding of human existence and how we should live together. I shall return to this matter in the following section, which is about a paradigm for the IIDE research, but first we need to look for a moment at another stream of thought that also came up as a reaction to the current situation of 'economy' and 'society' and the role of the business world.

■ From profit-maximising business to social business (Muhammad Yunus and others)

Around 2003 I became acquainted with social entrepreneurship as an emerging field of action and study. At that time, I spoke with some people with vast experience in business who as social investors wanted to sponsor meaningful initiatives for economic assistance to the poor. The central idea was to create possibilities for cross-fertilisation between the university with its core tasks of research and teaching and external parties who want to support innovative practices for providing economic assistance to the poor. This finally resulted in the establishment of the MDF with the idea to link research and teaching to concrete social entrepreneurial initiatives. Here I will discuss some general ideas underlying social entrepreneurship as a new field of study and action. It is not my intention, nor is it possible to provide a detailed overview and critical account of the literature. Instead I will focus on Muhammad Yunus, the well-known winner of the 2006 Nobel Peace Prize for his work for the poor in the Grameen Bank, and the vision that he articulated on the business world and the future of capitalism.[16]

The central problem for which Yunus has passionately sought a solution in his life and work is articulated in the main title of his book, *Creating a World Without Poverty: Social Business and the Future of Capitalism* (2007). As a small part of the world marches towards ever greater prosperity, why have so many been left behind? The negative impact of single-track capitalism is visible in many ways every day, such as exploiting cheap labour in poor countries (including child labour), pollution of the environment and deceptive marketing and advertising that promote harmful or unnecessary products. How should we address these problems? Many people believe that if the free market cannot solve the large-scale social problems of our age we should turn to the government and enforce rules that control and limit capitalism. Yunus agrees with that, and says that governments must indeed do their part to help

---

16. For further reading about social entrepreneurship, I refer to Bornstein and Davis (2010) for a first introduction and to Nicholls (2006) for a more scholarly presentation.

alleviate our worst problems, but it is clear that governments alone cannot do it. Many people, therefore, put their trust in non-profit organisations, NGOs and charitable foundations. Although this sector can do a lot of good work, given the very nature of these organisations they cannot be expected to solve the world's social ills.

What about multilateral institutions like the World Bank that have the elimination of poverty as their overarching goal? Like many others, Yunus is very critical of the development elite represented by such organisations, because they treat the poor as objects, and in this frame of mind they miss the tremendous potential of the poor as actors in their own right. The key to solve the problem of poverty is in the hands of the business world. The movement for corporate social responsibility (CSR) comes with good intentions, but they are not radical enough, because it leaves business life as it is. The fundamental problem that we have to tackle, according to Yunus (2007:17), 'lies with the very nature of business. Even more profoundly, it lies with the concept of business that is at the centre of capitalism'. The subtitle of his book – *Social Business and the Future of Capitalism* – therefore conveys the message that there is a need for a renewal of capitalism along with the rise of a new kind of business, the social business.

We should notice that Yunus is thus not opposing capitalism and the concept of the free market. His point is that capitalism is, as he says, just a 'half-developed structure' because the underlying concept of the free market is based on a too-narrow understanding of human nature. In conventional business theory people are seen as one-dimensional beings and the mission of the so-called entrepreneur is to maximise financial profit. This fails to capture the essence of what it means to be human. Nevertheless, the reality contradicts the theory. In real life people are multi-dimensional and seek to express the fact that in economic and business life as they do in other areas as well. This is why the new concept of social business enters the scene. This concept enables us to steer capitalism in a more humane direction in which 'not every business should be bound to serve the single objective of profit maximization' (Yunus 2007:19). Social business stays within the landscape of business because it cannot incur losses indefinitely. The difference is that the profit does not go to the investors but is reinvested in the business.

In the literature the terms 'social business' and 'social enterprise' are often used interchangeably. According to Yunus, however, a social enterprise is something different. For instance, a leading foundation in the social-entrepreneurship movement, the Ashoka Foundation, which was founded in 1980 by Bill Drayton in Washington DC, defines social entrepreneurs as (Ashoka n.d.):

> [/]ndividuals with innovative solutions to society's most pressing social problems. They are ambitious and persistent, tackling major social issues and offering new ideas for wide-scale change. Rather than leaving societal needs to the government

or business sectors, social entrepreneurs find what is not working and solve the problem by changing the system, spreading the solution, and persuading entire societies to take new leaps.[17] (n.p.)

Social entrepreneurship is thus a very broad idea that includes any innovative initiative to help people. In other words, in Yunus' view, all those who run a social business are social entrepreneurs, but not all social entrepreneurs are engaged in social business.

In my discussion of Hart and Prahalad, I made a critical comment about the need to take into account in business life, and also in the conceptualisation of the business firm the spiritual side of people. More than these authors, Yunus seems to be aware of the importance of this when he emphatically points to the multi-dimensional nature of humans; to their personal emotions, beliefs and cultural patterns. At this point, Yunus' thinking shows a clear affinity with that of T.P. Van der Kooy, a leading Dutch economist who worked at the Vrije Universiteit in Amsterdam in the 1950s. In an essay in which he develops some thoughts about 'Religion and society', Van der Kooy (1953) notes that a variety of norms – social, cultural, juridical, aesthetic and others – provide guidance for human action and have to be satisfied simultaneously. In his view, religion holds a key position in the multi-dimensional nature of human action. Religion gives human action a total, integral character. Directing action to the one God, the creator of the world, gives human life coherence, stability and harmony. However, people can also seek their orientation elsewhere and derive norms from idols. It seems that it is in the serving of the idols of our secular lives that the deepest problems of today come to the surface. If this is true, it is vain to expect that the business world and entrepreneurship can solve the problem of poverty.

■ On the disclosure of society

The reintegration of technology and economy implies different things for the different schools of thought and authors that have been discussed. Let me try to clarify this in light of the distinction that I made elsewhere among three fundamentally different approaches in development that I termed the instrumental-technical, participative-communicative and intercultural-disclosive approaches (Strijbos 2011c).

Facing the problems of our age, for Norberg-Hodge and others the way forward is to break with the trend of globalisation in which the 'developed world' imposes its modernisation programme on the 'developing world'. In their view we should return to a more locally focused world that cherishes the traditions and values of the old days. They search for the separate development

---

17. What is a social entrepreneur? See http://www.ashoka.org/social_entrepreneur

of cultures and societies alongside one another. Not 'become like us', but 'remain who you are and as you are' seems to be the credo of Norberg-Hodge and others. Prahalad, Hart and others point us in another direction. They agree that modernisation as such is not the solution but the cause of the problem of poverty. Therefore, they seek a way out in turning to the bottom of the pyramid and aim to make use of the potential of the poor themselves to create wealth for all. The mental attitude of this school of thought is one of humility and a willingness to learn. They reject an instrumental-technical approach and advocate a participative-communicative approach in enterprise development. The idea is that one should live in harmony with the poor and in this way learn how to co-create innovative business solutions in a so-called bottom-up process. The message is thus: 'you can remain who you are but together we will learn and succeed in dragging you into the framework of the global market'. Yunus and the social enterprise movement propagate another kind of business, which is social business or social enterprise. They believe that this new kind of business, next to the profit-maximising corporations of the current economy, provides the key to make poverty history. What strikes me is that in Yunus' view, the existing shape of capitalism is a 'half-developed structure'. Like the proponents of the participative-communicative approach he believes in the potential of the poor. The solution of the problem of poverty for Yunus, however, is not to drag the poor into the existing structure of capitalism, but to expand capitalism by launching the idea of social business.

These three schools of thought all oppose rigid modernisation programmes and are to a greater or lesser extent aware of the importance of 'culture and religion' to the shaping of economy and society. I found good elements in each of them that I want to acknowledge, but it seems to me that they share a common weak point that has remained unnoticed. The question for me is why one needs to regard 'culture and religion' and its broad diversity as a static given in development and enterprise development. Are they not open to a future in which humanity may discover new horizons? In answering this question in the affirmative I should like to introduce here the notion of disclosure that is also referred to in Chapter 10 of this book.

Disclosure, a dynamic process as we find it in living nature, is a term that refers to given structures and qualities that we should respect in our human interventions. What holds for the living world is in a particular way also valid for human affairs. Fundamental to the idea of disclosure, therefore, is the mindset that we do not construct our world out of nothing and are not its owners. Fundamental is that we are strongly aware that the world is given to humankind and humankind is given to the world. Because we live in such an *a priori* relationship we also should be aware that people and cultures are given to one another. In the encounter between peoples and cultures, we are not dealing with unchanging essences, nor with amorphous material. In short, the credo of the intercultural-disclosive approach is not 'become like us' or 'remain who you are', but 'have an openness to a process in which all those who are involved grow in human self-understanding and change together'.

■ Conclusion

What does this all mean to someone like David, whom we met at the beginning of this chapter? What has the notion of disclosure of society to do with his life, his situation of poverty and that of his household and the broader community of QwaQwa? What does it mean for economic support and the fostering of entrepreneurship as a normative social practice in such an environment, where different cultures encounter one another? We will suffice here with a single comment. First of all, we need to acknowledge the fact that entrepreneurship and economy are manifestations of human culture and express specific values. Economic support is, therefore, more than a technical affair. It implies a reciprocal learning process in which each participant is prepared to change. Secondly, disclosure requires the framing of relationships in which each party accepts its own responsibility and the accountability to the other party. In the third instance, a disclosive approach should take into account the specific qualities, resources and abilities that people and communities have. Finally, those who provide assistance in a disclosive approach should be aware that finding norms for a specific situation is not simply a matter of theory and thinking but usually requires a process of learning by doing in practice.

PART 1
Issues

Chapter 3

Energy transition challenges in South Africa: A study of residential coal use practices

Kristy Langerman
Department of Geography, Environmental Management and Energy Studies,
Faculty of Science, University of Johannesburg,
Johannesburg, South Africa

Farina Lindeque
Department of Geography and Environmental Studies,
Faculty of Science and Agriculture, University of Limpopo,
Mankweng, South Africa

Montagu Murray[a,b]
[a]The NOVA Institute,
Pretoria, South Africa
[b]Department of Religion Studies, Faculty of Theology and Religion,
University of Pretoria, Pretoria, South Africa

Christiaan Pauw[a,b]
[a]The NOVA Institute,
Pretoria, South Africa
[b]Department of Religion Studies, Faculty of Theology and Religion,
University of Pretoria, Pretoria, South Africa

How to cite: Langerman, K., Lindeque, F., Murray, M. & Pauw, C., 2021, 'Energy transition challenges in South Africa: A study of residential coal use practices', in A.S. Van Niekerk & S. Strijbos (eds.), *We cannot continue like this: Facing modernity in Africa and the West*, pp. 51–72, AOSIS, Cape Town. https://doi.org/10.4102/aosis.2021.BK283.03

■ Introduction

Access to affordable, clean and modern energy sources is key to the socio-economic development of any nation and is included as Goal 7 of the United Nations SDGs. Rapid progress towards this goal has been made – the proportion of the global population with access to electricity has increased steadily from 83% in 2010, to 89% in 2017 (United Nations 2019). In most developing regions, access to electricity does not mean an end to energy poverty. Many households are unable to afford electricity as their only energy source, and rely on multiple fuels to meet their energy needs (Balmer 2007; Naidoo, Piketh & Curtis 2014). This contradicts the 'energy ladder' model that assumes a linear transition from traditional energy carriers (e.g. wood, dung and crop waste), to transitional carriers and technologies (e.g. coal and paraffin) to modern energy carriers and technologies (e.g. electricity and gas). Households more often use the 'energy stacking' approach, choosing a combination of carriers and technologies at all levels of the energy ladder, depending on their preferences, fuel availability and affordability, and needs at a specific time (Israel-Akinbo, Snowball & Fraser 2018).

Biomass (e.g. wood, dung or other agricultural residue) is the most widely used solid fuel source globally, with residential coal use mainly confined to regions where it is mined and easily accessible (Hendryx, Zullig & Luo 2020). Coal as a fuel source is rarely used only for cooking purposes, but rather as the main source of fuel in regions where there is a simultaneous need for cooking and space heating. The use of coal for residential heating was widespread for centuries, but has steadily declined in most of the developed world (Kerimray et al. 2017). Today, the negative impacts of emissions from residential coal use on public health and the environment are well understood. Residential coal use dropped worldwide by 51% between 1990 and 2014, especially in developed regions and China (Kerimray et al. 2017). Despite this significant decrease, residential coal use is still prevalent in Asia (China, Kazakhstan, Mongolia, Republic of Korea), Eastern Europe (Czech Republic, Poland), Ireland and South Africa. In 2014, these countries represented 21% of the world's population, but accounted for 86% of the global residential coal consumption (Kerimray et al. 2017).

Emissions from residential coal and other solid fuel burning not only expose people to polluted indoor air but also expose people to polluted air in the environment near the household, where individuals spend most of their time (Smith et al. 2014). In contrast with wood, residential coal burning is a source of SO_2 and NOx (4% of SO_2 and 1% of NOx globally; WHO 2015). Toxic substances, particularly volatile organic compounds, and elements like mercury, lead, fluorine, arsenic and selenium, are also released into the air when coal is burnt. The WHO indoor air quality guidelines (World Health Organization 2014) strongly discourage the residential use of raw coal, based on evidence that indoor emissions from residential coal use are carcinogenic to humans (IARC 2010).

In the household environment, the most vulnerable populations include pregnant women, infants, young children and the elderly. Exposure to toxic air in the prenatal and early postnatal life stages can permanently alter organ function, resulting in an increased likelihood of acute or chronic diseases surfacing at any life stage, from infancy to old age (Rollin 2017). Strong evidence also exists to link exposure to household air pollution to severe and fatal acute lower respiratory infections in children under 5 years of age (Bruce et al. 2015). Health impacts of adult exposure to household air pollution include chronic obstructive pulmonary disease, lung cancer, cataracts, ischemic heart disease, stroke and cardiovascular disease (Bruce et al. 2015; Hendryx et al. 2020; Pope et al. 2014). Worldwide the major burden of these negative health impacts falls on the poor, increasing health inequities in already vulnerable populations (WHO 2015).

Of all the environments in South Africa, ambient concentrations of particulate matter are highest in solid fuel using areas (Hersey et al. 2015). Moreover, particulate matter levels can be almost twice as high indoors than outdoors in winter (Adesina et al. 2020; Wernecke et al. 2015).

Numerous initiatives to phase out residential coal use have been implemented, usually motivated by the harmful health effects of air pollutants released when coal is burnt. However, households that use coal usually have a choice of several energy carriers, and choose to continue to use coal. Coal use persists even in areas that have been electrified. Coal is abandoned by households only when they are sufficiently affluent to afford good quality housing and electrical appliances, and to spend a fair amount of money on electricity or gas. We assert that residential coal use needs to be understood as a satisfier of several fundamental human needs (Max-Neef 1991), in order to successfully design interventions to transition households away from coal use.

In this chapter, we address the question of where residential coal use still occurs in South Africa, and how the prevalence of residential coal use has changed in the last 15 years or so. Coal use practices are examined to understand the utility gained from coal use, and factors that influence when and how much coal is used. We scrutinise the reasons for the persistence of coal use, even when it is such a dirty fuel and has been decisively demonstrated to harm health. Our premise is that a full understanding of the utility provided by coal and how it affects the quality of life of the people using it can be used to design social policies and interventions to accelerate the transition away from coal to cleaner energy carriers more effectively.

In order to address these objectives, areas in South Africa where coal is used for residential heating or cooking purposes are identified, and trends in the proportion of households using coal are analysed on a provincial and local (suburb or village) scale. Coal-using practices are investigated using information collected in several studies related to the reduction of residential coal use implemented by the NOVA Institute on the South African Highveld over the last decade. Insights into the reasons for continued coal use are obtained from focus group interviews conducted with members of two coal-using communities in Mpumalanga. As the need for space heating is one of the main drivers for residential coal use, we examine housing conditions and the satisfaction of residents with their housing in the five coal-using communities, to determine the role that poor-quality housing plays in creating the demand for coal. Finally, we reflect on the personal, geographical and societal factors that affect decision-making and behaviour resulting in a person using coal, and how social policies and interventions can be informed by these factors.

■ Status quo of residential coal use in South Africa

Various factors influence household energy choices in South Africa. Rural/urban location, climatic conditions, quality of housing and proximity to coalfields all influence the availability, choice and amount of fuel burned. Rural households are typically more reliant on biomass fuels (mostly collected firewood) than those living in urban or peri-urban environments (Barnes et al. 2009; Wright & Diab 2011).

Geographical pattern of coal use

Residential coal use is not very high at the national level but remains prominent in many low-income urban and peri-urban settlements around South African coalfields. Figure 3.1 shows the areas in South Africa where more than 5% of households used coal as a preferred energy source in 2011. Areas are clustered around operating and abandoned coal mines in Mpumalanga, Gauteng, Free State and KwaZulu-Natal, with smaller clusters scattered in the Eastern Cape, Northern Cape, Limpopo and North West provinces. In the northern parts of Limpopo province, residential coal use is low despite the presence of active coal mines, because of a warmer climate, availability of wood and little need for space heating. Wood remains the preferred alternative fuel source for cooking in Limpopo (StatsSA 2019).

The Highveld region of South Africa is an extensive interior plateau. The Highveld and Witbank coalfields in this region account for approximately 75% of South Africa's total coal production (Department of Energy 2016). Because of the proximity to these rich coalfields, industrial activities and coal-powered electricity generation are also concentrated in this region, resulting in very

Chapter 3

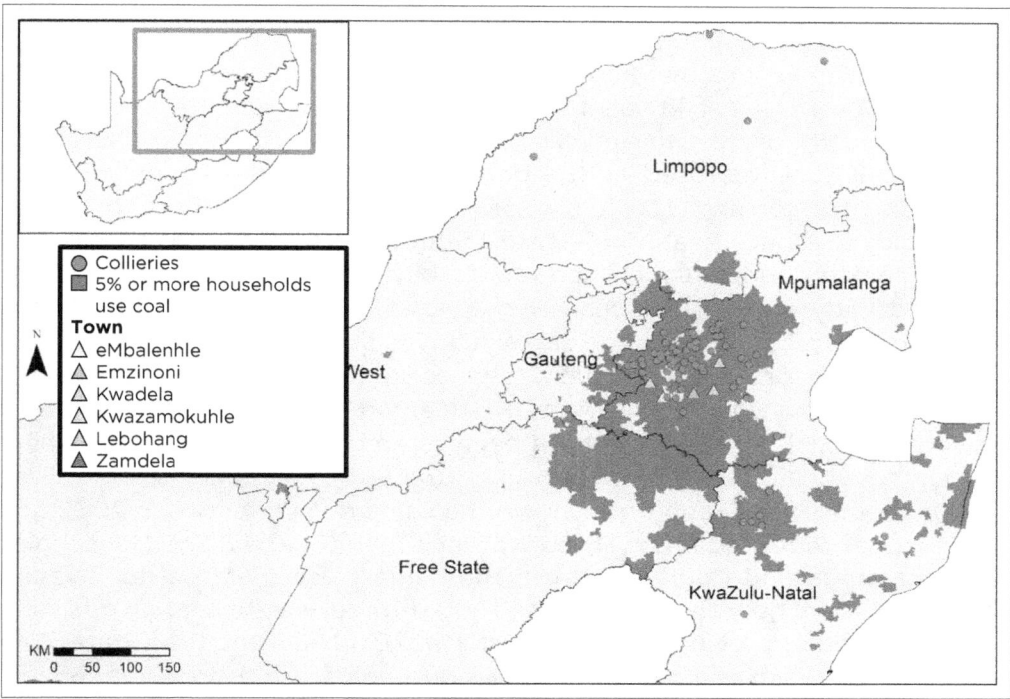

FIGURE 3.1: Map of regions in South Africa where more than 5% of households use coal as an energy source (from Census 2011) and active coal mines.

poor air quality that often exceeds National Ambient Air Quality Standards aimed at protecting public health (Feig et al. 2019; Govender & Sivakumar 2019). Meteorological conditions over the Highveld further exacerbate poor air quality, because of the prevalence of a subtropical high that leads to weak pressure gradients and the formation of inversion layers that limit the vertical dilution of pollutants (Wenig et al. 2003). These inversions are especially prevalent in the winter months, when low temperatures increase the demand for heating.

As an economic hub, large parts of the region are already densely populated and continue to attract both international and internal migrants looking for employment and other opportunities (Statistics South Africa 2015). As in the rest of Africa, the highest rates of urban growth are occurring in areas of existing poverty where access to basic services and decent housing are a challenge. Historical housing backlogs, continued urbanisation, immigration and natural population increase make meeting the growing demand for housing and basic services even more challenging. This can lead to an increase in solid fuel burning households in a region where air quality is already very poor (Mathee & Wright 2014).

National trends in residential coal use

Despite the challenges mentioned above, declining national residential coal use trends over the last 18 years are a reason for optimism. Residential coal use has steadily decreased annually as household electrification increased, and in 2018 coal was used as the primary energy carrier by only 1.2% of households for cooking, 1.0% of households for water heating and 1.6% of households for space heating (Statistics South Africa 2019). Residential coal use for cooking purposes declined rapidly between 2002 and 2013 and has remained fairly stable since then (Figure 3.2a). Electricity is currently the preferred energy source for cooking, with 77% of South African households using electricity for cooking in 2018 (Statistics South Africa 2019). Mpumalanga remains the province with the highest percentage of households using coal for cooking (3.0%), while there have been steep declines in provinces where coal use for cooking used to be prevalent (Gauteng, KwaZulu-Natal and Free State). Coal use for heating has shown the same decline between 2002 and 2013 and has remained relatively stable since then (Figure 3.2b). Households in Mpumalanga and Gauteng remain the highest users of coal for heating (7.9% and 1.4% of households, respectively), with coal use for heating declining over time in other provinces (North West, KwaZulu-Natal and Free State). The difference between the percentage of households using coal for cooking (0.2%) and heating (1.4%) in Gauteng highlights the important role of climatic conditions and the need for space heating in household energy choices.

Local trends in residential coal use

Considering the localised nature of residential coal use in South Africa, a better understanding of trends in local contexts is needed to truly understand changes in residential coal use. We have analysed here a series of 630 surveys conducted by the NOVA Institute in 181 distinct coal-using sub places located in 14 local municipalities (in five district municipalities and one metropolitan area), between 2009 and 2018. Sub places are delineated by Statistics South Africa and are suburbs, or zones of towns, wards or informal settlements. Only surveys of at least 20 households per subplace are included. For each sub place survey, we calculated the proportion of coal users and the associated confidence interval. We then calculated the year-on-year rate of change in the proportion of coal-using households in each sub place. We also analysed trends in the proportion of coal-using households at the 90% level of significance. The resulting summarised dataset contains the geometric mean and geometric standard deviation for each sub place group (i.e. all years measured for each subplace), as well as the p-value for the test for trend in proportions. Based on this, the trend for each sub place was categorised as either flat (no statistically significant trend), increasing or decreasing. These results were aggregated by district municipality.

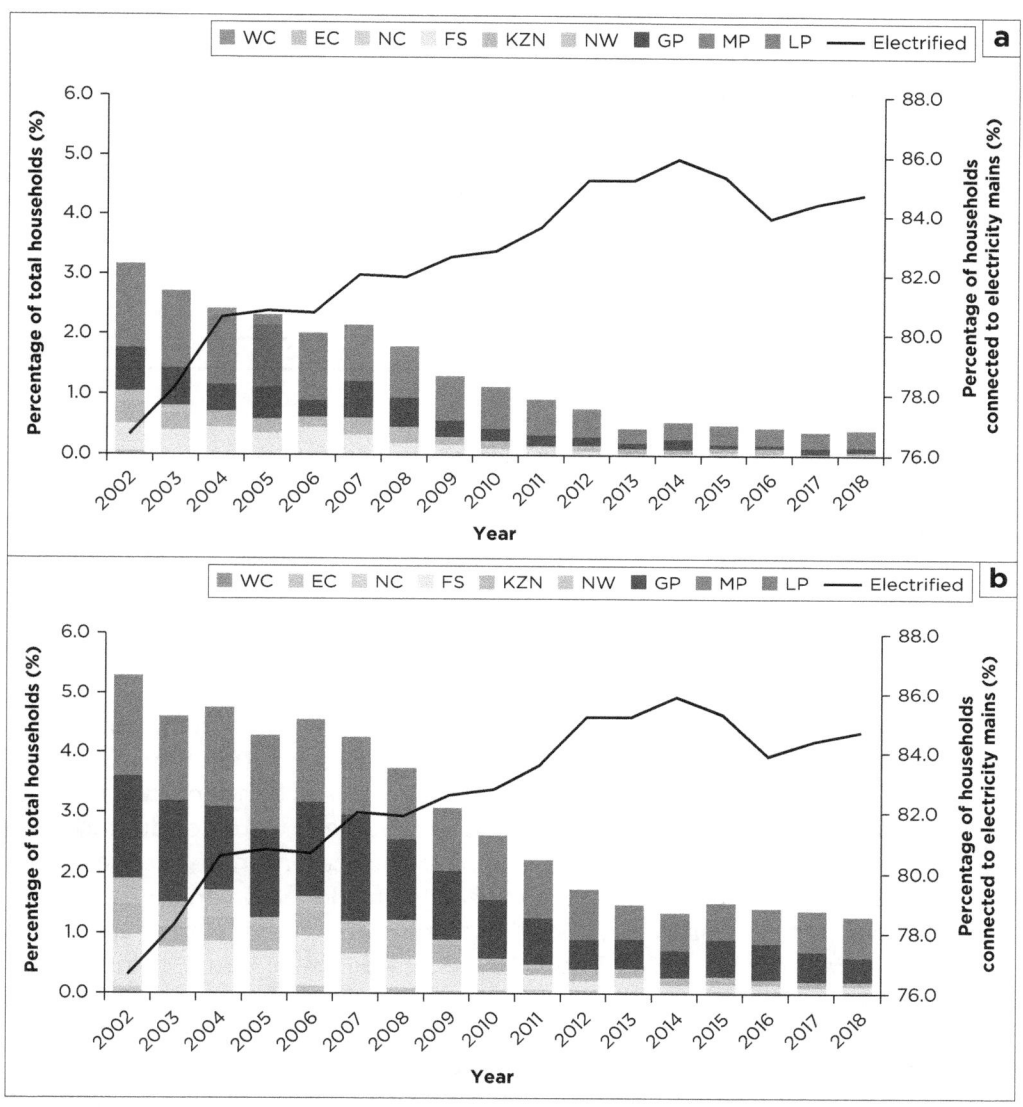

Source: Compiled from Statistics South Africa (2019).
FIGURE 3.2: Percentage of households connected to electricity mains per province (2002–2018) and households using coal for cooking (a) and heating (b).

In coal-using areas of South Africa between 2009 and 2018, no significant trend was detected in the majority (53.9%) of the 181 sub places surveyed. In 11.1% of sub places, an increasing trend was detected. In 35.9% of sub places, coal use declined over the observed period (Table 3.1).

There is a marked difference in trends between regions. Coal use declined rapidly and rather uniformly in South Gauteng, the Vaal Triangle and the northern Free State but much less so in the traditional heartland of coal use in

TABLE 3.1: Residential coal use trends in six district municipalities in coal-using areas of South Africa between 2009 and 2018, based on data collected in 630 household surveys.

District municipality	Province	Decrease (no. of sub places)	Flat (no. of sub places)	Increase (no. of sub places)
Ekurhuleni Metro	Gauteng	16 (26.67%)	36 (60.00%)	8 (13.33%)
Fezile Dabi	Free State	1 (50.00%)	1 (50.00%)	0 (0.00%)
Gert Sibande	Mpumalanga	14 (28.57%)	31 (63.27%)	4 (8.16%)
Nkangala	Mpumalanga	9 (31.03%)	15 (51.72%)	5 (17.24%)
Sedibeng	Gauteng	10 (71.43%)	4 (28.57%)	0 (0.00%)
Thabo Mofutsanyane	Free State	15 (55.56%)	9 (33.33%)	3 (11.11%)
Total		**65 (35.9%)**	**96 (53.0%)**	**20 (11.1%)**

South Africa, Mpumalanga (Gert Sibande, Nkangala and the north-eastern parts of Ekurhuleni). These findings reiterate the importance of fuel availability in household energy choices. A greater in-depth analysis of residential coal use practices in these areas is discussed in subsequent sections of this document.

■ Coal use practices

Insights into how and when coal is burnt are obtained from General Household Surveys conducted in five coal-using communities on the South African Highveld in 2013 and 2016, and Detailed Energy Surveys conducted in three of these communities in 2016. General Household Surveys were conducted from August to October 2013 in 1085 households in four communities at the centre of the coal-using region on the South African Highveld: eMbalenhle, Lebohang and eMzinoni in the Govan Mbeki Local Municipality and Kwadela in Msukaligwa Local Municipality (Figure 3.1). These towns are all low-income communities that originated as townships adjacent to Secunda, Bethal, Leandra and Davel, respectively. In June–August 2016, General Household Surveys were conducted in 751 households in Zamdela, a low-income community near Sasolburg in the northern Free State. Zamdela provides an interesting comparison with the other towns because it is on the periphery of the coal-using region and wood, rather than coal, is the primary solid fuel used. The surveys were conducted by fieldworkers who were recruited from within the study region and provided with intensive theoretical and practical training. The population and household size, location and number of households surveyed in each of the communities are shown in Table 3.2. The General Household Survey results have a confidence level of 95% and a margin of error of 5%.

The general survey information was supplemented with Detailed Energy Surveys conducted in 675 households in eMbalenhle, Lebohang and Zamdela between July and October 2016. As part of this initiative, temperature sensors

TABLE 3.2: The population, location and number of households that participated in the General Household Surveys for the five low-income, coal-using communities on the South African Highveld.

Town	Population (year)	No. of households (year)	No. of households surveyed	Local municipality	District municipality	Province
eMbalenhle	125 213 (2013)	37 059 (2013)	559	Govan Mbeki	Gert Sibande	Mpumalanga
Lebohang	34 778 (2013)	9943 (2013)	198	Govan Mbeki	Gert Sibande	Mpumalanga
eMzinoni	43 821 (2013)	11 094 (2013)	185	Govan Mbeki	Gert Sibande	Mpumalanga
KwaDela	3624 (2013)	1148 (2013)	143	Msukaligwa	Gert Sibande	Mpumalanga
Zamdela	98 902 (2016)	30 284 (2016)	751	Metsimaholo	Fezile Dabi	Free State

were fitted close to the chimneys of 13 households in eMbalenhle (16 July 2016–28 February 2017) and Zamdela (20 July–06 October 2016) to monitor the frequency of fires made.

It was found that between 36% and 66% of households in the Mpumalanga communities use coal for heating (Table 3.3). The proportion of coal-using households is much lower in Zamdela (10% in 2016), because it is on the periphery of the coal-using region.

The numbers in brackets are the number of household respondents. Coal-using households are identified based on all the energy carriers that households reported using for heating.

The majority of coal-using households in Mpumalanga use cast iron stoves and, to a lesser extent welded stoves, which are usually made by local entrepreneurs and have poor burning efficiency (Table 3.3). Mbaulas (braziers), which have poor burning efficiency, are fortunately not widely used at all in Mpumalanga. In contrast, the majority of coal-using households in Zamdela (71%) use a welded stove, and mbaulas are still used by a substantial proportion (14%) of households. Coal fires are typically lit using the traditional or bottom-up method. Evidence of previous Basa Njengo Magogo roll-outs (initiatives to teach people to make fires using the top-down method, which uses less fuel and produces significantly less smoke) is seen in eMalahleni and eMzinoni, where 14% and 17% of households, respectively, use the top-down method.

Most households in Mpumalanga buy coal in a big bag, while in Zamdela coal is generally bought in a small bag, and to a lesser extent in a tin (Table 3.3). Interestingly, there is one reported case in Zamdela of a household making their own coal out of coal dust and clay. The median price for a big bag of coal in 2013 was R90. Most households buy coal on an ad hoc (49% of total households) or monthly basis (41%), with only a few buying it every fortnight (2%) or weekly (7%).

TABLE 3.3: Proportion of coal users, coal buying formats, device types and ignition method in eMalahleni, Lebohang and eMzinoni in Mpumalanga and Zamdela in the northern Free State.

Category	Sub-category	eMbalenhle 2013	Lebohang 2013	eMzinoni 2013	Kwadela 2013	eMbalenhle 2016	Lebohang 2016	Zamdela 2016
Coal-using	Yes	35.6% (199)	53.5% (106)	63.2% (117)	65.9% (91)	33.2% (77)	49.3% (109)	9.5% (21)
	No	64.4% (360)	46.5% (92)	36.8% (68)	34.1% (47)	66.8% (155)	50.7% (112)	90.5% (201)
Format	Big bag	73.9%	97.2%	90.6%	98.9%	94.8%	89.9%	0.0%
	Small bag	16.6%	0.9%	9.4%	0.0%	3.9%	8.3%	81.0%
	Tin	5.0%	1.9%	0.0%	1.1%	1.3%	0.9%	14.3%
	Large drum	2.5%	0.0%	0.0%	0.0%	-	-	-
	Self-made coal	-	-	-	-	0.0%	0.0%	4.8%
	Other	2.0%	0.0%	0.0%	0.0%	0.0%	0.9%	0.0%
Device	Cast iron stove	52.3%	50.0%	84.6%	82.4%	49.4%	55.0%	14.3%
	Welded stove	44.7%	50.0%	13.7%	15.4%	49.4%	45.0%	71.4%
	Mbaula	2.5%	0.0%	0.9%	0.0%	1.3%	0.0%	14.3%
Ignition method	BnM/top-down	14.1%	0.0%	17.1%	0.0%	-	-	-
	Traditional/bottom-up	78.4%	100.0%	82.9%	100.0%	-	-	-
	Hybrid or 50/50 method	7.5%	0.0%	0.0%	0.0%	-	-	-
Purchase frequency	As needed	62.3%	48.1%	29.1%	47.3%	-	-	-
	Monthly	27.1%	46.2%	65.0%	36.3%	-	-	-
	Fortnightly	1.5%	2.8%	1.7%	2.2%	-	-	-
	Weekly	8.5%	2.8%	3.4%	14.3%	-	-	-
	Other	0.5%	0.0%	0.9%	0.0%	-	-	-

The proportion of households that use coal in summer is dramatically lower than that for winter in all towns (Table 3.4). In Lebohang and Zamdela, the proportion of households that use coal in summer drops to less than 5%. In both eMbalenhle and Zamdela, the average monthly household consumption drops to roughly half of the average monthly winter consumption.

Coal is used for cooking, space heating and water heating, very often simultaneously. The peak coal use hours coincide with hours before mealtimes, before warm water is needed for washing and especially those times when space heating is needed. This means that a morning and afternoon peak in coal use is typically expected. The reported frequency of fires is shown in Figure 3.3. The morning ignition peak starts slowly after 04:00 and increases after 05:00 to reach its peak after 06:00 and then decreases rapidly. A slight increase in the frequency of ignitions is reported around midday. The evening peak starts with a sharp increase in ignitions after 16:00 continuing with decreasing frequencies until about 18:30.

TABLE 3.4: Seasonal differences in residential coal consumption (kg) in eMbalenhle, Lebohang and Zamdela in 2016.

Location	Winter		Summer	
	Coal users (% of total households)	Monthly consumption (kg)	Coal users (% of total households)	Monthly consumption (kg)
eMbalenhle	33.2	220.4	11.2	92.3
Lebohang	49.3	207.2	2.3	220.4
Zamdela	9.5	112.45	3.3	50.0

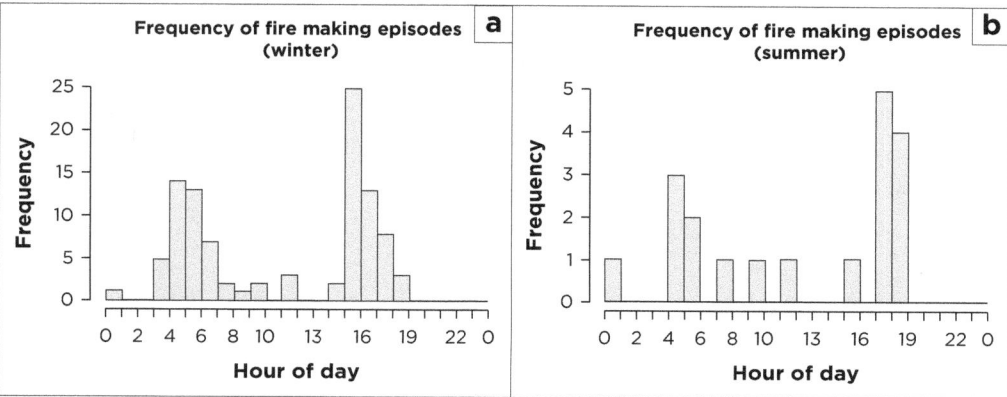

FIGURE 3.3: The frequency of fire making episodes in (a) winter and (b) summer measured in 19 households in eMbalenhle and Zamdela between July 2016 and February 2018.

The characteristics of the coal burnt by households is highly variable, even within one town. Table 3.5 shows the calorific value, ash content and sulphur content of 25 coal samples collected from five different coal merchants in KwaZamokuhle, Mpumalanga, in winter 2015 (five samples per merchant). It is generally assumed that lower quality coal is used by households, but as can be seen by the coal sold by merchants 1 and 3 in particular, that is not always the case. As a reference, the thermal coal used by Eskom's coal-fired power stations in South Africa in 2018/2019 had an average calorific value of 19.2 MJ/kg and average ash content of 31.0% (Eskom 2019).

Despite the prevalence of coal use in low-income communities on the Highveld, electricity is the most popular energy carrier in all the study communities, although there are differences in each town in the way households stack fuels. The area of each circle in the Venn diagrams in Figure 3.4 is proportional to the number of respondents who indicated that they use a particular energy carrier. Coal-burning households in eMbalenhle and Lebohang are also likely to use wood, probably because wood is used to ignite the coal. The pattern of concurrent coal and wood use does not hold for Zamdela, where the majority of wood-using households do not use coal.

Energy transition challenges in South Africa: A study of residential coal use practices

TABLE 3.5: Characteristics of coal sold by five coal merchants in KwaZamokuhle, Mpumalanga, in winter 2015.

Merchant number	Calorific value (MJ/kg, as received)	Ash content (%m/m, air dried)	Total sulphur (%m/m, as received)
1	28.8 (28.1-29.6)	13.2 (11.9-15.0)	0.55 (0.43-0.72)
2	22.4 (20.6-23.6)	31.9 (29.5-34.8)	1.11 (0.37-1.55)
3	27.2 (27.0-27.7)	16.2 (15.1-16.7)	1.29 (0.19-2.58)
4	23.8 (23.1-24.6)	25.0 (22.8-26.4)	0.79 (0.20-1.89)
5	25.7 (21.1-28.6)	20.9 (12.4-31.8)	0.81 (0.17-0.56)

Five samples were collected per merchant. Average, minimum and maximum values are given.

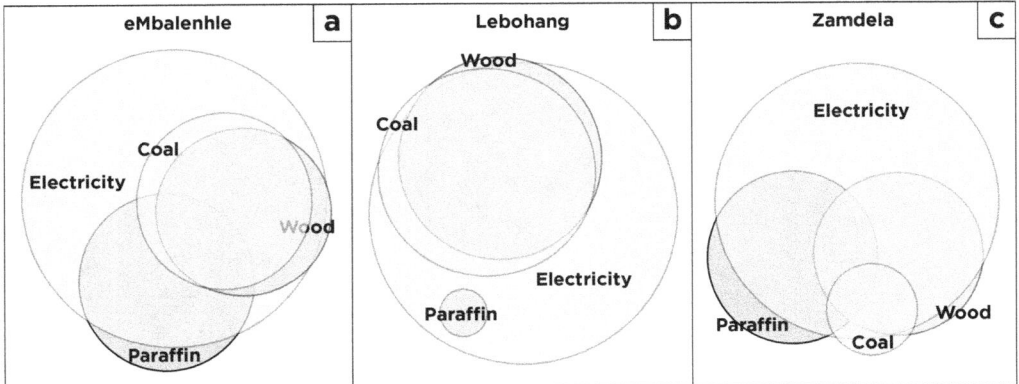

FIGURE 3.4: Simultaneous use of energy carriers by households in (a) eMbalenhle, (b) Lebohang and (c) Zamdela.

While only 9.5% of households in Zamdela reported using coal, 32.9% reported using wood on least some occasions. In all communities, the paraffin-using households are largely a separate group from those who use coal and wood. The widespread use of electricity shows that the lack of access to electricity is not the reason for use of solid or liquid fuels.

Qualitative insights into coal use

Valuable insights into how coal is perceived by low-income communities were obtained from focus group interviews conducted in 2013. Two group discussions were held in eMbalenhle, one with six men and one with seven women, and two focus groups were held in Kwadela, one with four men and one with 12 women. The discussions were held in English (with translators supporting). The groups were asked the following questions:

- What do you think causes people to prefer using coal when they cook or for warming up the house?
- What could be a reason that can make people stop using coal?
- What are the reasons that make people continue to use coal?

The discussions quickly evolved into debates about the relative merits of coal and electricity. The relative affordability of coal is one of the main reasons it is used. A woman from eMbalenhle explains:

> '[...] coal is good, you don't use a lot of money like with electricity. Electricity you can switch on the kettle and use the iron but I'd spend more than when I use coal. With coal I can cook, boil water, iron and still not spend a lot. You find that in a month I buy one bag of coal but electricity I buy maybe four times'. (Participant, female, eMbalenhle)

The cost of buying electrical appliances is prohibitive for some: 'others don't have money to buy an electric stove, so they end up using coal'.

The multi-functionality of a coal stove, which can be used to cook food, warm up the house, heat water and even heat an iron, is a great advantage. A man explains, 'some people prefer to use coal because when it is cold they want the children to keep warm at the same time while they are cooking'. A woman from Kwadela further states:

> 'Sometimes we go back to the coal because on the coal stove you can cook on it and keep warm while with the electricity you'll have to get a heater and the stove separately'. (Participant, female, Kwadela)

Coal is superior to electricity for space heating: 'with coal the fire can burn the whole night and the house becomes warm'. A woman from Kwadela elaborates:

> '[/]f you have lit the coal stove in your house, its heat it's different from that of a heater because the heater if you are using it to warm up maybe in the house it can end up causing flu and the coal stove you warm up nicely'. (Participant, female, Kwadela)

Many people prefer to cook on a coal stove because it cooks at a steady pace and the temperature is optimal. A woman from Kwadela explains:

> 'I like cooking on the coal stove because when you cook on the coal stove it does not rush you like an electric stove because the electric stove sometimes when you adjust it, it becomes too on and too off, it interrupts you but with the coal stove you can relax and cook your food without rushing'. (Participant, female, Kwadela)

Also: 'on the coal stove you can never find that your food is burned, perhaps you have turned the stove too high like you would do with the electric stove'. People prefer the taste of food, particularly pap (a thick maize meal porridge), cooked over coal. A woman from eMbalenhle describes, 'The pap cooked on electricity becomes sticky but the one cooked on a coal stove ripens nicely'.

Older people tend to prefer coal stoves, but working women prefer electricity because it is faster. A woman from Kwadela explains:

> '[A]t my home there is a grandma who is old and maybe in that home we are all not working and we are maintained by the granny and we are dependent on the pension money. We know that grandmothers like coal stoves they can't stay in a house unless it's warm, so on that little money we get we have to prioritize and buy the coal. We can't buy coal and electricity that would be a waste, so that is why we cook on the coal stove'. (Participant, female, Kwadela)

On the other hand, an electric stove is more convenient for people who have less time, as another woman from Kwadela says:

> 'I live alone. You'll find that I'm working and I arrive at home at six so when I get home at six it is better for me to use an electric stove so that I can cook fast'. (Participant, female, Kwadela)

Even if people prefer to use electricity, they are forced to resort to coal when the electricity supply is unreliable. A woman from eMbalenhle states:

> '[T]he other thing that makes people to use coal more is because we have a problem of load shedding [*when electricity delivery is suspended for a period of time*], so others prefer to have coal. There is electricity but they still use coal. That is the biggest problem we have, we do like using electricity so as to avoid air pollution but in our area I don't know maybe it's because we are in the township so electricity just goes as it pleases, and they don't even give the reason why they take electricity they just take so it's safer to have coal'. (Participant, female, eMbalenhle)

On the negative side, as alluded to in the previous paragraph, coal is perceived by some as being dirty. A woman from Kwadela complains:

> '[T]he coal stove is not right, it makes the house dirty and you'll find that there's too much smoke in the house. Electricity is good because it doesn't make the house dirty'. (Participant, female, Kwadela)

A shack dweller in Lebohang feels strongly about how dirty coal is: 'With coal our hands get dirty, they get cut and they even become coarse … coal is actually filthy'. A few people realise that coal smoke is harmful to their health. A woman from Kwadela propounds:

> '[F]irstly the smoke of the coal is dangerous and others are killed by it, and secondly the smoke of the coal causes the air that we breathe to be polluted and then we have lung illnesses'. (Participant, female, Kwadela)

With regard to moving away from coal, the men feel that both better-quality houses ('proper houses') and a shift to electricity are causing people to use less coal. However, the women from eMbalenhle are adamant that coal use will continue because electricity is unreliable and more expensive:

> '[…] it is impossible to stop using coal, we rather say we can stop using electricity because it's always gone. Even this morning it could go; that's why I think Eskom can terminate but coal will always be there'. (Participant, female, eMbalenhle)

Question from interviewer: 'Coal will always be there?' All: 'Yes'. With regard to the cost of electricity a woman from Kwadela explains 'with electricity you can go buy electricity for R20 and end up getting R6 so obviously what are you going to use? Coal instead of electricity!' (Participant, female, Kwadela).

To sum up, coal promotes a better quality of life in coal-using communities because a coal stove is multi-functional, it heats more effectively than an electric heater does, many people prefer the taste and experience of cooking on a coal stove and coal is more affordable. Coal is also a more reliable source of energy, in light of frequent electricity outages in low-income areas.

The only downside of coal use raised by coal users is the air pollution, which makes houses dirty and potentially causes illnesses.

■ Housing conditions in coal-using areas

The high energy demand for heating in winter in coal-using areas is exacerbated by the fact that government-built and informal housing is usually not insulated and often badly constructed. In the great majority of houses in eMbalenhle, Lebohang, eMzinoni, Kwadela and Zamdela, for example, there were no ceilings in any of the rooms in 2013/2016 (Table 3.6). eMzinoni had by far the greatest percentage of houses with a ceiling (21%), but in Kwadela a mere 5% of houses had ceilings in at least one room in 2013 (prior to the insulation retrofits).

A high proportion of households in these communities live in informal dwellings (usually poorly built using corrugated iron on a wooden frame). In 2013, eMbalenhle had the largest number of shacks, with 54% of all houses being informal structures. The number of informal dwellings in eMbalenhle compares fairly well with the value in the Census of 2011 (41.7%), but NOVA's 2013 survey found a significantly higher number of informal dwellings in eMzinoni (44.6%) than the Census 2011 figure of 24.3%. This could point to an increase in the number of informal dwellings between 2011 and 2013. Households living in informal dwellings are particularly reliant on coal because they are usually not connected to grid electricity, have very low or no income and have a high energy demand for space heating in winter because of highly conductive building materials used.

Qualitative insights into perceptions of housing

All the coal-using communities surveyed are fairly dissatisfied with their housing conditions, with mean satisfaction scores ranging between 6.3 (out of 10) in Lebohang and 5.1 in Kwadela (Table 3.6), despite the fact that a lower proportion of Kwadela residents live in informal dwellings compared to other towns.

TABLE 3.6: Housing conditions and satisfaction with housing in coal-using communities: eMalahleni, eMzinoni, Lebohang, Kwadela and Zamdela.

Category	Sub-category	eMalahleni 2013	eMzinoni 2013	Lebohang 2013	Kwadela 2013	Zamdela 2016
Housing	% informal structures	53.8% (50.1, 57.4)	44.6% (38.4, 50.9)	30.1% (24.6, 36.2)	11.5% (7.3, 17.6)	37.6%
Ceiling in at least one room	% of houses	11.2% (9.1, 13.7)	21.3% (16.6, 26.9)	10.6% (7.3, 15.2)	5.4% (2.8, 10.3)	14.4%
Satisfaction with house (1-10)	Mean	5.4 (5.2, 5.7)	6.1 (5.8, 6.4)	6.3 (5.9, 6.7)	5.1 (4.9, 5.3)	–

The 95% confidence interval is given in brackets.

Government-built subsidy houses (called RDP houses) have many problems, but people generally feel they are better than shacks. Most people are grateful that they have received their house, and a few have no complaints, but there are also many who are not happy at all. Residents complain that the RDP houses are poorly built and do not maintain a comfortable temperature. They grumble that 'dust gets in, the windows are of a bad quality, they always open up all on their own at night when there is a lot of wind'; 'the roofing is damaged' and 'rain comes in'; 'there is no ceiling' and 'there are cracks'. A resident describes, 'the house goes with the weather conditions, if it is hot, it gets hot inside, if it is cold, it also gets cold'.

Residents of informal houses are much unhappier with their dwellings. One respondent in eMbalenhle articulated his experience as follows:

> '[B]ut the shack will always be the shack. When it is raining there will be leaking inside the shack, when there is wind the wind comes and put all the dust inside and your furniture and clothes will be full of dust [...]. When it is cold, it is cold and when it is hot, it is hot. It goes along with the weather [...] our houses want to move or fly away if there is a wind'. (Participant, gender not specified, eMbalenhle)

Informal dwellings are very cold, especially on winter nights. It is reported that '… we are always cold, how can that make us happy?', and fires do not warm the whole shack: 'Yes, we make fire in the stove … but it becomes warm in the kitchen only, in the bedrooms it's cold. Air comes in everywhere else in the shack'. Dwellings leak, and are windy and dusty:

> 'When it is raining we have to wake up at night to place buckets where there are leaks even when we try to close the leaks the water still comes in'. (Participant, gender not specified, eMbalenhle)

> 'We tried to install the ceiling but it's the same as nothing, because the dust can get in, even though we have cleaned, when it's windy it looks like we have not cleaned'. (Participant, gender not specified, eMbalenhle)

Moreover, there is a fear of fire: 'Zinc [corrugated iron] is not safe, if a mistake happens it burns quickly, the shack is not safe' (Participant, gender not specified, eMbalenhle). Almost everyone complains about rats and mosquitoes.

■ Personal, geographical and societal context of coal use

In light of the insights into coal use practices and perceptions described above, we explore the phenomena related to human decision-making and behaviour that result in a person using coal, by considering three aspects of being a person living in a coal-using community:

- being a person in a coal-using community
- being in the place of a coal-using community
- being a resident of a coal-using community as part of a larger local, national and global society.

We write with reference to the coal-using households and communities considered in this chapter.

Being a person in a coal-using community

We consider two aspects of being a coal-using person: how the use of coal (and the fire it makes) is related to meeting fundamental human needs; and how subjective perceptions of reality influence decisions or behaviour that result in coal use.

Common to all human beings are fundamental human needs such as subsistence, protection, affection, participation, understanding, creation, idleness, identity, freedom and transcendence (Max-Neef 1991). The concept of human needs has become popularly known through the human needs theory of Abraham Maslow, particularly his hierarchy of needs (Maslow 1943). Although Maslow did not necessarily see his hierarchy of needs pyramid as a fixed order, Maslow's theory contributes in our opinion to the false perception sometimes found among government officials and affluent communities that they have progressed to higher levels of need actualisation, whereas the poor still struggle with basic needs (see Hofstede 1984). The work of Manfred Max-Neef, Chilean Economist, and the Latin American scholars on Human Scale Development (Max-Neef 1991) is a more useful framework within which to consider the meeting of human needs in low-income communities. Max-Neef (1991) proposes that there are nine fundamental human needs that are the same across all cultures and all historical periods. These needs are met through satisfiers that change over time and across cultures. Living in a house, for example, satisfies the need for subsistence and protection at a minimum, and probably also the need for creation and identity, to some extent.

Nova's detailed quality of life surveys that investigated 250 fundamental human needs and household element interfaces in eMbalenhle and Zamdela support Max-Neef's (1991) assertion that there is no hierarchy of human needs. Although people struggle to obtain basic necessities such as food, clothes and proper housing, and to attain a clean, unpolluted environment, they report that they are satisfied with the higher needs in Maslow's hierarchy: most interviewees find the positive meaning of their daily existence in their relationships with fellow household members or other members of the community and their faith in God. The implication for community project development is that low-income households should not be approached with a preconceived idea that their basic needs should first be met and thereafter higher needs become important.

Fire has played a central role in human life for long (cf. Niele 2005:44–45). A cooking and space heating usage pattern is not merely regarded as a clinical action to get food in one's stomach or keep one's body warm. The act of cooking itself is a cultural event that leads to a meal that can be described as a symbolic experience of intimate participation between people who identify with each other. Sitting around a coal stove in the winter to keep warm has an important social meaning. Coal usage needs to be understood as a satisfier of fundamental human needs when developing initiatives to reduce coal use, so that alternative behaviours that are more beneficial to general well-being and quality of life can be designed together with households.

In the coal-using communities considered in this study, both traditional as well as modern patterns of behaviour are identified. Some people ascribe value to the coal stove itself (e.g. the stove brings the family together), whereas the social need of others is rather to watch television and they prefer quicker ways of cooking, space heating and water heating. In some cases, using a modern appliance and modern energy carriers is part of a person's identity.

In addition to satisfying physical and social human needs, the decision to use coal is influenced by the knowledge that people possess, their subjective perceptions of reality and values which determine how they integrate the knowledge when making decisions and personality traits of individuals. Consider that very few residents of coal-using communities in South Africa identify their own coal stoves as a source of air pollution or greenhouse gases. There is also not a good understanding by coal users of the long-term health effects of household air pollution. In this case, lack of knowledge about the indirect effects of coal use may impede the move away from coal.

The ways in which people weigh decisions and impacts in terms of available options and immediate needs are complex. For example, someone in an electrified shack who feel very cold might decide to light a coal or wood fire, depending on what is available, because of the immediate dire need to stay warm. Even after a household has switched to cleaner energy carriers, they can revert to a dirtier fuel if the cleaner energy sources become unaffordable or unavailable. The residential energy usage patterns in low-income households are a combination that residents choose from the possibilities that are available in terms of affordability, accessibility and adequacy of the energy combinations.

Individual personalities also influence decisions and preferences. Different people have different preferences and varying willingness to change from one energy usage pattern to another. Someone who tends to be conservative might be more hesitant to switch to a new way of doing things. Human beings are multifaceted and there are numerous personal aspects that can influence decisions and preferences.

Being in the place of a coal-using community

Residential coal use in South Africa is restricted to areas where there is a need for space heating in winter because of cold temperatures (and often poor housing quality), and where coal is readily available because of proximity to coal mines. On the South African Highveld, minimum temperatures frequently drop below 0°C in winter and lower income households that reside in uninsulated RDP housing or informal dwellings are particularly exposed to the cold. Changes in housing quality or dwelling type over time may affect the prevalence of residential coal use. For example, in Zamdela, 19.5% of all housing structures were informal structures or shacks in 2011. By 2016, the proportion of informal structures had increased to 37.6% of all structures. These additional shack-dwellers are likely to be impoverished households that have a great need for space heating in winter, and who will probably resort to using solid fuels.

Poverty related to limited employment and education opportunities in low-income communities on the South African Highveld may prolong the persistence of residential coal use. The average per capita income was ZAR18.60 (US$2.00) per person per day in eMbalenhle in 2013, and in Zamdela in 2016 the per capita income was ZAR20.52 (US$1.40) per person per day. In situations like this, it is possible that people will return to using cheaper energy forms and slide back on the energy ladder. If, for example, the price of electricity increases and cheap or free wood is available, people might choose to use wood for cooking, space heating and water heating.

Being a coal-user in a larger local, national and global society

In the previous paragraphs we looked at individual human needs and at the geographical factors that need to be considered to gain a better understanding of coal use. There are also broader societal phenomena that influence local behaviour, including economic activity, science, ethics and politics.

South Africa has abundant coal resources. Coal is one of the foundations of South Africa's economy. Coal was used to generate 86% of South Africa's electricity in 2016 (Statistics South Africa 2018), is exported for foreign income and powers many industries. Coal is also made available for residential use in regions around coal mines.

Globally, there is an energy transition underway, moving from a reliance on fossil fuels to renewable sources of energy. The energy transition is largely driven by the concern that greenhouse gas emissions are changing the climate, and the other harmful impacts of fossil fuel use are on the environment and human health. At grid level, this transition to non-dispatchable renewable energy is enabled by technologies of the Fourth Industrial Revolution, such as information and control technologies that monitor network use and allow for enhanced control of power system (MIT Energy Initiative 2016). The extent to which low-income communities such as those discussed in this chapter may benefit from the technologies of the Fourth Industrial Revolution is questionable, however, considering the lack of infrastructure like high-speed internet and the generally low skill and education levels (Ayentimi & Burgess 2019).

Within this broader context, there have been numerous initiatives in South Africa to assist households to transition to cleaner sources of energy, including connecting households to the national electricity grid through the national electrification programme, providing a Free Basic Electricity subsidy, the RDP housing programme and various programmes to provide households with cleaner fuels or cleaner burning combustion devices. However, the efforts have been hampered by the persistent poverty of low-income communities. Reliance on solid and liquid fuels persists because cleaner sources of energy are unaffordable for energy-intensive uses like heating.

Political decisions impact on coal use. In South Africa, residential coal use falls within the sphere of the Department of Mineral Resources and Energy, which has promulgated policies like Free Basic Electricity and Free Basic Alternative Energy, and is spearheading the electrification programme; the Department of Environment, Forestry and Fisheries which is concerned about the impact of emissions from coal burning on ambient air quality; the Department of Health which deals with the illnesses resulting from the inhalation of coal burning emissions; and indirectly the Department of Human Settlements that regulates housing standards. There is seldom coordination between these departments when addressing coal use.

When it comes to the local municipality, there are many ways in which the political environment and performance of the local government impact on coal use. For example, in areas that experience a rapid influx of people and where construction of government housing and electrification do not keep up (such as is happening in both eMbalenhle and Zamdela), the residential use of coal may increase.

■ Conclusion

In South Africa, coal use for residential purposes is limited to urban and peri-urban settlements on the Highveld in proximity to coal fields – western Mpumalanga, north-eastern Free State, Ekurhuleni and parts of northern KwaZulu-Natal. Residential coal use declined until 2013 and has remained relatively constant since then. Coal use remains particularly persistent in Mpumalanga, the traditional coal heartland of South Africa. Coal is usually burnt in cast iron stoves or stoves welded by local entrepreneurs, using the conventional top-down method. Considerably more households use coal in winter than in summer. Most coal fires in the winter are lit in the morning between 04:00 and 06:00 and in the late afternoon between 15:00 and 17:00. The quality of the coal used is highly variable and not always as low quality as is generally assumed.

Coal offers great utility value because it is a dense form of energy, is highly effective in space heating and can be simultaneously used for cooking and water heating. Burning coal in the home improves the quality of life of many low-income households, especially those living in informal and/or poor-quality housing during winter months. Coal stoves not only satisfy physical needs for sustenance and warmth but also have important social and cultural meaning to many users.

However, considering the negative health effects of emissions from coal burning, transitioning households to cleaner sources of energy needs to be promoted. Despite the professed fondness for coal stoves, most households abandon coal spontaneously as they become more affluent. Electricity is more convenient and cleaner, and there can be a stigma of poverty attached to coal use. Consequently, there has been a significant decline in residential coal use in most areas where it was once much more prevalent until 2013. Nevertheless, coal use prevails, even in households that are connected to the national electricity grid. Two main reasons for this persistent use of coal in electrified homes have emerged: the unreliable electricity supply, which forces households to resort to coal, and the fact that coal is cheaper than electricity where space heating is required. Any project that seeks to accelerate the move of households away from coal needs to address both of these issues in order to completely eliminate coal use.

The availability and quality of housing also remain persistent drivers of residential coal use, especially during the winter months when there is a need for space heating in poorly insulated houses and informal dwellings. Urbanisation rates are expected to rise and will further impact existing backlogs in the provision of housing and other infrastructure. More households will have to resort to constructing informal dwellings in areas where basic services are not yet available, increasing the reliance on solid fuels such as coal. Ensuring access to good quality housing with adequate insulation is critical to any efforts aimed at promoting household adaptation to cleaner sources of energy.

Fuel use choices are not only made out of necessity; a complex mix of psychological, geographical and social factors all influence decision-making and fuel-use behaviours. Human beings are multifaceted, and there are numerous personal aspects that can influence decisions. Different people have different preferences and varying willingness to change from one energy usage pattern to another. Managing residential coal use will never have a 'one-size-fits-all' solution.

The surge in extreme poverty is one, if not the most important, metric to monitor in the post-COVID-19 world. Cilliers et al. (2020) predict that '[…] while the recession, infections and hospitals dominate the current daily headlines, the personal economic consequences of the virus are what will linger'. An increase in extreme poverty can reverse much of the progress made in the last decades to reduce household dependence on solid fuels. An increase in poverty can unleash a whole set of evils that could worsen the air quality situation. It will increase the backlog in quality housing, could lead to accelerated urbanisation with more people residing in informal settlements on the fringes of urban areas, and further deterioration in service delivery.

From our analysis, we conclude that, although there has been a decline in coal use in some of the areas we have monitored, there is a marked difference in trends between regions. If poverty increases in the years to come, it can be expected that in areas where coal is available and affordable, low-income households living in structures with suboptimal thermal protection will continue to use coal as part of their energy mix. In some areas, it is likely that a number of households will revert back to coal if electricity is unreliable or unaffordable.

Residential coal use satisfies a number of fundamental human needs. Because domestic coal use is multi-utility and a pervasive part of everyday life in low-income communities on the South African Highveld, it needs to be addressed through a comprehensive suite of social policies. A well-constructed house with some level of insulation, access to a clean and convenient source of energy like electricity and poverty alleviation in some form, whether it be in the form of employment (preferably) or a subsidy, are necessary but not necessarily sufficient to facilitate a transition away from domestic coal use.

■ Acknowledgements

The general household surveys and detailed energy surveys were funded by Sasol. Nova coordinators and fieldworkers conducted the surveys. Siyabonga Simelane compiled the map showing the location of coal-using households and coal mines, and Eskom performed the KwaZamokuhle coal analysis.

Chapter 4

Towards a complementary approach in sustainable food production

Betsie le Roux[a,b]
[a]Food and Water Research (Pty) Ltd,
Pretoria, South Africa
[b]Centre for Faith and Community, Faculty of Religion and Theology,
University of Pretoria, Pretoria, South Africa

Mike Howard[a,b]
[a]Food and Water Research (Pty) Ltd,
Pretoria, South Africa
[b]Centre for Faith and Community, Faculty of Religion and Theology,
University of Pretoria, Pretoria, South Africa

■ Introduction

Sustainable food production is increasingly becoming a problem, especially in developing countries. It is estimated that agricultural outputs have to increase by 60%–70% by 2050. This increase in demand for agricultural products is driven by population growth, by the change from plant-based diets to increased meat consumption, by growing markets for biodiesel from grains and urbanisation and improvement of infrastructure that allow for increases in consumption of more perishable foods (Silva 2018).

How to cite: Le Roux, B. & Howard, M., 2021, 'Towards a complementary approach in sustainable food production', in A.S. Van Niekerk & S. Strijbos (eds.), *We cannot continue like this: Facing modernity in Africa and the West*, pp. 73–91, AOSIS, Cape Town. https://doi.org/10.4102/aosis.2021.BK283.04

According to the current dominant paradigm the solution to food production lies with intensifying production on large-scale industrial farms, to conserve natural ecosystems by reducing the footprint of agriculture in terms of space and to provide job opportunities to rural people. Previous advances in productivity on industrial farms have created an optimism that human ingenuity and Western technology can do miracles and increase productivity indefinitely, despite limited resources (Roodt 2021). However, the impacts of industrial agriculture have become clear through climate change, water pollution, loss of biodiversity, social instability etc. (Bezner-Kerr et al. 2012; Food and Agriculture Organisation 2017; Mazoyer & Roudart 2006).

In this chapter we argue that previous advances in food production, though they have solved many problems over the short term, have most likely led us up to the pinnacle of a pyramid, with no way forward and, because of population growth, we cannot go back down along the same route. And the long-term impacts will increase as consumption grows. We briefly discuss some impacts of industrial agriculture and evaluate a number of adjustments that are presented to mitigate existing negative impacts.

We argue that regenerative farming and a switch to integrated agriculture are essential elements of a viable solution for a sustainable food security in future. However, to change the impacts of industrial agriculture, we need something more impactful than just to substitute it with regenerative agriculture within the current framework of centralised food production. Regenerative agriculture is more viable on a small scale, and we argue that what is needed is not just a reduction in consumption, but cultural changes to produce food at home on a small scale to supplement centralised food production. This will not just have the benefit of taking advantage of domestic resources such as space, compost, grey water and rain, it will also give people a sense of and respect for what it takes to produce food. When food is produced locally, the relationship between the consumer and the farmer provides a more natural environment for feedback mechanisms; people may be less likely to waste food or to consume too much and they can more easily influence decisions that are made in the production process. Decentralisation, if practiced efficiently, will help people to become less dependent in terms of their food requirements.

In a modified world we need a diversity in agricultural approaches, small- and larger- scale, to address future food security. But all agricultural systems must focus on increasing sustainability as well as productive outputs.

Characteristics of sustainable production
Perspectives on sustainable food production

The concept of sustainable food production has originated from different schools of thought for various reasons. The diverse ways of approaching, thinking about and understanding sustainable food production, therefore, make it difficult to define and use the concept in a consistent way. Several studies have been undertaken to review the various approaches and to find a useful definition. Hansen (1996) classified different definitions of sustainable food production as:

- Sustainability as an ideology: Emphasis is on the values and philosophies of sustainability.
- Sustainability as a set of strategies: Emphasis is placed on sustainable technologies and practices, such as sustainable sources of nutrients and pest control.
- Sustainability as the ability to fulfil a set of goals: Emphasis is placed on the outcomes of sustainable agriculture, such as improved quality of the environment and human life.
- Sustainability as the ability to continue: Emphasis is on the sustainability of technologies over the long-term.

Brklacich, Bryant and Smit (1991) identified three perspectives and six approaches to define sustainability. Two of these approaches originate from an ecological perspective, two originate from an economic perspective and two originate from a social justice perspective:

- Ecological perspective:
    - *Environmental accounting*, which identifies agricultural production limits by quantifying the impacts of chemicals such as fertilisers and pesticides and distributions of ecological degradation, such as soil erosion, climate change etc. (Brklacich et al. 1991).
    - *Carrying capacity*, which describes the number of animals that can be sustained by the natural ecosystems. Gunderson and Holling (2002) warn against using the concept of carrying capacity in the way that one tries to impose limits to a dynamic ecosystem. They also, however, admit that this view is not always incorrect, but can be incomplete.
- Economic perspective:
    - *Sustained yields* to understand and address decreases in yields because of environmental degradation. It is a common phenomenon that yields tend to decrease after several years of farming a certain field (Stirzaker 2010).

- - *Production unit viability* focusses on the ability of farmers to withstand and adapt to stress. Currently, this is a particularly relevant issue for South African farmers who are confronted with various problems, including an ongoing drought, impacts of COVID-19 pandemic and a lack of government support (Van der Walt 2020).
- Social justice:
  - *Production supply and security*: According to the Food and Agriculture Organisation (2006), a person is food secure if food is consistently available, if he/she has access to the food and if the food is utilised in a way that promotes general well-being.
  - *Equity*: It includes both intergenerational (equal distribution of food over generations) and intragenerational (equal distribution of food over the world) equity (Brklacich et al. 1991).

Being an extremely complex subject, it is not possible to say that any of the above is incorrect. Natural ecosystems are remarkably sustainable, as long as all species within it remain within their natural limits. As humans we are not able to reduce the number of people in order to bring them within the natural carrying capacity of the earth. Therefore, it is difficult to achieve sustainability in all of the above conditions. However, the ecological concepts of recycling and feedback mechanisms remain extremely important principles to achieve sustainability. These concepts are essential irrespective of any other modifications that can and should be made in future food production systems.

Upscaling production versus sustainability

Complex systems such as ecosystems operate at multiple scales. This concept is particularly well illustrated in the panarchy theory (Gunderson & Holling 2002). It is a common occurrence that systems work well on a small scale, but that complex problems then arise at a larger scale. On a larger scale, more role players become involved, and the interplay between the social, ecological and economic systems can become extremely difficult to manage. Different models for food production work better on different scales.

Establishing feedback mechanisms

Feedback mechanisms ensure the sustainability of ecosystems by inducing remedial responses to a negative event or impact. The physical distance between consumers and the commercial industrial farms that produce their food makes it difficult for consumers to respond to the indirect impacts that they have on the environment through the products they buy. Therefore, the scale at which a system operates affects the efficiency of feedback mechanisms. Water footprints (WFs) aim to provide a feedback mechanism that indicates to consumers their indirect impacts on water resources when purchasing a product. However, the fact that the ISO standards on WFs (ISO 14046:2014) were unable to specify how WFs can be used for product labels or raising consumer awareness highlights the complexity of interpreting the data.

■ Analysing the current food production system

This section describes an analysis of the food production system, which is summarised in Figure 4.1. Food production is a complex problem and responds to several drivers, including resource availability (this could include natural or artificial resources) and the market, which again is influenced by population growth and consumer demands. These drivers put pressure on the food production system and in response several options are available to produce the required food. These options include various agricultural methods that

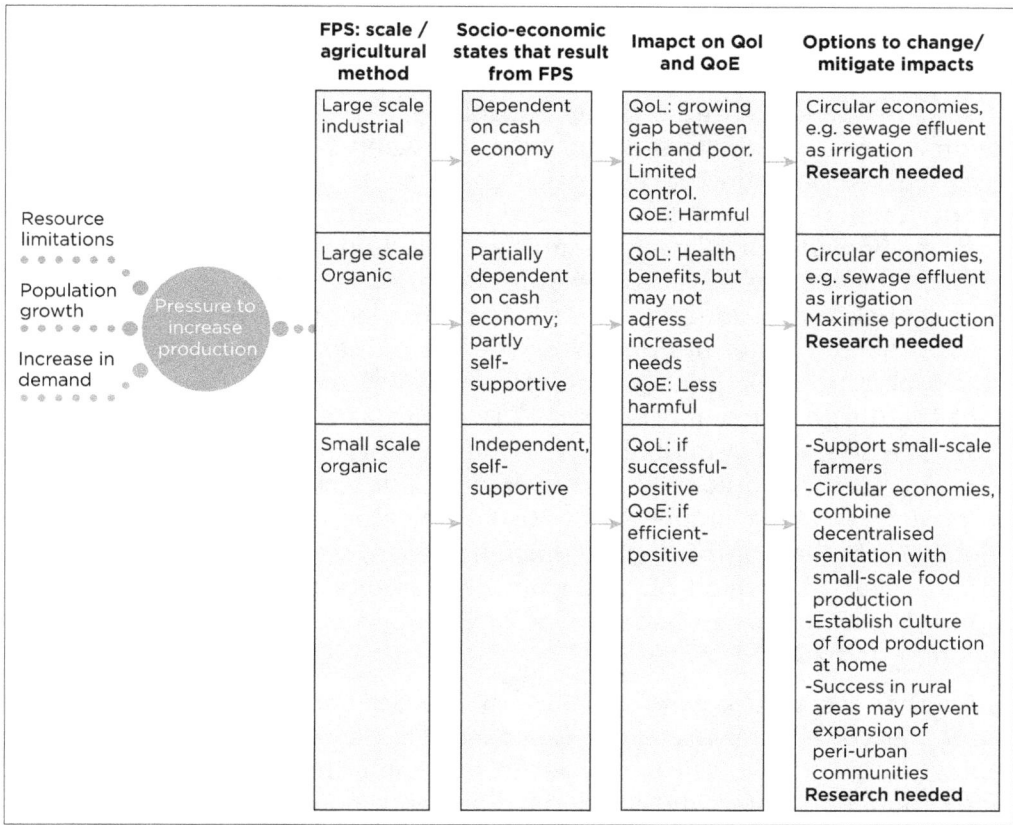

FPS, Food production system; QoL, Quality of life; QoE, Quality of ecosystem.
FIGURE 4.1: Analyses of the current food production system.

could be practiced on different scales. The different methods and the scales that are chosen for food production have implications, they affect socio-economic states and ecosystems in different ways. Each of these options will have a role to play in food production in the future. Research related to each of these options is needed to improve sustainability and/or efficiency.

Drivers

The drivers of the food production system include increased demands (i.e. the 'market') and resource availability. Increasing demands and decreasing resources put pressure on food production.

The 'market' is a strong driver in food production. Increases in demands are not just because of population growth. Wealthy people tend to consume more meat and more food in general. They are more particular about the appearance of the food they eat, which is evident from the high wastage of 'unmarketable vegetables' at commercial farms (Le Roux et al. 2018). Markets could dictate even small details in the management decision taken by farmers, and in some cases, it has negative ecological impacts.

Resources could also be considered a driving force, which is most clear when it becomes limited. Locally and globally, the availability of water is becoming more and more of an issue. Between 2015 and 2020, a water crisis was among the top five risks identified by the Global Risk Report (World Economic Forum 2020). In the future, water scarcity is expected to intensify because of climate change as well as population and economic growth. The increase in future water scarcities is one of the factors that make global food production an issue of particular concern. Current sources of good quality water are declining; therefore, the maintenance of current food production becomes a problem and it will be even more difficult to meet the future demands (Postel 1999). South Africa is a dry country with a low average annual rainfall of 490 mm (World Wildlife Fund 2016). The variability of rain regionally and over time adds compounding factors to water supply (Binns, Illgner & Nel 2001; Department of Water Affairs 2011). Annually, an average of 49 000 million m^3 of water flows through South Africa's rivers, of which 50% is from catchments that occupy 8% of the country's surface area (Department of Environmental Affairs 2012; World Wildlife Fund 2016).

Another resource is land. In 1960, the globally available arable land per capita was 0.42 hectares, and this is expected to decrease to 0.19 hectares per capita in 2050 (Silva 2018). In order to overcome this dilemma, the present food production system must change: more land should be made available, or more food must be produced on current land, or food distribution and storage must change, or eating habits must change, or all of these must change. Making more arable land available may be at the expense of natural ecosystems. If productivity is to be increased per surface area, low-productivity systems will have to be transformed. This should provide the opportunity for the utilisation of other resources, such as grey water and sewage, which are currently wasted.

Food production alternatives

To address the problem of sustainable food production, we need to consider and evaluate the various approaches. Current approaches to food production range from industrial to regenerative agricultural methods and also from large-scale to small-scale production systems.

Regenerative versus industrial agriculture

Many consider intensive production on industrial farms as the only possible solution to future food production because of the quantities of food that can be produced on a relatively small space and at very low costs. In reaction to the problems of industrial agriculture (refer to 'Consequences resulting from various food production alternatives'), regenerative agricultural methods are proposed. Several methods exist that aim to produce food in a more 'natural' way, for example, organic agriculture, conservation agriculture, agro-ecology et cetera, and we refer to all of these as 'regenerative agriculture'.

Regenerative agriculture focusses on enhancing biological diversity by preventing harmful agricultural practices such as tilling. It presents important alternatives to regenerate rather than to degrade natural resources during food production. Organic agriculture is one form of regenerative agriculture that has been adopted by many large-scale farmers (Reganold, Elliott & Unger 1987; Scialabba 2007).

The classic definition of organic farming proposes a set of strategies to minimise the negative impacts of industrial agriculture. In terms of crop nutrients, organic farming prescribes the use of natural sources such as manure and crop rotation with legumes that are able to fix atmospheric nitrogen. The primary focus of organic farming is to maintain a healthy soil, assuming that it will necessarily produce healthy crops. Reganold et al. (1987) reported that soils under organic agriculture had more organic matter, deeper topsoil and less soil erosion. However, organic farming has also received much criticism. Studies have shown that compared to conventional farms yields on organic farms are on an average 20% lower where vegetable crops are combined with animal production and 33%–45% lower where only vegetables are produced

(Kirchmann & Ryan 2004). Lower yields are a result of poor nutrient uptake and periods of no production on fallow lands (Kirchmann & Ryan 2004). Connor (2013) argues that upscaling organic farming is a key issue that hampers its potential to feed the growing world population. Commercial farmers in general, with a few exceptions, say that organic farming is not possible on a larger scale. Stirzaker (2010) said that, although he practiced organic agriculture on a small scale, he was not able to apply those principles on a large commercial scale.

According to Kirchmann and Ryan (2004) nitrate leaching under organic agriculture can exceed that of conventional agriculture, because of less efficient absorption of the nutrients by the crops. Organic agriculture often depends on manure from commercial farmers for their nutrient requirements (Nowak et al. 2013). Kirchmann and Ryan (2004) criticise organic farming for excluding waste water as a source of nutrients, which will become an important source in the future as new technologies are developed. Although the philosophy behind organic agriculture is sound, the rules that are formulated from it can become an aim in itself, sometimes missing the original goals (Kirchmann & Ryan 2004). The classic definition of organic farming, which prescribes a set of rules, is often too restrictive and may be the cause for many of the complaints against it.

As part of the debate around regenerative agriculture, it must be kept in mind that the population has grown in response to artificial resources. These resources have created an artificial carrying capacity, and it is not necessarily possible to keep on supporting the current population without the artificial resources. It does not mean that the concept of regenerative agriculture should be rejected. For example, artificial nutrients that are already in the system, i.e. sewage, can be recycled as fertilisers, rather than being discarded.

From the above, it becomes clear that the principles of the different kinds of regenerative agriculture are not incorrect, and that these methods work on a small scale. The problems may arise when they are used on a larger scale. However, the premise that a healthy ecosystem gives rise to healthy crops remains important in finding a sustainable future for food production.

◻ Small-scale/subsistence versus large-scale

With the rise of commercial agriculture, the number of small-scale farms has declined globally. In 1935 the number of farms in the United States was 6.8 million, but this reduced to 1.9 million in 1997 (Stam & Dixon 2004). The number of farms in Europe is falling by 3% annually and this trend is also observed in developing countries like South Africa (Boyce 2006).

There are widely diverging opinions about what kind of farming system is most suitable to achieve sustainable food production. According to Phalan et al. (2011) there is a lack of empirical data to fully understand whether, in terms of ecological conservation, it is better to separate agricultural land, in the form of intensive industrial farms, from protected ecosystems, or to integrate farm land with ecosystems, as found in smaller scale agriculture. Intensification, which aims to maximise production per surface area, is often considered to be the only viable option, considering the constraints in making more agricultural land available and the competition for land with the expansion of urban areas and other land uses (Silva 2018). However, we now realise that our full environmental footprint is not just the space we occupy, but extends to other areas through carbon and WFs etc. Others claim that small-scale farms incorporating more diverse habitats and supporting greater biodiversity are ecologically more sustainable (Altieri 2008).

Small-scale farms usually support a higher diversity of crops and crop varieties (Nærstad 2007). According to the Food and Agriculture Organisation (2012), 80% of agricultural land in sub-Saharan Africa and Asia is farmed by small-scale farmers working on less than 10 hectares, and 80% of the food is supplied by them. They play an important role in maintaining biodiversity by keeping alive many natural and resilient varieties and breeds that are adapted to local climates. It may be that smallholder farmers will be in a better position to implement farming methods that reduce carbon emissions than commercial farmers, as well as adaptation to climate change (Bezner-Kerr et al. 2012). According to Kruger (2020), rural households in Makhathini are able to produce all the vegetables and fruits they need in gardens that are less than 200 m^2 in size. Some people are able to generate a notable income of up to ZAR2000 per month in homestead gardens, if they farm intensively with high value crops. In order for a household of five people to be self-sustained in terms of their grain requirements, a garden of about 2500 m^2 is required (Kruger 2020). Household-based farming increases resilience of a household. It was observed during the COVID-19 pandemic that rural households in Makhathini that produced food in their gardens were better able to provide food for their families (Kruger 2020).

Small-scale farms are criticised for their lower yields, thus increased surface area requirements, but by applying sustainable intensification principles, it has been shown that smallholders can become very productive (Food and Agriculture Organisation 2012).

Consequences resulting from various food production alternatives

As mentioned in the previous section food production can be practiced on a large scale either as industrial or regenerative agriculture. Food production can also be practiced on a household scale. The scale of the chosen food production system and the agricultural method, namely, industrial or regenerative, contribute to the development of different socio-economic states and ecological impacts.

The impacts of agriculture differ according to the agricultural method used and the scale at which agriculture is practiced. Impacts of household farming are limited, because the space that will be used is likely to be some kind of garden, as opposed to natural areas. However, the agricultural activities at the household level could become destructive if chemicals are used, over-irrigation occurs without proper management and soil erosion could result from poor soil management. Industrial agriculture has a negative impact on the socio-economic and ecological environments, which are discussed further. Regenerative agriculture aims to reduce the ecological impacts.

☐ Socio-economic states that result from food production systems

Many rural people in South Africa still engage in subsistence farming and some are self-supportive in terms of food production (StatsSA 2013). On a spiritual and social level, the successful subsistence farmer can create a wholesome environment, where ecological impacts are minimised and children can engage with the process while parents are at work. Grandparents can participate and teach the children how to farm. By harvesting and eating fresh food from the garden, children and adults develop a healthy relationship with the earth. Being connected to the earth is an important need in African traditions (Van Niekerk 1992). However, rural–urban migration is proof that many people are not satisfied with their rural lives. This could partly be because of the highly attractive lifestyle in the urban areas, or because of difficulty in competing with industrial farms, or actual poverty and suffering (Mazoyer & Roudart 2006). According to Tsegay, Rusare and Mistry (2014), most people in rural areas are dependent on a cash economy. Many small-scale farmers are struggling to survive and are not able to follow a healthy lifestyle, which requires further research and highlights the importance of support and extension services to these families. Very often rural subsistence farmers will give up this practice and start working on an industrial farm for a minimal income. In these cases, the rural people become dependent on industrial farms or grants for both their income and for purchasing their food.

In the densely populated peri-urban communities, garden space for food production can be limited and people are mostly dependent on a cash economy. Again, the attractive lifestyle of the urban areas is impacting on the lives of these people; those who have gardens often plant ornamental plants and lawns, and they have a habit of sweeping the ground to bare soil and dust, rather than using their energy, space and water for food production (Van Niekerk 2008).

People in urban areas in South Africa have relatively large gardens that could have been used for producing a percentage of their food requirements, but urban households are mostly fully dependent on commercial farms. Some people have vegetable gardens, but this is inhibited by the absence of a general culture of producing food at home. Instead, gardens are used for ornamental plants and lawns. Without intending to, wealthy urban people play a role in catalysing the process of rural and peri-urban communities to give up small-scale farming and become more dependent in terms of food security (Van Niekerk 2008).

Therefore, people in all parts of the country are dependent on a cash economy and centralised food production system, while most people can produce some of their own food and some could also be completely self-supported.

☐ Carbon footprint

According to the IPCC, agriculture contributed 10%–12% of total greenhouse gas emissions in 2005. These emissions included methane (CH_4) from animal husbandry and nitrous oxide (N_2O) from agricultural soils. Nitrous oxide is an intermediate compound in the natural denitrification of nitrates in fertilisers to N_2 gas (Smith et al. 2007).

A carbon footprint is also found along the supply chain of resources and chemicals used in agriculture, such as the production of fertilisers. Nitrate (NO_3), which is an important nutrient in fertilisers, is produced through the Haber–Bosch process, by fixing N_2 gas in the atmosphere into ammonia (NH_3), and then converting NH_3 to NO_3. The Haber–Bosch process is an energy-intensive process that requires constant pressure above 100 bar and high temperatures of about 500 °C (McPherson & Zhang 2020). Currently, ammonia production through the Haber–Bosch process contributes 1.4% of global CO_2 emissions (Capdevila-Cortada 2019). To put this in perspective, total carbon emissions in 2020 were at 34 billion tons (Global Carbon Project 2020), and 1.4% is thus 476 million tons, which is equivalent to about 105 million cars.

However, different agricultural systems have different impacts on climate change. Large-scale industrial agriculture contributes to the majority of agricultural greenhouse gas emissions, whereas smaller scale farms that incorporate regenerative agricultural principles that generate less carbon emissions can potentially become a carbon sink (Bezner-Kerr et al. 2012). The major differences between large-scale industrial farms and small-scale regenerative agricultural farms that influence the difference in carbon footprints are given as follows:

- Large-scale industrial farms are more energy intensive, while small-scale farms are generally more labour intensive.

- The two systems differ in terms of their use of resources such as fertilisers and crop-management choices.
- Large-scale industrial farms require more transportation of inputs, outputs and products, while small-scale farms generally use more local resources and access more local markets (Bezner-Kerr et al. 2012).

Water quality impacts

Human activities are also impacting on the water quality in South Africa. Nutrient waste through the now much increased sewage production of the current human population represents the main impact at the end of the fertiliser life cycle. Increased nutrient levels from wastewater treatment plants and fertilisers from agriculture enrich river systems through a process called eutrophication (DEA 2012). Eutrophication causes the following impacts on water quality (DEA 2012):

- High nutrient concentrations result in an increase in aquatic plants and harmful algae that deplete dissolved oxygen in the water, causing ecosystem degradation and reduction in aquatic species diversity.
- Algal toxins are released in eutrophic waters and are a risk to human and animal health if consumed. Toxins from cyanobacteria can be taken up by fish that will become a health risk if consumed by humans. If ingested, these toxins can cause respiratory and gastrointestinal problems, skin rashes, ear pain and eye irritation, liver and nerve damage.
- The smell and appearance of the water that reduce the recreational value of a dam.
- An increase in the cost of purifying the water to drinking water standards.

The South African aquatic environment is phosphate limited, meaning that any addition of phosphates is usually the driver of eutrophication. Nitrates also have potential human health impacts, causing methaemoglobinaemia, which is especially hazardous in infants (Department of Water Affairs and Forestry 1996). It has been reported that nitrates can also be converted to carcinogens in the body, but conflicting claims have been published and further research is needed on this topic (Chowdhury & Das 2015). Although the environmental interactions and crop genetics complicate the process of nitrate uptake by plants, it has been observed that increased application rates result in nitrates being stored in leaf vacuoles.

Therefore, there is a risk of consuming toxic levels of nitrates through fresh vegetables, especially leafy vegetables, that have been grown using too much nitrates (Blom-Zandstra 1989; Chowdhury & Das 2015; Maynard et al. 1976; Qiu et al. 2014). Elevated nitrate levels in animal feed can also be lethal for livestock (Stanton & Whittier 2006). Eutrophication and accumulation of nitrates in natural water resources may, therefore, become another threat to future food production.

Globally, nitrate accumulation in aquatic ecosystems because of agriculture is a concern. It has been found that the nitrate accumulation in the vadose zone of agricultural lands across the world is highest in North America, Europe and China, partly because of the thickness of the vadose zone and because of the long agricultural histories in those countries. This means that nitrate leaching from these areas will have a longer lag effect, once more sustainable agricultural practices are implemented to reduce nitrate inputs (Ascott et al. 2017). The problem of nitrate pollution of water resources in the Netherlands, which is one of the largest food producing countries in the world, is particularly severe. Stokstad (2019) warns that the pollution caused by nitrates in the Netherlands is now a crisis that threatens the environment and the economy. Permits for construction projects, expansion of pig, poultry and dairy farms were frozen and the Dutch Government is even considering other measures to reduce nitrogen pollution, such as lowering of speed limits on highways (Stokstad 2019).

In South Africa, the poor state of wastewater treatment works (WWTWs) is currently a major cause of nutrient accumulation in aquatic ecosystems. According to the 2012 Green Drop Progress Report, which is the last report on the condition of South African WWTWs published by the Department of Water and Sanitation (DWS), 39% of all municipal WWTWs deteriorated from 2011 to 2012 and 44% of all municipal WWTWs can be categorised as at high or critical risk. More recently, AfriForum (2019) evaluated the WWTWs of 124 towns in South Africa and found that 52% did not comply with the required water quality standards. According to the World Wildlife Fund (2016), approximately 25% of South Africa's largest rivers are 'critically endangered'. Twenty nine of the 100 major dams in South Africa have a health risk, because of high nutrient levels or toxins dangerous to humans. According to the Department of Water Affairs (2012), 88% of South African freshwater resources have unacceptable levels of orthophosphate concentrations, mainly because of poorly functioning WWTWs. The discharge of poor-quality waste water into the aquatic environment poses numerous risks to public and environmental health.

The question is: how urgent is the situation? Impacts that are currently experienced and reported are mostly ecological degradation and sometimes polluted water affects the recreational industry. Recorded cases of human health impacts and acute toxicity are scarce. However, the chronic impact of long-term exposure to polluted water is a concern. Nutrients and organic chemicals accumulate in water bodies and are not removed; therefore, the problem will escalate over time. It would be wise to manage this situation proactively.

Because of the availability of fertilisers, nutrients are currently not regarded as an important limiting factor in agriculture. However, the ecological impacts of chemical fertilisers on water quality and in terms of climate change make it a very relevant topic when considering sustainable food production. Considering all the impacts of nutrient accumulation in water, using sewage water for irrigation may provide a viable solution.

Quality of ecosystems

Unsustainable agricultural practices have resulted in a decrease in ecological integrity, with the loss of biodiversity and ecosystem services, such as pollination and beneficial insect predation (Kumaraswamy & Kunte 2013). Industrial agriculture is also criticised for its dependence on fossil fuels, low crop diversity, impacts on ecosystems and high requirements for external chemical inputs such as fertilisers and pesticides (Altieri 2008).

Pathways into sustainable food production

Finding a sustainable way of producing food in the future has become a very complex problem. We discuss three important changes that are needed to reach the goal of producing food sustainably.

Creating circular economies, for example, by reusing sewage effluent for crop production

Despite the massive challenges to keep up with the increasing waste flows and the threats to the environment, sewage effluent is also a rich source of water and nutrients, and could potentially become an important resource to farmers. If these nutrients are recycled it will reduce environmental impacts at both the supply end (climate change impact and depletion of resources) and of the final wastage generated through the fertiliser life cycle. Reusing nutrients in sewage effluent presents an opportunity for both small- and large-scale agriculture to become more sustainable. Using treated effluent from dysfunctional WWTWs for irrigation potentially has the following benefits:

- assisting farmers to maximise production in areas with limited water availability or during dry seasons
- creating job opportunities
- reducing the amounts of expensive fertilisers required and subsequently the impacts on climate change
- improving the water quality of the region
- reducing the rate at which a limited resource like phosphorus is depleted.

Irrigation with sewage effluent is a common practice throughout the world and a number of studies have been conducted to determine the safety of irrigating with sewage effluent. The impact of irrigating with treated sewage effluent on soil properties, crop yields, nutrient uptake and leaching was found to be insignificant (Musazura et al. 2015). Insignificant levels of leaching could, however, possibly be because of very precise irrigation scheduling done for scientific experimentation, and this risk may require management under normal farming conditions. Risks of using sewage effluent for irrigation were low in terms of certain human pathogens, especially if the water is disinfected (Chale-Matsau 2005) or if the crop is cooked before consumption (Al-Lahham, El Assi & Fayyad 2003). Heavy metal accumulation has been studied and may pose some risks that require monitoring and management (Ogbazghi et al. 2015).

During a Water Research Commission (WRC) project, a small feasibility study was conducted at the Rooiwal Agri-park, north of Pretoria, South Africa, South African Agri-parks aim to provide land and support to small-scale previously disadvantaged farmers. During the research, treated effluent from the adjacent WWTWs was used to irrigate a field of cabbage. The purpose of the research was mainly to assess the willingness of Agri-park farmers to use sewage effluent for irrigation. During the course of the project, the farmers were introduced to several technologies that could assist them with improving water use efficiency, including user-friendly soil moisture sensors such as the Full-Stop wetting front detectors and chameleon sensors (Stirzaker 2014; Stirzaker et al. 2017) and good agronomic practices such as mulching and weeding. Soil moisture sensors were relatively poorly accepted and remained unused in the fields, while mixed reactions were found regarding mulching and weeding practices. In contrast, the Agri-park farmers and all visitors to the farm came over as completely comfortable and enthusiastic about using sewage effluent for irrigation. The Agri-park farmers not only cooperated but also worked very hard to establish and maintain the trial. They even gave some of their irrigation pipes and tanks for the trial. Some bystanders mentioned that sewage effluent is nothing to be concerned about, because it really is just 'human manure' (Le Roux et al. 2021).

The South African Government is considering ways to decentralise sanitation. The decentralisation of sanitation in South Africa can be linked to small-scale agriculture in rural areas. Research is needed to develop safe domestic practices with rural households for reusing sewage effluent in food production. More research is also still needed to investigate some potential risks to better understand and manage the safety of consuming crops grown with effluent water. Over-irrigation and leaching of sewage effluent, which are more likely where farmers are uneducated, would result in the pollution of groundwater. This could be prevented by applying sewage water in a hydroponic system, a practice that requires further research. Organic pollutants are an important health risk to consider when using sewage effluent, which is currently not well understood. Helmecke, Fries and Schulte (2020) said that numerous organic pollutants could potentially be found in sewage effluent, and it is still unknown whether these are taken up and accumulated in the edible portions of the crops. Information on the transmission of enveloped type viruses like COVID-19 through water is limited. Therefore, despite the potential benefits of reusing sewage water, there are some important risks that require further research.

From a social perspective, the irrigation with effluent could address sustainable food production in terms of food security and equity, because sewage waste is freely available to all people, and poor people have continuous access to this resource. From an economic perspective, the practice could help to achieve production unit viability, because the consistent supply of sewage can make production units more resilient to stresses.

Addressing consumer behaviour and household cultures

Many scientists are investigating ways to achieve the targeted 60%–70% increase in production. However, it is probably more important to prevent this increase in demand. Consumer behaviour must be directed towards more sustainable limits. Excessive consumption of animal products and of food in general must be discouraged and food wastage must be addressed. Yet, even current food production is unsustainable, and it is worth re-considering the systems that have led us to this point.

In the modern world food production moved away from the household, which created problems that are difficult or impossible to solve. We argue that what is needed is not just a reduction in consumption, but cultural changes to produce food at home or on a small scale in rural and urban communities. Food production at a small scale fundamentally presents the least complexity, for example, by making the consumer more independent and more in control of the food production process. If rural areas become more successful and self-supported through small-scale agriculture, it may prevent further rural–urban migration. Currently, regenerative agricultural principles are more feasible for smaller scale farms, or farms using the concept of hubs with mixed agriculture. The fact that there is still significant production of food on small-scale farms in African countries, indicates that the opportunity exists to develop small-scale food production. These small-scale farms are not as productive as they could be, and with proper support they can become a key role player towards more sustainable organically produced food. Such households and farms must be supported to use regenerative agricultural principles and still achieve optimal food production and remain viable production units.

Most people in urban areas do not have enough space available to produce all the food they need, and will always be dependent on commercial farms. However, with arable land becoming more limited, urban gardens present an opportunity to contribute to food production. Grey water coming from an urban household and the rainfall that falls in the garden are potential water resources that can be used in food production. If urban households can grow a percentage of their food requirements, it will reduce the pressure on commercial farms. It may also give people a sense of and respect for what it takes to produce food and possibly create a feedback mechanism where people will be less likely to waste food, or consume too much. There is also a good possibility that such a culture will motivate lower-income communities to make use of their garden space and resources for food production.

Diversifying food production responses

In the section on 'Food production alternatives', different kinds of food production systems were discussed. Although it is clear that industrial agricultural practices are far from sustainable, finding a better alternative can be rather complex when practicing agriculture on a large scale. For example, although regenerative agriculture provides important goals for sustainable food production, it presents problems on a larger scale. Issues in terms of sustainability arise when agriculture is practiced on a large scale, not just because of the increased need of external inputs, but also because of the distance between the farmers and the consumers. Developing a general culture among people in rural, peri-urban and urban communities to produce at least some of their own food locally, on a small scale, is considered to be an important strategy to apply regenerative agricultural techniques, obtain feedback mechanisms within the system and to reduce the pressure on large-scale agriculture.

However, industrial agriculture, with its efficiency to produce food for many people will probably be with us in the foreseeable future. Communities that lack the space and time to produce all their own food will be dependent on industrial farms to at least a certain extent. In a modified world we need a diversity in agricultural approaches, small- and larger- scale, to address future food security. But all agricultural systems must focus on increasing sustainability as well as productive outputs.

■ Conclusion

Local and small-scale food production is an appropriate scale to reach sustainable food production, because regenerative agricultural methods of farming are possible on this scale, feedback mechanisms can occur more naturally, when people are able to observe the impacts of the production of their food, and communities can become more independent in terms of food production. The current trends in rural–urban migration and poor production on small-scale farms indicate that currently farmers are struggling to produce on a small scale, and this needs to be addressed in future research. The concept of hubs where several small-scale farmers are supported by a central body, which is what South African Agri-parks aims to be, can perhaps become a good model to improve production outcomes on a small scale.

Working towards a more sustainable food production system will require changes from all people at all levels of society:

- On a household and community level at least three important practices need to be adopted:
    - Food production within the homestead and communities that make use of the available land, organic waste and water resources in order to reduce pressure on commercial farms.
    - Consumption patterns in developed countries and communities must change. This includes preventing over-consumption and changes from consuming large quantities of meat towards more plant-based diets, which have a lower carbon and WF.
    - Extension services should be made available at the community level, to ensure maximum production, and minimise food losses on household and community level farms.
- On a small-scale farm it is important to use all available waste products and work according to regenerative agricultural principles, while maximising production. Extension services must also be provided at this level.
- On a larger scale, farmers must develop practices that minimise the losses of nutrients from their fields and to reuse nutrients.
- Future research is necessary to:
    - Develop safe practices of recycling nutrients from sewage effluent. Different technologies will be suitable for industrial, small-scale and homestead food production.
    - Co-design, with rural households, effective household-based farming practices that will ensure maximum production, food security and a good quality of life for all the people in the household.

■ Acknowledgements

This research originated from a project initiated, managed and funded by the Water Research Commission (WRC project No. K5/2823//4): Evaluation of the management and impact of the quantity and quality of water for Agri-parks in Gauteng Province, South Africa.

Chapter 5

Partnerships that flourish or fail: A case study of social entrepreneurship in the Eastern Free State, South Africa

Deidré van Rooyen
Centre for Development Support,
Faculty of Economic and Management Sciences, University of the Free State,
Bloemfontein, South Africa

Willem F. Ellis
Centre for Gender and Africa Studies,
Faculty of Humanities, University of the Free State,
Bloemfontein, South Africa

■ Introduction

Since the turn of the century, social entrepreneurship has been a significant focus of dialogue and engagements worldwide by social activists, policymakers, academics, big business, entrepreneurs and the media (Mair & Marti 2006; Nicholls 2010:756; Zahra et al. 2008). Furthermore, social entrepreneurs and social enterprises are rising globally, as is their influence and impact

How to cite: Van Rooyen, D. & Ellis, W., 2021, 'Partnerships that flourish or fail: A case study of social entrepreneurship in the Eastern Free State, South Africa', in A.S. Van Niekerk & S. Strijbos (eds.), *We cannot continue like this: Facing modernity in Africa and the West*, pp. 93–118, AOSIS, Cape Town. https://doi.org/10.4102/aosis.2021.BK283.05

(Urban 2008:347). In the United States of America, Canada, Korea, South America and the United Kingdom, such organisations have been fundamental in planning social and environmental opportunities and helping to restore economic prosperity. In the developing world, social entrepreneurship is also entrenched in providing public services on a small local scale – from solving poverty and social problems (i.e. co-operatives) to functioning as quasi-governmental in social development and employment (Nicholls 2010:756). Dees (1998) suggests that society has always had social entrepreneurs, even though they might not have been referred to as such in the past. There are several examples of best practice social entrepreneurship in South Africa. Every day more are being 'discovered' – the reason being that many have not been operating under the formal terminology of social entrepreneurship.

Something all relevant research seems to agree on is that social entrepreneurship is a complex phenomenon not yet well understood (Massetti 2008:7), and therefore, the research agenda for this field is also not yet clearly defined (Nicholls 2010; Short, Moss & Lumpkin 2009). Much of the literature on social entrepreneurship centres on defining the concept (Corner & Ho 2010:635; Mair & Marti 2006, 2009; Peredo & McLean 2006), with a heavy focus on conceptual over empirical research (Dacin, Dacin & Matear 2010:38; Short et al. 2009). Despite the interest in social enterprise, the concept has not been researched as extensively as conventional business or charity cases (Galera & Borzaga 2009:210). According to Bull and Crompton (2005), social entrepreneurs can be seen as part of the third sector – the not-for-profit sector, comprising social enterprises, non-profit businesses, civil society organisations and NGOs. These terms are used interchangeably, which also makes the industry challenging to understand (Doherty et al. 2009:2). Still, the prevailing theoretical view on social entrepreneurship refers to entrepreneurial behaviours employed to address social challenges through financially viable and self-sustainable entities (Defourny & Nyssens 2010). Saebi, Foss and Linder (2018) add that social entrepreneurs display characteristics similar to commercial entrepreneurs in identifying and taking advantage of existing opportunities, mobilising resources and using innovative approaches to create new ventures. Social entrepreneurs engage in these activities to achieve a social mission (Austin, Stevenson & Wei-Skillern 2006; Zahra et al. 2009). However, it is noted that the opportunities identified by social entrepreneurs trace their source to social problems that plague societies, an approach that is different from that usually taken by commercial entrepreneurs who are solely driven by the bottom-line of profit maximisation (Zahra & Wright 2016).

Social entrepreneurship success stories show up frequently in the media (Bloom 2009:129); are referred to in the public sector; have become a shared subject of debate on university campuses (Martin & Osberg 2007:30) and inform the future planning of numerous prominent social sector organisations. Research on social entrepreneurship is filled with examples of 'success stories', yet the study of entrepreneurial failure is just as crucial to understanding the potential viability and sustainability of social enterprises (Bloom 2009:133; Dacin et al. 2010:51; Light 2009).

Although many social enterprises aim to become financially self-sufficient in their operations, they may need various income streams like donations, grants, public funding and self-generated profit (Doherty et al. 2009:28). In attaining this status, it has become even more critical to partner with a wide variety of role players active in the social entrepreneurial space – some of them very similar to the social enterprises themselves, but others frighteningly different and originating from domains very dissimilar to their own. The skills and diplomacy of partnership formation and the ability to 'fuse' the interest of entities from divergent realms has thus become crucial, adding yet another challenge to the viability of social enterprises in general (Bull 2018).

This chapter presents a case study that will highlight the importance of healthy partnerships in social entrepreneurial endeavours. It concerns a 'story of failure' – about the MDF, an initiative in which several divergent parties entered a partnership to support small-scale entrepreneurs in the QwaQwa region, one of the most impoverished areas in South Africa. The discussion will focus on the dilemmas of collaboration and the challenges that the MDF faced. The chapter is divided into three main parts, a concise summation of theory relevant to partnership formation in the social entrepreneurial context, related to that perspective, a description of the story of the MDF, followed by a review of lessons learned and their importance for partnership formation.

■ Partnerships in the social entrepreneurship space

According to Mohr and Spekman (1994), partnerships are defined as:

> [P]urposive strategic relationships between independent *firms* who share compatible goals, strive for mutual benefit, and acknowledge a high level of mutual interdependence. They join efforts to achieve goals that each *firm*, acting alone, could not attain easily. (p. 137)

There are no fixed characteristics of a good partnership but Lister (2000:230) and USAID (1997) mention a few examples like:

> [M]utual trust, mutual support, willingness to negotiate, reciprocal accountability, financial transparency, joint decision-making, two-way exchange of information, long-term commitment articulated goals, equitable distribution of benefits and liabilities, a clear outline of responsibilities, shared perceptions of the outcomes, and a process of adjudicating disputes. (pp. 20–23)

Botes and Abrahams (2008:121) highlight the fact that partnerships are beneficial not only to the process (a means to an end) but also to the outcome (an end in itself). They then note a few advantages like seeing issues through the eyes of others, sharing information that could enhance participatory development and foster open communication. Partnerships improve access to funding, human, physical and social capital and link value chains. Partners may bring various aspects to the table like finances, technicalities, employment, resources and services (Choi et al. 2018). Partnerships can help develop strategic direction on a scale that is almost impossible for a single actor independently, with collaborations between social enterprises and larger corporations proving beneficial for both parties. The social enterprises involved attract extensive business resources for sustainable business, while the larger corporations gain public interest because of the fulfilment of their social responsibilities (Park, Hwang & Kim 2018).

The lateral capacity of a partnership network is linked to the number of partners in the network. As the lateral scale increases the network, the number of contracts within the greater partnership also increases. Therefore, more resources and other networks become available. A more extensive network then also helps gain access to more markets, equipment, products and services. However, the more extensive the network of partners, the higher the cost of building and managing the network, sometimes causing greater uncertainty (Choi et al. 2018). Organisations should, however, each be strong enough to gain the benefits of the partnership network.

London and Rondinelli (2003) described three emotional barriers that often undermine the formation of partnerships: mistrust, fear of losing control and misunderstanding of each partner's motivations and intent. Diverse sectors have alternative values, governance structures and missions (Googins & Rochlin 2000), explaining the misinterpretation of purpose and goals. Therefore, partnerships are complicated, miscellaneous and delicate relationships, which change with time, but they are also essential for executing the development chain (Morse & McNamara 2006:321). Collaborations have been a common occurrence to secure funding and portray a progressive persona. Botes and Abrahams (2008:117) mention that a partnership is crucial in bridging the gap between the developed and undeveloped, the rich and the poor and the prosperous and the disadvantaged.

The concepts of developmental partnerships were, at the time of the creation of the MDF, one of the eight-millennium development goals (MDGs) adopted by the United Nations in 2000: *'develop a global partnership for development'* (World Bank 2015). With the MDGs being superseded by the SDGs in 2015, the importance of partnerships did not fall by the wayside. The SDG 17 aims at revitalising the global partnership for sustainable development. SDG target 17.17 particularly envisions partnerships between the government, the private sector and civil society (Global Goals for Sustainable Development 2021). The importance of partnerships can be seen in initiatives such as the 2030 Agenda Partnership Accelerator. The Accelerator is an initiative by the United Nations Department of Economic and Social Affairs

(UN DESA) and The Partnering Initiative – collaborating with the United Nations Office for Partnerships (UNOP), UN Global Compact and the UN Development Coordination Office. The initiative aims to significantly help accelerate and scale up effective partnerships supporting the SDGs (Stibbe & Prescott 2020).

Although they acknowledge that the field is still wide open for further research, Littlewood and Holt (2018) acknowledge the fact that social enterprises around the world is definitely contributing to the attainment of the SDGs – relating to the goals in a variety of ways as far as positioning in value chains and operational activities are concerned. As far as the role of social entrepreneurs in the attainment of the SDGs are concerned, Vujasinovi, Lipenkova and Orlando (2019) assert that although very few social enterprises clearly link their activities to the SDGs, they do offer an all-encompassing and innovative way of addressing local and global challenges – offering contextual business models.

Consequently, collaboration across sectors can provide innovative solutions to social problems (Maase & Bossink 2010:68). Hence, building successful stakeholder relationships with the targeted disadvantaged groups is also key to the success of social entrepreneurial ventures – the effective ones establishing high degrees of trust (Doherty et al. 2009:32). Sako (1992) identified three components of faith: competency trust, contractual trust and goodwill trust. Competency trust refers to the 'skills, competencies, and characteristics that enable a party to influence within some specific domain' (Mayer, Davies & Schoorman 1995:717). In other words, the partners trust each other to perform their duties as anticipated. This is a trust that is entirely based on prior experience. On the other hand, contractual trust is rooted in contracts developed and signed by each partner to uphold the agreements (Curtis, Herbst & Gumkovska 2010:194). Finally, goodwill trust refers to a willingness to do more than is formally expected. Indeed, goodwill trust is when one partner is willing to put other partners' interest above their duties (Sako 1992).

Sonenshine (2018) acknowledges that organisations working on social, environmental and economic impact are under pressure to form partnerships to be most effective, especially for social entrepreneurs. Partnerships do contribute to the delivery of impact at scale but can be pretty challenging to put together. It is time consuming, resource-intensive and brings the challenges of marrying up skills, motivations and organisational cultures. Several suggestions in this regard are forthcoming from Sonenshine (2018):

- A clear understanding by all organisations of their motives, goals and objectives when entering into a possible partnership.
- Goal alignment among prospective partners, quantification of outcomes and role-clarification is paramount and can be cemented in the compilation of partnership criteria and action plans.

- Complimentary skills should be identified to strengthen the combined effort and skills gaps addressed.
- Regular reviews of partnership efficiency are crucial – partnerships might change as they evolve but cannot move beyond the original mission parameters.

Partnerships are not always straightforward because they often encounter managerial challenges and are impacted upon by complicated interpersonal relationships (Park et al. 2018). Furthermore, if any of the partners are not willing to commit and do not have the capacity to execute the duty allocated to them, the probability of the partnership failing significantly increases. The lack of competency and commitment from partners increases uncertainty and the likelihood of partnership failure (Choi et al. 2018). In many cases, asymmetrical power relations can also cause resource dependence and an 'unbalanced' partnership structure. Partnership creation for social enterprise between a social entrepreneur and other organisations from various sectors could be inhibited by conflicting interests and diverging speed of partners on the one hand, and by the conflicts that originate from the opportunity-seeking behaviour of the social entrepreneur and the risk-avoiding behaviour of the organisations on the other (Maase & Bossink 2010).

There are several differences between commercial and social entrepreneurial partnerships. The main difference is that social entrepreneurs endorse social value and development instead of economic value (Maase & Bossink 2010; Martin & Osberg 2007). Considerable research has been conducted on commercial partnership creation between existing organisations in business, and the non-profit public to public situations. Yet, most publications do not explicitly focus on socially-driven entrepreneurial partnerships, in which the social entrepreneur acts as a 'man or woman with a dream' (Maase & Bossink 2010:72).

Considering the above-described dynamics and especially the challenges related to forming enduring social entrepreneurial partnerships, the following case study will elucidate the MDF as an effort to align the agendas of several development role players into a viable social entrepreneurial initiative. The section will render a broad background to the formation and activities of the MDF, the interest and roles of its different participants and the dynamics relevant to its operation and ultimate closure.

The MDF. Taking the lead from this term, the main aim of the MDF was to create a revolving development fund in terms of which identified budding entrepreneurs in the QwaQwa region of South Africa could be assisted through the provision of financial means and ongoing business support. Not only were identified entrepreneurs to be supported with low interest loans but they were also to be mentored through training, advice and consultation interventions for a specific period.

The MDF was a combined effort of the International Institute for Development and Ethics (IIDE), the University of the Free State (UFS) and a Dutch consortium of donors consisting of the Noaber[18] Foundation and CHR Investments BV. The distinct origins of the prospective partners made for a partnership structure with a myriad of possibilities and eventually made it much more challenging to communicate effectively in forming a cohesive partnership vision, with accompanying 'fusion' of agendas and clarification of roles.

Location of the Moahisane Development Fund

The MDF was operationalised in the central Free State Province of South Africa in an urban/peri-urban area called Phuthaditjhaba. Phuthaditjhaba is the urban centre of a previously semi-autonomous region called QwaQwa and serves as the administrative head office of Maluti-A-Phofung Local Municipality. Surrounding Phuthaditjhaba are rural villages established on land governed by a variety of local indigenous leaders. The area forms part of the Thabo Mofutsanyane District Municipality (Figure 5.1). It covers the Eastern part of the Free State province, bordering the KwaZulu-Natal Province of South Africa and Lesotho (Thabo Mofutsanyane District Municipality 2010).

At the time of the existence of the MDF, the population of Thabo Mofutsanyane District Municipality accounted for 25% of the people of the Free State province, with most of the population in the district situated in the Maluti-a-Phofung Local Municipality (55.5% of the district population and 13.8% of the provincial population). The district is the second smallest contributor to the Free State's gross domestic product, with community services, financial services and wholesale, retail and trade being the main contributing sectors (Maluti-a-Phofung Local Municipality 2010). The population is relatively young, with almost 65% of the population younger than 29 years. Maluti-a-Phofung Local Municipality is rated as the most poverty-stricken area in the Free State province, with about 67% of the population living below the subsistence level (less than ZAR800 per month). Only about 26% of the workforce was employed, with the government sector is the largest employer in the municipal area (Business Trust and Department of Provincial and Local Government 2007).

The partners in the Moahisane Development Fund

As said, the MDF partnership was between three major role players. Firstly, the IIDE, represented by both its South African and European offices, is an innovative scholarly institute researching the extent, nature and normative

---

18. 'Noaber' is in the Twente dialect of Dutch which means neighbour.

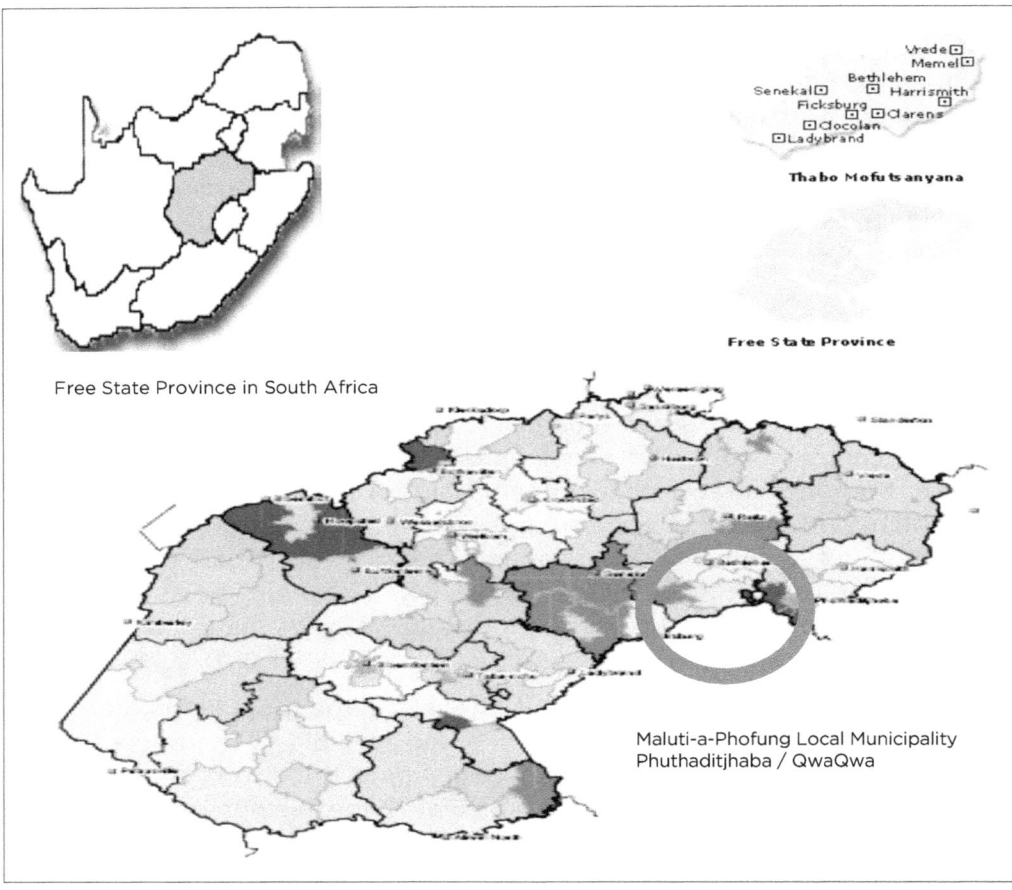

Sources: Business Trust and Department of Provincial and Local Government (2007) and Thabo Mofutsanyane District Municipality (2010).

FIGURE 5.1: Region where case study plays an important role – Eastern Free State.

aspects of poverty, inequality and injustice through local, regional, national and international channels. It had been created in 2003 through the initiative of several Dutch and ultimately South African scholars and had, at the time of the creation of the MDF, already initiated research projects on the topic of the role of religious actors in development initiatives as well as the publication of a book entitled '*From our Side – Emerging Perspectives on Development and Ethics*' in 2008. At the time of the creation of the MDF, the IIDE had mainly acted as a 'catalyst' of initiatives, a 'facilitator' of discourse and the 'initiator' of research interventions. The MDF would be the IIDE's first effort at facilitating the creation of a 'home-grown' initiative that would enable it to research some of the practical and ethical aspects of development initiatives that it had only grappled with within the academic realm before. It would also be the first time that the IIDE had ventured into social entrepreneurship as a permutation of many developmental models that had gained favour at that time. Originating in the domain of development research, the IIDE's interest in the creation of the MDF and its successful operationalisation were as follows (MDF 2008a):

- The creation of a 'real-life' social entrepreneurial venture aimed at uplifting identified entrepreneurs through which the IIDE could research issues of ethical development, especially the effect of the MDF as a development initiative in the QwaQwa environment. This would be done through the creation of a 'committee for ethical development' (CED) made up of community members within the operational area of the MDF.
- The compilation of research reports in this vein, in cooperation with the UFS, and the publication of scholarly articles on lessons learnt from social entrepreneurial interventions of this kind and their influence on communities involved in such interventions.
- The building of good practice networks among donors, practitioners, scholars and community members to learn from each other and disseminate lessons and best practices in this field (Free State's Regional Steering Committee, 2010). The vision of the IIDE that an intercultural approach in development interventions should be developed was paramount in this regard – ensuring that Western development ideas and practices did not dominate but that a development model could be created that was operationally and culturally acceptable in QwaQwa – ensuring its future viability. The CED was to play the lead role in this vital endeavour – acting as a conduit between the community and its needs and the MDF partners and their capabilities. The ideas mooted by Strijbos (2012:160–161) regarding the importance of diverse approaches to development are essential in this regard. The idea of 'a reciprocal process of cultural co-evolution' with development partners underpins what was envisaged with the concept of the CED.

Secondly, a Dutch donor consortium, The Noaber Foundation, was a foundation with a public benefit goal based in Lunteren in the Netherlands. The organisation consisted of two parts, namely, Noaber Ventures, an impact investment vehicle, and Noaber Philanthropy that funded development projects by providing donations. Projects and investments that purported to have solutions to social problems were identified by Noaber and targeted for assistance through financial investment or the provision of loans. Based in Rotterdam in the Netherlands, CHR Investments also made investments in social engagements, with the MDF being its first venture of this kind outside of the Netherlands. The company was managed by an individual businessman who had been a very successful insurance broker, working with highly influential business people in Europe, but with minimal knowledge of the dynamics of the developing world. In their introduction in the build-up to the MDF, CHR Investments and the Noaber Foundation had also not previously cooperated in any developmental initiatives. This consortium, finding its cue from the domain of development finance, aimed at the following:

- The successful creation of a revolving development fund based on their initial financial investments that would assist identified entrepreneurs and provide them with small loans – with the repayment of the loans and concomitant interest forming the basis of the next round of funding.
- Through cooperation with Northern and Southern partners, setting up a record of good practice that could be adopted by other impact investors and financial actors wanting to become involved in initiatives of this kind.
- Broadening their portfolios of successful development interventions outside of the Netherlands – especially in the case of the Noaber Foundation (MDF 2008a).

Thirdly, from an academic origin, the UFS. The UFS was a natural partner for the MDF endeavour as it was the pre-eminent educational institution in the Free State province with a campus in the QwaQwa region. The IIDE-Africa office was also hosted by the UFS and had strong links with the institution, especially the Chief Directorate Community Service (currently the Directorate Community Engagement). Even though the MDF was never formally institutionally linked to the above directorate, its proposed activities naturally slotted into the aims of this directorate in that it brought the UFS closer to the QwaQwa community and allowed the UFS to capacitate both its staff members and its surrounding community through the implementation of the MDF – an earlier interpretation of the 'engaged scholarship' approach currently driven by this directorate at the UFS (UFS 2020). Adding to the possibility of a viable intervention in QwaQwa was the fact that the QwaQwa campus of the UFS hosted the Unit for Entrepreneurship (UE), a small unit aimed at building capacity among students and related role players in the QwaQwa region. The UE formed part of the Department of Business Management under the UFS Faculty of Economic and Management Sciences (EMS). The UE offered expertise in entrepreneurship development, training and mentorship of small businesses. Broadly, operating from the domain of academic inquiry, the UFS and the entities designated to assist in operationalising the MDF had in mind the accomplishment of the following aims in participating in the MDF:

- The creation of a community engagement intervention that would allow for the creation of good practice learning in the setting up and operationalisation of a development intervention such as the MDF.
- Allowing the UE to contribute in a practical way to building capacity among entrepreneurs in the QwaQwa region and establishing itself as a competent role player in entrepreneurial development in the QwaQwa region (MDF 2008a).

- Participating in a prestigious partnership with international donors would enhance capability among staff members of the UFS and expose them to a multi-disciplinary development intervention.

From the above, it is clear that all prospective partners had a range of interests at play in setting up the MDF – some of them unique to their organisations and mandates and others complementary and overlapping. These varying interests, mandates and agendas lay at the root of successful partnership formation.

Over and above the interest shown in the operationalisation of the MDF, all parties were to play specific roles in the setting up and operationalisation of the MDF – some directly linked to the stated interests and others of a broader nature. Even though this could be elucidated upon much more, it will be kept brief for the case study. The roles of each of the organisations are highlighted in Table 5.1 and reinforced by the organisation's structure in Figure 5.2.

Table 5.1 clearly specifies the roles of each of the partners. Figure 5.2 further highlights the 'organisational structure' of the MDF in terms of the broader scope of its management, with the entrepreneurs represented in the lower block entitled identified projects.

This naturally brings to the fore the question…what about the chosen entrepreneurs as the fourth leg of the partnership? Where can their voice be heard? The absence of a dedicated section in this case study, dealing with the personal experiences of the entrepreneurs that had participated in the MDF possibly reflects (again) some of the weaknesses in the setting up of the MDF from its inception until its demise. This issue is commented upon in more detail later.

The QwaQwa region was scanned for applicable entrepreneurial ventures with growth and development potential. These entrepreneurs had to complete a comprehensive application process, and a selection matrix was developed to determine whether the venture was feasible and viable. The entrepreneurs who were chosen during the existence of the MDF are listed in Table 5.2 followed by photographs of some of the manufactured products (Figure 5.3).

Upon acceptance into the project, a brain profile analysis determined whether the individual entrepreneur was the 'correct fit' for the venture proposed and the training (financial, marketing, management, general or entrepreneurial creativity/innovation training and computer literacy) needed for the entrepreneur to succeed in this venture (see Figure 5.4). A mentoring programme was initiated and tailor-made to the individual entrepreneur's needs – aimed at assisting the entrepreneur on an ongoing basis with marketing, financial control and management (MDF 2008a). Loans were also granted to the individual entrepreneurs in terms of separate loan agreements to meet the needs of each enterprise.

TABLE 5.1: Partners in the Moahisane Development Fund.

Partners	Role
Dutch donor consortium (Noaber Foundation & CHR Investments)	• The provision of funding for the utilisation of small loans in the MDF • Financing of some of the operational aspects of the MDF through donations to administer the MDF • Participation in decision-making and monitoring through its representation on the Supervisory Board of the Fund
University of the Free State (Chief Directorate Finances; Chief Directorate Community Service; Office of the Dean of Economic and Management Sciences)	• Hosting the entity (and its legal operation) within the financial structures of the UFS • Coordination of all the procedures and administration for financial transactions from the allocated financial entity (A dedicated UFS account) • Hosting of the bank account with special tariffs applicable to the MDF's bank costs • Responsibility for the facilitation of the audit procedure by independent auditors at the end of every financial year • Participation in decision-making and monitoring through its representation on the Supervisory Board of the Fund
Unit for Entrepreneurship (UE)	• The operational management of the Fund • Scanning the QwaQwa region for applicable entrepreneurial ventures with growth and development potential for possible assistance • Establish a specific entrepreneurial approach as a business coach with every potential entrepreneur for representation to the Fund's board for approval • Manage the whole entrepreneurial approach and being responsible as a business coach for every entrepreneur according to the specific strategic plan of that entrepreneur • Reporting annually on the progress of each entrepreneur to the Supervisory Board • Reporting annually, after the audit report made by an accountant, on the financial and operational state of the Fund to the Supervisory Board • Reports quarterly to the Funders about the progress made during the quarter according to a template developed in close cooperation between the Fund and the Funders • Participation in decision-making and monitoring through its representation on the Supervisory Board of the Fund
International Institute for Development and Ethics (IIDE Europe and IIDE Africa)	• Ensuring 'monitoring' over the input of a variety of role players in the environment of development (in this case QwaQwa and the MDF) • Explore an approach where a 'guarantor' of ethics and good governance is involved to ensure maximisation of the positive impact of the intervention of the MDF and the limitation of the adverse effects of the MDF– also providing good 'social returns' • Acting as the convenor of the Committee for Ethical Development (CED) • Participation in decision-making and monitoring through its representation on the Supervisory Board of the Fund

Source: MDF (2008a).
MDF, Moahisane Development Fund; UFS, University of the Free State.

Although, new and existing entrepreneurs entering the MDF were exposed to a number of training modules and capacity building interventions (as described in Figure 5.4), it was all very technical in nature and little attention was given to the 'human' factor of being part of such an initiative. Too little attention was perhaps given to the experiences of the chosen entrepreneurs in the project and the transformation (personal and professional) occurring within the lives of the entrepreneurs chosen. This was to be the focus of the to-be-created CED. Quite some energy was put into the creation of such a committee, and high hopes were held for its successful inclusion in the broader project.

Chapter 5

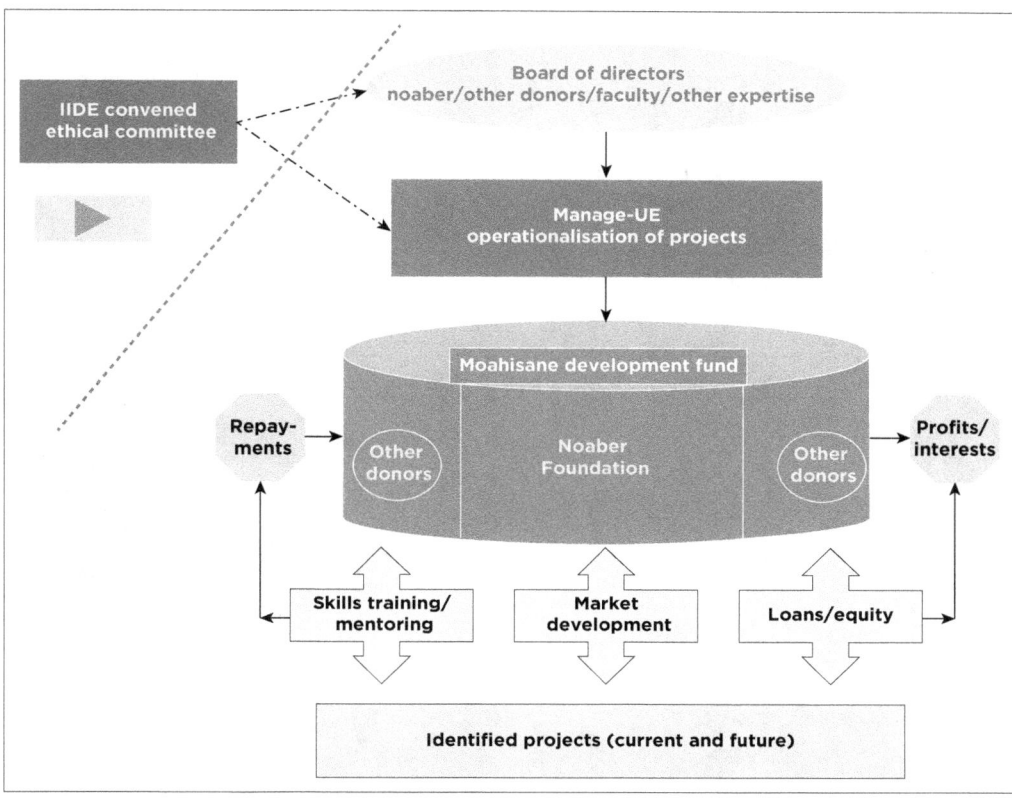

Source: Moahisane Development Fund (MDF) (2010).
FIGURE 5.2: Moahisane Development Fund organisational structure.

TABLE 5.2: Summary of entrepreneurs assisted by the Moahisane Development Fund.

Entrepreneurs	Name	Business
2008 Entrepreneurs	Palesa Collections	Handmade cards for specific target markets like funeral services, anniversaries, weddings, other functions, with an own identity and a personal touch
	Thaba Blinds	A grass weaving project, producing blinds and other hand-woven products of excellent quality at an affordable price
	Simon's Cars	Manually manufacturing cars from wire and metal, producing life-like models with an own identity
	Ilholomelo's	Jewellery produced from copper wire
2009 Entrepreneurs	Lydia Thetha	Manufacturing school uniforms, jerseys, socks for school in QwaQwa
	Modise's Steel and Window Frames	Manufacture window frames, burglar bars, gates and washing line poles
	Rebecca Motuang Weavers	Ornaments, necklaces, hats (Traditional Basotho hats) from grass
2010 Entrepreneurs	MyStore	MYstore Holdings (Pty) facilitated the renting of shipping container-based outlets for entrepreneurs selling consumer goods to the local community
	Ramon Naroodien Printing	Printing service for all types of printing on different objects
	Happy Nappy	To produce nappies of all sizes for the clinics and the local hospital in QwaQwa

Sources: MDF (2009, 2010).

105

Partnerships that flourish or fail

Source: Photographs taken by Willem F. Ellis, published with permission from Willem F. Ellis.
FIGURE 5.3: Some of the products delivered by the 2009/2010 batch of entrepreneurs, (a) Palesa collections – Event cards and printing, (b) Thaba blinds – Grass woven window blinds and room dividers, (c) Simon's cars – Toy cars, (d) Ilholomelo's – Copper jewellery, (e) Nteffeleng Sibeko's shoes – Shoes from recycled materials, (f) Modise's steel and Window Frames – Steel products for the home.

The Moahisane Development Fund in action and the role of the Committee for Ethical Development

A critical role in the operation of the MDF was envisaged for a CED. The CED was a guarantor to foster an ethical and intercultural approach in development (MDF 2011a) and eventual ownership of the possible development brought by entrepreneurship by those impacted upon in QwaQwa. Moreover, it favours recognising new needs and more effective exploitation of the resources of a given locality – human, economic, cultural and environmental (Galera & Borzaga 2009:218). Various other disciplines such as law, medicine and accounting have 'governing bodies', but this seems to be absent from the 'development' environment – except when the mentioned disciplines

Chapter 5

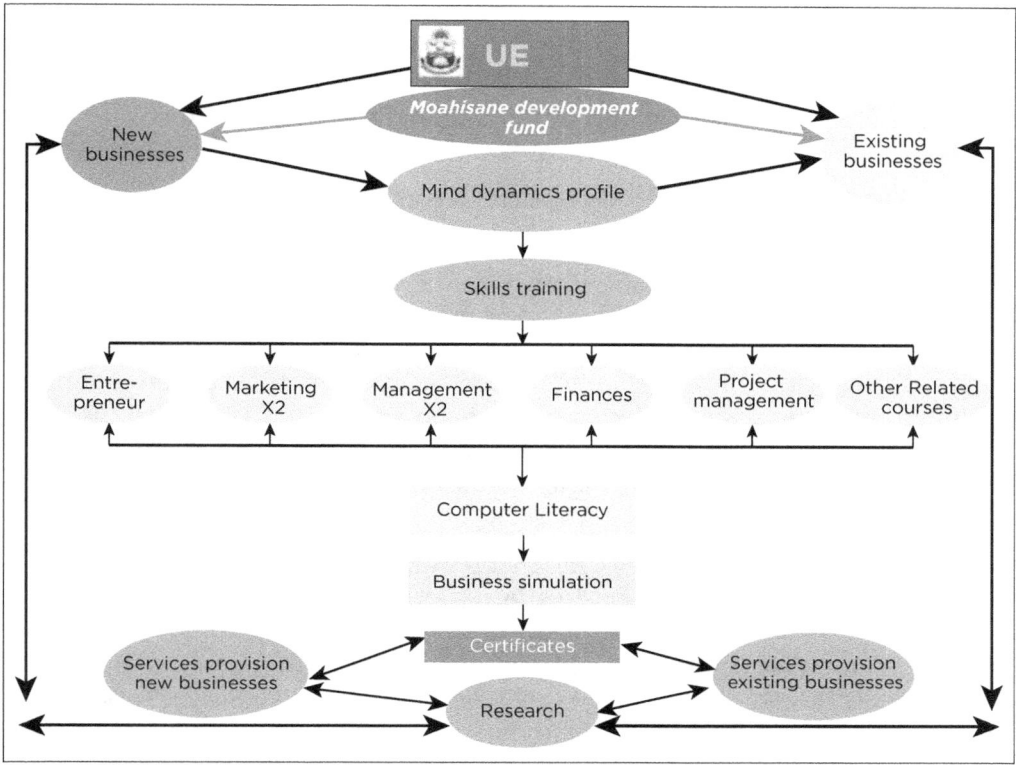

Source: Moahisane Development Fund (MDF) (2010).
FIGURE 5.4: The capacity building undergone by Moahisane Development Fund entrepreneurs.

become involved in development in their specific roles. It can be said that the involvement of local stakeholders allows approaching the community's interest as a whole, as it contributes to enhancing trust relations.

The role of a CED convened by the IIDE was a novel approach aimed at ensuring 'monitoring' of the input of various role players in the environment of development (in this case, QwaQwa and the MDF). The IIDE envisaged this committee playing a crucial facilitative role within the growth process of the entrepreneurs in making and keeping them aware of the effect of their activities on the communities surrounding them. They acted as a 'bridge' between the entrepreneurs and the communities they operated in, keeping their entrepreneurial activities 'rooted' in the peculiar needs of their surrounding social environment. This relationship would also then be utilised to develop and roll out a tool designed to measure the social return on investment of the whole MDF venture – over and above the standard measurement of financial returns for the entire project.

With the lack of success in getting the CED fully operational before the demise of the MDF, such best practices and research fell by the wayside – robbing the initiative of extremely valuable information and wisdom for future

107

generations of development practitioners. After the demise of the MDF, no effort was made to do a thorough post-mortem of the project with the affected entrepreneurs. In hindsight, this lack of follow-up possibly encompasses the biggest lapse in ethical development practice in the whole project.

☐ The demise of the Moahisane Development Fund

Several environmental factors elucidated below caused the MDF to take off slowly, causing some frustration among the members of the Dutch donor consortium. They wanted to see quicker results in the setting up of the MDF and the empowerment of the identified entrepreneurs. In addition, the differences in operation between a commercial venture as an agent of implementation and an academic entity such as the UFS (with the UE as an agent of implementation) did cause some frustration at first. Still, they were primarily addressed – although this could have been the first cracks in the partnership edifice.

Another common problem experienced was that the business did not prove to show growth and expansion in the period of involvement. Furthermore, several entrepreneurs had been supported through government grants too. They could not always differentiate between the rendering of a grant with few returns expected and the provision of a 'soft' loan that had to be repaid over a reasonable period. Therefore, the most critical overarching factor leading to the ultimate demise of the MDF was the fact that the fund never reached its status as a 'revolving' fund. This was because none of the identified entrepreneurs was able to pay back their loans within the designated times – because of a variety of factors such as constantly changing business plans; entrepreneurs absconding from their places of operation; misunderstandings in terms of the differences between grants and loans and a lack of explicit control and fund management from the UE. This led to much frustration among the members of the Dutch donor consortium, with a high level of anger and distrust emerging among the partners of the MDF. Again, in retrospect, the possibility of non-payment by entrepreneurs is a factor that should have received more attention in the run-up to the creation of the MDF – especially in informing the Dutch donor consortium of the dynamics of the micro-loan environment in South Africa. The almost complete absence of the traditional South African banking sector from this 'business space' should have raised red flags regarding the risk of operating in this 'space'. This risk would be much more significant for a new and inexperienced partnership consisting of entities not at all experienced in operating in this 'space'. No amount of enthusiasm and good intention could make up for the lack of previous exposure to this operating environment. This is an excellent example of an operational factor not well-foreseen during planning, ultimately negatively impacting the focus and coherence of the partnership.

This led to the activation of an evaluation-based early-exit clause in the MDF partnership contract, which allowed for a cessation of financial contributions by the donors and a complete withdrawal from the MDF (MDF 2008a). In terms of an agreement reached between the partners all activities of the MDF were ceased, and an agreed-upon amount of already received funding was repaid to the donors. Later, the UE tried to reclaim some of the budget allocated to entrepreneurs using mediated discussions and legal efforts – largely without success.

Few of those involved in development interventions, successful or not, will argue that hindsight is 20/20. Yet, when looking back mainly at unsuccessful interventions, the warning signs should have been clear for all to see. If visible and clearly understood at that time, proactive measures could have been put in place to head off possible challenges, unforeseen circumstances and unintended consequences. But alas – that is looking back when it is too late to act, but never too late to learn.

The demise and lack of impact of the MDF could, in our view, partly be ascribed to unforeseen and accidental circumstances but primarily to partnership-related challenges – all contributing to the closure of the initiative. Nevertheless, the effects of the environmental circumstances upon the MDF should not be underestimated. Although it is not the primary aim of the chapter to review these factors, but rather to look at the partnership problem, these factors made it much more difficult to operate – causing the MDF to lose momentum and be subsumed by technical and management challenges, rather than those of development practice.

■ Environmental factors

The first environmental factor having an influence was the financial systems of the UFS becoming unfit for purpose in terms of the newly promulgated *National Credit Act*, No. 34 of 2005 and the *Consumer Protection Act*, No. 68 of 2008 that came into effect just as the MDF was taking off. The ability of the UFS to act as a 'lender' to prospective entrepreneurs was severely curtailed by the new legislation– making it difficult to provide funding for prospective entrepreneurs (RSA 2005, 2008). This had two unexpected results. To keep the entrepreneurs going, the UE started buying raw materials for entrepreneurs instead of providing funding for them to do it themselves. Again, the buying of raw materials did not fit in with the existing leeway given by the financial structures of the UFS, which were tailor-made for the provision of academic material and not for the bulk buying of tools, steel, grass (for weaving), wire and textiles (MDF 2011c). The bureaucratic and logistical burden on the UE became unbearable and led to a drop in the focus and morale of those involved. This further led to the inability of prospective entrepreneurs to be skilled in financial management and the art and skill of bulk buying and the bookkeeping processes that went with it, largely negating an important part of the training and mentoring impact of the empowerment effort. As mentioned above, this did lead to frustration among the members of the Dutch donor consortium as it delayed the operationalisation of the MDF and the shorter-term impact of the initiative.

Secondly, the academic staff member who was heading the UE was transferred from the QwaQwa campus of the UFS to the Bloemfontein campus of the UFS – 300 km away. He had built up an excellent network of contact with entrepreneurs previously because of the location of the UFS QwaQwa campus close to the industrial areas of Phuthaditjaba and the ability to consult and do capacity building easily. The transferral to a location 300 km away negated the effectiveness of the network and his ability to converse with and build the capacity of the identified entrepreneurs. Contact time between the academic as a mentor and the prospective entrepreneurs became severely limited with the concurrent knock-on effect of less time being spent on training, support and mentoring. Because of the limited human resources of the UE, no one with the necessary expertise could follow in the footsteps of the transferred academic staff member. The necessity of regularly travelling 600 km to and fro to support entrepreneurs also added unexpected cost to an already frugal budget – leading to anger over the repayment of funding received by the UFS to the Dutch donor consortium after the demise of the MDF (MDF 2011c).

As previously described, the three partners entering the MDF all had differing interests, mandates and capacities at the genesis of the venture. Although, as stated, there were also complimentary and overlapping focus areas. In addressing the role that partnership dynamics (or the lack of it) played, the satisfaction of the ultimate interests of each of the partners will be elucidated – hopefully clarifying the partnership conundrum ultimately contributing to the demise of the MDF.

■ Partnership-related factors
The position of Institute for Development and Ethics

The fact that the facilitation of the setting up of the MDF was primarily driven by the IIDE as an 'initiator' was initially positive as it was well-intentioned and was able to bring together all the role players at first. The IIDE was able to act as the 'driver' of the process and, at first, saw itself as the glue keeping the partnership together. This 'outsider' facilitation role was hardly a novel concept, but the fact is that the role and influence of the IIDE and its interests later largely fell by the wayside. Not being one of the main implementing parties in the partnership trusted with either funding the whole process (as done by the Dutch donor consortium) or being a primary implementing agency (as done by the UE as part of the UFS) led to the IIDE being relegated to a secondary role – that of setting up the CED and monitoring the effect of the MDF as a development initiative. Novel and commendable as the idea of the CED was, it never was the primary aim of either of the other two partners, with little of their focus and energy being devoted to it. The creation of the CED might have been viewed as a 'soft' intervention, whereas the funding and implementation of the MDF were seen as the 'hard', visible part of the intervention – actions that could be seen and measured in the shorter term. Even though the IIDE was represented in the supervisory board of the MDF, its efforts at proving its worth and its ultimate contribution to the more significant influence of the MDF were not always well understood and appreciated (IIDE, 2012). This ultimately impacted the success of the IIDE in reaching its other goals, as ensconced in its participation in the partnership. Even though initial meetings of a 'prototype' CED were held, the MDF did not last long enough for the IIDE's idea of an ethical guarantor to take root – both in the community of QwaQwa or even among its partners (MDF 2011a).

Even though the IIDE was successful in forging cooperation between many differing Northern and Southern actors, it might have been guilty of the crucial mistake sometimes made by development practitioners – that of introducing 'solutions' to communities and not co-creating 'solutions' *with* communities (Social Innovation eXchange [SIX] 2020). Even though it was clear to all who had followed the discourse on development in the QwaQwa region that it was in dire need of assistance, the idea of the MDF should have been allowed to organically grow within the community – gaining support, legitimacy and ultimately efficacy. In retrospect, the CED should possibly have been the first product of the MDF initiative, paving the way for its introduction into the impoverished community. Unfortunately, ongoing consultation with the community of QwaQwa by all role players lacked – including the UFS, UE and the IIDE (IIDE 2013). Even though the Dutch donor consortium did show an understanding of the concept of the CED, as proposed by the IIDE, and was not ignorant of the possible academic fruits to be harvested from the MDF in the form of teaching and learning; research and community service, they made it clear that they had little interest in these outcomes and wished to concentrate on the funding and capacity-building effort (IIDE 2012). In the end, none of their interests in the MDF partnership was met – except for lessons learned.

In an almost domino-like effect, the interests that the IIDE had in the MDF and the results that it had strived for became casualties of the lack of success of the MDF. The short life of the MDF and the unsuccessful effort to get the CED operational scuppered chances of reaping the research results necessary for contributing to good practice in the development field. The lack of transparent cooperation in this regard with the UFS is glaring in hindsight –

none of the core aspects of teaching and learning; community service (as it was then), or research conducted by UFS students and staff members were adequately negotiated before the commencement of the MDF and was approached on an ad hoc basis (IIDE 2013). The UE as implementing agents were not primarily interested in these issues and saw its role as limited to identifying and capacitating entrepreneurs – not students and academic staff.

The position of the Dutch donor consortium

As mentioned earlier, the Dutch donor consortium was made up of the Noaber Foundation, which had experience in development interventions across the world and CHR investment, which lacked any such experience. As can be expected of any donor willing to put their money where their mouths were, they were pretty excited to become involved in the MDF and contribute to a development intervention in the global South. This fact was proven by their willingness to fund and host preparatory consultations in the run-up to creating the MDF. Both the principals of the consortium partners visited the MDF and were introduced to its activities and the budding entrepreneurs. Looking back, the slow uptake in the operationalisation of the MDF because of, among others, the environmental factors mentioned above might have sown the initial seeds of doubt in the minds of these donors. The doubts harboured came to fruition when the concept of a revolving fund did not get off the ground, because of the lack of repayment of the loans offered and the inability of the MDF to become a truly 'revolving' fund where the repayment of loans and the interest on the loans would act as the funding basis for the next round of entrepreneurs (IIDE, Europe 2012). The consortium partners originated from the Northern business sectors and were possibly not ready for the intricacies and challenges of development interventions in the global South.

Again, when looking back, it is clear that the donor consortium was eager for quick and visible results where the upliftment of entrepreneurs could be 'showcased' (IIDE, South Africa 2012). However, even though some positive results were shown initially, the lack of impetus in the MDF and a growing unease by the donor consortium in the ability of the UE to manage the MDF lead to the implementation of an early exit clause in the contract of donorship – leading to the closure of the MDF, in our view prematurely.

The position of the University of the Free State

Lastly, the UFS and its implementing agent, the UE. From the beginning, the UE was ideally placed to act as the primary implementing agent and was unfortunately also the entity most heavily impacted upon by the environmental factors stated above. This was unfortunate as there was no QwaQwa-based alternative to take over the task of the UE, and it had to continue trying to implement the project over a distance – quite a complex undertaking where a direct hands-on approach seemed to be a *sine qua non*. The holistic approaches that the UE utilised in identifying and capacitating budding entrepreneurs were novel and exciting at first. Still, the lack of buy-in and accountability of entrepreneurs also later showed its weaknesses. This issue might have been addressed if all partners had seen the results of it in a possible pilot project (IIDE 2012). Even though the UE indicated that it saw its role as capacitating entrepreneurs and managing the operations of the MDF, the lack of a clear vision from the UE regarding the CED and the possibilities of involving students and academic staff in MDF related to teaching and learning; research and community service, left a gap that had to be filled by the IIDE on its own as described earlier.

The then management of the UFS welcomed the creation of the MDF. It involved senior management members at the institutional and faculty level – welcoming the donors and hosting celebratory functions. However, even though the UFS facilitated the hosting of the MDF within its operational and financial systems (as managed by the UE), it left the MDF partners to their own devices as far as operational issues were concerned. Creating a broader foundational support base for the UE within the UFS Faculty for EMS structures might have contributed to the more successful operation of the UE and, ultimately, the MDF. Such a structure that might have included more sources of expertise and experience was, however, never created – again highlighting some possible shortcomings in the readiness and capability of the EMS to support the UE in its operational endeavours.

Only when the MDF wound down, and the donors exited the agreement, the senior and faculty management of the UFS became involved again (IIDE 2013). Back to the 20/20 vision – it is now abundantly clear that the MDF, as a community service-aligned initiative, should have been anchored far stronger within an academic entity of the UFS – the Centre for Development Support (CDS), conducting socio-economic research for instance. Even though the Chief Directorate Community Service supported the MDF, it could not act as an academic 'home' for the MDF – a role that the UE could and would not play. Again, this came back to haunt the IIDE as it had no academic home at the UFS to anchor its research work. With community service being a primary concern of the UFS, it missed an opportunity to kick-start its social engagement in the QwaQwa community at that time.

■ Learnings from the Moahisane Development Fund

How do we utilise that evasive 20/20 vision that we now have? What learnings do we take from the MDF – about 10 years after its demise? Some of the learnings will be generic and will apply to development interventions in general while others will be specific to the MDF. How do they relate to the formation of partnerships and how will others learn from a partnership that did not work in the end?

As far as the environmental factors were concerned, none of the MDF partners had any degree of influence over national legislation and could do nothing to change the imagined legal and financial environment. Even though the UFS did have control over the career planning of the manager of the UE, his transferral away from the QwaQwa campus was a promotion, and it might have been unfair to elevate the operation of the MDF over the career path of an individual. Perhaps succession planning should have been scheduled and not specifically around an individual but rather in terms of an institution. However, the partnership should have been more resilient and have considered the adverse environmental factors, acknowledging the fact that partnerships change with time (Morse & McNamara 2006:321) and that the early adjudication of disputes arising from the environmental factors should have been addressed as Lister (2000) and USAID (1997) advises.

Most of the learnings for the future originated in the partnership formation-related environment. The concept of partners' interest in a development intervention is elucidated above – both in theory, shared and in the summation of the positions of all parties. It is done with an apparent reason. The identification and sharing of the positions, interest and needs of prospective partners when setting out on the road of partnership is crucial. This is true in widely diverging interest and closely related interests – maybe even more so in the latter case. Even though 'fusion' of interests is not always possible, it should be openly shared and debated among prospective partners – looking for future challenges and current synergies.

The most important lesson that needs to be carried over to such endeavours in the future is that the agreement and expectations of all parties should be highlighted upfront (MDF 2008b, 2011b). The partnership, in this case, was an almost incompatible relationship because of all the diverse expectations and interests of the partners. One of the donors was a philanthropist and a social venturer who needed to return on their investment (be it social or monetary). The UFS did not have specific expertise in social entrepreneurship initiatives per se and had to deal with unexpected environmental and partnership-related challenges – something that the UE was not equipped to do. The IIDE who facilitated the concept brought unique ethical dynamics to the table, which complicated facts even more. It is recommended that when starting such a miscellaneous partnership, all organisations need to 'speak the same language' and have a common goal and vision for their purpose. The competency and contractual trust mentioned earlier were established during this relationship; what was lacking was the goodwill trust for doing more than what is expected from each partner to assist the well-being of the other partners (Sako 1992). The MDF clearly shows a partnership where partners knew or thought they knew the complete positions, interest and needs of their prospective partners – only to see very few of the interests met during the implementation of the MDF. The eventual lack of an academic base for teaching and learning, research and community engagement propagated by the IIDE is a clear example.

Secondly, the partnership should have gone through more formal role-clarification exercises and skills audit to review who would be responsible for what exactly and ensure that all motivations and interests were synchronised. Even though all of the parties forming the partnership got on well and understood the intentions of the MDF, the relationship should possibly have been thrashed out better – enabling the MDF to withstand the environmental pressures that time put on it later in its existence. Participation encourages stakeholders to express their views and goals and then share common goals between the partners (Galera & Borzaga 2009:218). Each of the role players had different expectations when entering the agreement. Furthermore, some of these visions changed slightly as the fund developed. This is entirely predictable because they did not operate in similar situations and had completely diverse business outlooks. Seitanidi and Crane (2009) highlight that a critical phase of a social partnership is partnership selection. MDF was an excellent initiative that could be successful if the expectations and realities of all the parties (including the entrepreneurs) were highlighted upfront and that the partnership or relationship was set up correctly. This case study just proves that even though the correct type of role players (donor for the money, university for the training and area in dire need of employment opportunities) have been included in a partnership with good understanding and trust, it still does not mean that this endeavour can be successful if each of the parties has their agendas and expectations. Botes and Abraham (2008:121) highlight that partnerships are beneficial not only to the process (a means to an end) but also to the outcome (an end in itself). The MDF partnership should perhaps have been more closely aligned to the definition of a partnership as described in the Community Service Policy of the UFS (2006):

> A partnership can be defined as a collaborative effort between two or more parties sharing a similar vision, aimed at reaching a common goal by devising and implementing a cooperative modus operandi while maintaining their respective identities and agendas. A partnership entails the pooling and sharing of skills and resources, as well as risks and benefits, thus enabling such partnerships to accomplish goals beyond the capability of the individual parties. (p. 26)

Thirdly, the mistake of the partnership taking a top-down approach could also be seen as a contributing factor to the demise of the MDF. Even though it is sometimes challenging to give time for the 'organic' growth of a bottoms-up approach, the partnership should have spent more time eliciting the advice and experience of the role players in the entrepreneurial environment of the QwaQwa region – inclusive of community members and prospective entrepreneurs. As stated above, the idea of possibly having created the CED as a precursor to the actual MDF now seems logical – creating a conducive environment for the launching of a development intervention such as the MDF, with the community as a full partner from the onset and entrepreneurs not seen as 'clients' of the MDF. This more organic growth approach could have given the CED and ultimately the MDF time to 'settle in' in the QwaQwa community and solidify its presence, strategy and impact. In this case, the effort to create an intercultural approach to this specific development intervention failed utterly. 'Western' concepts as a revolving fund enjoying pre-eminence and not enough attention being given to local concerns and possible utilisation of more indigenous approaches to empowerment efforts as the MDF.

'We can't solve problems by using the same kind of thinking we used when we created them' (attributed to Albert Einstein in Sud, Sandt & Baugous 2009:201). Therefore, the last thought arises, which is entirely a different debate altogether: The developmental world has proved that the best projects that work effectively are usually from the bottom up (letting the community take ownership). There are three levels of participation: firstly, passive participation allows the community only to do what you want them to do, and the donor or government controls the information; secondly, quasi participation when the community can make certain decisions about the consultation, incentives and mobilisation; and lastly, active participation when the community is completely imbedded in the project design, planning, implementation and monitoring and evaluation (Isidiho 2016). The top-down method involves respecting the culture of the local people and their economic lifestyle. So, if this partnership was successful and the MDF was an excellent initiative – would it work because it follows the top-down (with very little community participation) approach? Perhaps, good examples to follow are partnerships between Starbucks and Conservative International (London & Rondinelli 2003); IKEA and Doi Tung (Wangsirilrt & Simon 2017), as well as JUMP and Hyundai Motors Company forming a collaborative platform called H-JUMP (Park et al. 2018). Furthermore, in Latin America, a tripartite partnership involving partners from the public, private and social sectors form collaborative frameworks at community, regional and national levels to revitalise urban areas (Fox et al. 2005). These partnerships are called 'social partnerships'. These partnerships can contribute to mutual gain and address social issues by combining resources into a common goal. Social partnerships 'address issues that extend beyond organisational boundaries and traditional goals and lie within the traditional public gain' (Waddock 1989:79). Persaud, Dixon and Thorlby (2017) suggest a few practicalities in building on the failure of social enterprise initiatives. These include identifying and mitigating everyday small losses as part of the regular project review, finding new ways of open and honest discussion, and sharing best practice stories and failed processes and programmes.

■ Conclusion

Chapter 2 introduced us to the theoretical approach encompassing an intercultural approach to 'small enterprise development' – the MDF was indeed an effort to give shape to a North–South partnership doing precisely this. Although challenging to share a story of ultimate failure for those who were involved in the MDF almost a decade ago, the effort of doing so is significant. In striving for what the world calls 'good' and 'best practice', there needs to be a reflection on 'not-so-good practice' as well. In analysing the travails of the MDF, essential lessons can be learned – especially as far as partnership formation is concerned. The sharing of a common goal and vision is fundamental. A bottom-up active participatory approach will allow all the stakeholders and partners to be part of each step of a project in decision-making and building trust. It should also be acknowledged that creating such a shared vision can take time and should not be rushed. There should be space and time for 'learning by doing'. This way of learning is crucial not only for those that participate in development interventions such as the MDF but also for those reflecting on it from the various domains they originate from – as happens in this chapter, this book and other future attempts at learning from past 'good' and 'not-so-good practice'.

It is at this late stage that the dreaded 'So what' question needs to be posed – by the authors as participants in the MDF to themselves. What difference will the introspection done in this chapter make?

So, was it difficult for the authors to expose participation in a project that failed in many aspects – yes it was. Mohanan (2017) posits that the fear of negative publicity and the concomitant reaction by supporters and donors will often incentivise development practitioners not to delve too deeply into aspects of failure – where robust interrogation of the failed project would have contributed much more in the longer run. This tendency is definitely not limited to development practitioners, but also applies to academics allergic to sharing publicly, and in high-profile publications, their participation in such failed ventures – especially when a compendium of failures could have added much more value than very similarly reported success stories (Mohanan 2017).

Will it make a difference to new development initiatives undertaken – either by the authors or any other readers of this chapter – we do not know – it depends on what they learn from it. The mistakes made, especially in the field of partnership formation as dissected above, has happened and continues to happen in development practice as we speak. What, and how do we learn (constructively) from our mistakes – seems to be an art in itself. Edmondson (2011) states that it is an incontrovertible fact that we can learn from mistakes, but that few organisations do so successfully. Without delving into the theory pertaining to the 'learning organisation' too much, it is, however, important to visit some of the reasons why Edmondson (2011) holds this position:

- Introspection often leads to fault-finding and blaming, negatively impacting on the ability to constructively dissect reasons for failure (this was indeed the case in the latter stages of the MDF with the EU being blamed for shortfalls in execution).
- The causes of failure can often be much more sophisticated than practitioners might admit, and process-complexity might be primary among reasons for failure (the relative inexperience of most the participants in the MDF relating to practical development interventions could also have been a factor in this regard).
- Organisations do not always credit those who 'fail at the frontiers' – trying to experiment with new approaches and methodologies – leading to a reluctance to innovate (the unsuccessful effort at setting up the CED could possibly be seen in this way).

Enter the concept of *deliberate reflection* as the departure point for analysing experiences and the accompanying tension between theories, values, norms, relationships and expectations held by individuals and entities participating in development activities. This entails systematic and deliberate reflection through exploration and analysis of failure in practice – only in this way can we really develop insight into the tasks accomplished and improve the way we approach our practice (Laksov & McGrath 2020:1–3).

So, what can the reader learn from the author? If only to keep on learning, then we have been successful in our endeavour. Only then will the future 'Simon's Cars' travel a road leading to viability, agency and human development…failures and all.

Chapter 6

Stones, bricks and windows: Searching for a sacred place

Willem Jan de Hek
Department of Practical Theology,
Faculty of Theology, Protestant Theological University,
Amsterdam, the Netherlands

■ Introduction

Amsterdam has been my hometown for several years. My family and I lived in an early 20th century apartment in Oud-West; we spent hours relaxing with friends in the Vondelpark; I worked as an architect and urban planner on projects in the Netherlands and oversees and on Sundays we worshipped in the Jeruzalemkerk, a church building from the 1920s in De Baarsjes. We left Amsterdam some years ago for Utrecht, where I started working as a minister in the Jacobikerk, a historic church in the inner city. As an architect who studied theology and a theologian who studied architecture, I am currently engaged in a research project that binds architecture and theology together. I wonder what can theology learn from the observations of an architect and vice versa, what can urban planning and architectural design learn from the thoughts of a theologian? Obviously, one of the themes bridging these two professional interests concerns the church building and its importance for community life. But more broadly, one can also think of the identity and role

How to cite: De Hek, W.J., 2021, 'Stones, bricks and windows: Searching for a sacred place', in A.S. Van Niekerk & S. Strijbos (eds.), *We cannot continue like this: Facing modernity in Africa and the West*, pp. 119-136, AOSIS, Cape Town. https://doi.org/10.4102/aosis.2021.BK283.06

of a sacred place in our contemporary city. My research project focusses on a sacred place in the urban environment, with field research being executed in the city of Amsterdam.

As a starting point for my reflections on a sacred place in this chapter, I take the work of the British theologian Philip Sheldrake, who published a thorough study on 'the spiritual city' (Sheldrake 2014). Sheldrake uses a description of successful cities throughout history from a provocative study of the American geographer Joel Kotkin. According to Kotkin, successful cities always did three things: they provided security to its citizens, they hosted a range of commercial activities and they created all kinds of sacred space. 'Historically, the latter has been expressed by religious buildings, cathedrals, temples, and mosques, which embody a transcendent horizon in and for the city' (Sheldrake 2014:4). But what about today? Where are we to find a sacred place in our contemporary city? And what contribution could a sacred place make for a sustainable future urban environment 'beyond modernity'? It seems to me that in actual discussions on the future of cities the topic of a sacred place is often absent. For example, in *The New Blackwell Companion to the City* (Bridge & Watson 2011) one can find contributions about neoliberal urbanism, gentrification, the liquid city and many more topics. There is an entry on a sacred place too, but this contribution has a rather narrow scope, portraying religious buildings as merely assertions of the power of religion, as something of the past. They are like 'containers of belief', locating faith within a bounded space and serving as a 'trap for the gaze' (Hill 2011).

This chapter is written from my personal conviction that there is more to say. Institutional religion is currently in decline and sacredness might indeed be experienced less institutional nowadays. However, I am convinced that it is certainly possible to find sacredness outside the walls of the 'containers of belief'. Sacred places are not merely about stones and bricks, but rather about windows, offering a glimpse into an otherworldly reality. These windows might take any form. For example, imagine looking at a sacred place from the perspective of social interactions and relationships. This is what Sheldrake does. He essentially views the city as a 'public arena' that is 'characterised by the interaction of strangers'. He sees cities as urban environments that can be distinguished by their considerable size, their population and their social, cultural, ethnic and religious diversity. These factors give cities the potential to play 'a vital role in shaping the human spirit for good or for ill. [...] Their future is not merely a social or economic matter but is also a profound spiritual challenge' (Sheldrake 2014:2-3):

> [C]ities reflect and affect the quality of human relationships. The fact is that in the context of urban environments we cannot separate functional, ethical, and spiritual questions. If places are to be sacred, they must affirm the sacredness of people, community, and a human capacity for transcendence. (p. 7)

Sheldrake argues that cities should be places that embrace the functional, ethical and spiritual dimensions of human life. Cities should reflect and affect the quality of human relationships, because human life is sacred rather than solely a biological phenomenon. Sheldrakes conclusion: 'We need human contexts that offer access to the sacred (however, we understand it) – or, better, relate us to life itself as sacred' (Sheldrake 2014:13).

But what can such a human context look like? Over the course of this chapter, I will focus specifically on a Christian sacred place, and reflect on that question with the first sentence from an 8th century Latin hymn as a framework. 'Ubi caritas et amor, Deus ibi est'. The text was written by Paulinus of Aquileia and states that: 'Where charity and love are, there is God'. Imagine a place – either traditional or unconventional, either indoor or outdoor – where a community that feels inspired by Jesus' command is gathering (Mk 12):

> [L]ove the Lord your God with all your heart and with all your soul and with all your mind and with all your strength. And love your neighbor as yourself. (vv. 30-31)

Can we see such a place as a window, opening new dimensions, guidelines and fresh expressions for life in the city and in general?

In this chapter I will take the reader with me on a stroll through Amsterdam. On our stroll we will find out how sacredness is all around us, and while looking at the city I will bring architecture and theology in conversation with each other. Doing so in my research project, requires that the project involves both. As an architect I want to know where people experience sacredness in their urban environment and why. Section 1 (Sacred Place) explores some of the reflections and experiences of a group of people I took with me on a stroll through Amsterdam, walking in an almost straight line from the southwest right into the city centre. This straight line – in fact a stripe, about 100 m wide – forms the research area for a series of articles that I am currently writing. It will sort out that sacredness *happens*. Sacredness can be seen as something that is experienced by people in such a way that it involves many senses. It is about feeling, seeing, hearing and so much more. In Section 2 (Holy Place) several theological perspectives will be highlighted to set the stage for a theological framework that helps evaluate the observations from my field research. I will look at the work of the Roman Catholic theologian Joseph Ratzinger, the Anglican theologian John Inge and the Reformed theologian Craig Bartholomew. I will make the choice for a theological framework that allows sacredness to happen inside church buildings – but just as well outside. It happens in traditional places – but just as well in unconventional locations. Sacred places are like seeds in the field of the city. In Section 3 (Storied Place), I will show how places are always storied places, and they are layered with meaning. Every place has one or more stories to tell, and these stories are related to personal experiences and are often a window to a particular worldview as well. What is the story that a Christian sacred place tells? What is the narrative layer that a Christian sacred place adds? The chapter ends with some concluding thoughts, in which I will briefly touch on what all of this could possibly mean for the overarching theme of this volume: the search for 'sustainability beyond modernity'.

■ Sacred place

In 2017, as part of the field research for my master's thesis, I took a group of people with me on a stroll through Amsterdam, to see and understand how they experienced places in the city. In their study on the good city, the British theologians Elaine Graham and Stephen Lowe pay attention to the idea of strolling through town as a method for researching the city (Graham & Lowe 2009):

> [F]or some urban theorists and theologians, the device of narrating the personal impressions and experiences of simply walking through a city or neighbourhood has been a powerful and eloquent toll. Such writing draws out how space and place evoke – indeed are saturated in – rich associations of memory and meaning; and how the immediate, the specific and the concrete provide tangible and living examples of deeper values, stories and power relations that are perhaps less easy to realise in more abstract terms. (p. 51)

For my research project I took several peer-groups with me on a 6-km photo-walk through the Eastern part of Amsterdam. I walked this route with various groups, whereby the participants were asked to take photographs of sacredness in the urban environment. I specifically asked them to take pictures of those locations that – according to their experience – were somehow related to a sacred place. I wanted to find out what my participants were thinking of, when discussing sacredness, holiness and sacred place. What locations, artefacts or human behaviour would they come up with?[19]

Surprisingly, one of the locations they came up with quite often was a park. Park Frankendael is the only remaining historic so-called 'buitenplaats' ('place out of town') in the Watergraafsmeer in the city of Amsterdam. Strolling several times through this area with my group of respondents, it appeared

---

19. This field research was carried out over the first half of the year 2017. The participants walked the route in three separate stages, with a discussion intermezzo after every leg. The transcriptions of these group discussions form the major source for the research data for this project, together with my own memo's and almost 1000 photographs that were taken during the walks. Two so-called focus groups consisted of three respondents each, accompanied by me. Apart from this, I walked the route a number of times on my own and twice with a single respondent. The participants were selected, based on their professional or personal engagement in place-making in Amsterdam. All of them knew the city well. Their background varied: like place of residency (Amsterdam, periphery), field of expertise (Theology, Real Estate, Photography, Architecture, Psychology, Geography, Journalism, Government), core personal religious belief (Christian, Agnostic, Atheist) and gender (female, male). Preliminary results of this research project, including a brief description of methodology and theoretical framework, have already been presented or published elsewhere (De Hek 2017b, 2021).

that they often related this park with sacredness. Park Frankendael (Figure 6.1) can be seen as a connecting-place: it has the full potential for citizens to connect with one another in several ways. From drinking coffee in an outdoor environment to engaging in a public sports event. The park can also be seen as an enjoying-life-place, because it is full of potential to relax. As the park has quite a history, it can also be seen as a commemorating-place, full of potential to discover the history of this area. Originally planned as a place away from the city, this location has always been a tranquil escape from the hustle of Amsterdam. One of the respondents puts it this way during our walk:

> '[/] really think that Frankendael is a fantastic spot [...] as is the Frankendael-house. Indeed, it is a historical place, but at the same time it is also a place of today. But also, because they made it accessible [...] for artists and for meeting places.' (Respondent, gender unspecified, exact location unspecified)

Most of the participants were convinced that the traditional worshipping places along the walk have a great potential as a more-a-less 'conventional' sacred place, meaning either as a meeting place or as community centre. Their potential lies, for example, in their urban dominance: they often literally take a lot of space and draw attention with their towers and architectural details. But having said that, we also came along worshipping places that were somehow camouflaged – such as an apparent mosque at the Plantage Middenlaan and Hillsong Church in the Tropentheater. It raised the question: Who knows how many 'conventional' worshipping places we have passed without knowing of

Source: Google Maps (n.d.a).
FIGURE 6.1: Areal view Park Frankendael in Amsterdam-East.

their existence? It also raised another rather interesting question. Can we also find a sacred place right in front of us on the street or in the bushes by the side of the road? Where exactly did the respondents experience some form of sacredness as well?

One observation shared by the respondents was that place is produced over time. This happens through smaller or bigger physical interventions, and also by personal experiences, stories and memories. The city changes from place to place, but it evolves over time as well. That became quite clear to me, when walking along the exact same route several times during the research period. Amsterdam looks very different on King's Day – the national celebration of the Dutch King Willem-Alexander's birthday; when everyone has a day off, is clothed in orange outfits and is in a festive mood – compared with an average working day. But also walking the route with others had a big impact on my perception of the city. The places along the route became richer the more often these places were passed through, because my fellow walkers kept sharing stories about these places with me. Places and cities are dynamic and layered. Actually, that is a good thing – because it makes the city very vital.

In the words of one of the respondents:

> '[T]his city has proven to be very resilient. Every time a new layer is placed over it, with new residents, new functions and so on [...] Well, apparently the city can move along with it.' (Respondent, gender unspecified, exact location unspecified)

In Park Frankendael this is actually quite visible. It was constructed around 1660 as a 'buitenplaats', a place out of town to escape the buzz of the inner city. Later, and until the 1990s, it was used as a nursery garden. And since then, it has been used as a public park (Kruizinga 1995:347–348) One can find a variety of different architectural styles when examining the buildings in the park. The old chimney of a small factory building that was once functioning here, and that is now a restaurant. The dilapidated housing on an island, that is now used as a place for reflection. The marble fountain with statues of Neptune, Amphitrite and Arion. It all adds to the charm of this place. Does it also add to the potential of this park for sacredness to happen or occur?

Analysing the research data, it turned out that the experience of sacredness can be connected to the experience of two opposite categories of feelings: distastes and desires. Respondents expressed their distaste for the commercial, for seclusion, for indefiniteness, ugliness and chaos. Starting in a more-or-less quiet neighbourhood and walking right into the buzz of the very city centre, they felt increasingly uncomfortable with the hustle of the city as they experienced it. The city in fact became to feel less 'sacred' along the way. Would it be different when walking the other way around, from the city buzz into the relative quietness of the outskirts of the city? In any case, this experiment helped me to get to know some of the desires that my respondents connected to the notion of sacredness. Some of their desires were clearly antipodes of the distastes mentioned above, such as their desire for authenticity, accessibility, fine texture, beauty and tranquillity. However, they also mentioned other desires. For example, a desire for social community – for being connected, engaged and in interaction with other people in a certain place. Respondents emphasised the need for social interaction that transcends the boundaries of generation, race, gender and cultural background. Another desire that often has been referred to, was the desire for nature, by which respondents expressed their longing for those phenomena of the physical world that are not man-made – although most of these phenomena sorted out to be part of bigger-scale man-made projects, such as parks and waterfronts. Both direct natural phenomena (such as trees, water and sunlight) and indirect phenomena (like wooden things, artificial green and fountains) fell within this category. A third desire that has often been mentioned was the desire for symbolism, in which respondents expressed their admiration for symbolic places, that somehow point to immaterial, ideal or otherwise intangible truths or states. Places that remind of another domain, distinct from the everyday city, such as the way a sculpture in the park points at stories from the past or at myths or religious narratives.

To sum it all up: respondents referred to their desires for beauty, symbolism and tranquillity when discussing sacredness. They quite often connected their desires for community, diversity and accessibility to a sacred place. Also, their conviction that a sacred place should be accessible (although it somehow contradicts their desire for tranquillity) was remarkable. And, quite remarkably as well, the existing churches along the route were not that frequently identified as sacred places. Respondents were far more open to find sacredness in the green areas along the route. As one respondent said:

> '[F]or me it expresses something like a longing for paradise. It is [...] nature, but it is not wild nature. It is ordered. It is a place where one can distract oneself. Where one can find a place that is removed from the hustle of the city, which I believe has something to do with sacredness.' (Respondent, gender unspecified, exact location unspecified)

And another respondent puts it like this:

> '[/]t breathes history. But it is not about history alone. A lot *happens* over there. People come to the park and a diversity of people does a diversity of things. [...] It comes closest to sacredness of everything we have seen thus far.' (Respondent, gender unspecified, exact location unspecified)

As I have been arguing before, sacredness seems to be something that is experienced by people in such a way that it involves many senses. It is about seeing, hearing and so much more. Sacredness comes into the picture when people feel that a place has the potential to fulfil their desires. Sacredness *happens* when certain human desires are fulfilled. And it seems that some places are better equipped for doing so than others (De Hek 2021)

Holy place

In the former section we have seen how my respondents found sacredness happening in parks and on squares in the city. But what about the traditional, the 'conventional' sacred places? How to value those structures? One would expect that from a more-or-less functional perspective, these would be the places where sacredness should be found first and foremost? One of the traditional church buildings in my research area is the Hofkerk – officially named the H.H. Martelaren van Gorcumkerk (Figure 6.2). It was built between 1927 and 1929 as a Roman Catholic church in a traditional architectural style and designed as part of a larger complex: the Linnaeushof, comprising a school, a monastery and residential housing (Kruizinga 1995:640) An information panel at the exterior tells visitors that this urban courtyard once aimed to function as a catholic enclave within a majorly protestant area. Today, this cluster of buildings no longer functions as such an enclave – or at least not as a 'religious' enclave. Citizens living here express their feelings that one of the good things about this area is precisely this, that it comes with the feeling of living in a secure and safe neighbourhood, on a 'sacred' island a little off from the hustle and bustle of the city. In the meantime, the Hofkerk is still in use as a consecrated holy place, separated from its 'profane' surroundings by its thick stone walls. The building is permanently dedicated to the sacred by prayers, rites and ceremonies. It is interesting to note that my respondents, when strolling through town, were

Source: Google Maps (n.d.b).
FIGURE 6.2: Areal view Hofkerk and its surroundings.

somewhat hesitant to point at obvious church buildings as sacred places. Even though they might suspect that buildings like the Hofkerk, De Bron and the Koningskerk are sacred on the inside. However, the inaccessibility of these buildings was perceived as unpleasant.

A somewhat different, but interesting case emerged to be the Tropentheater, a structure that has been a venue for concerts, dance performances, theatre and films from around the world since 1975. The theatre formed part of the Royal Tropical Institute, an institute aiming to collect and spread knowledge about the Tropics and Subtropics. It was forced to close its doors on 01 January 2013. Since then, the three halls in the building have been rented out for events, with one of the recent tenants being Hillsong Amsterdam, a branch of Hillsong Church – a charismatic megachurch based in Australia with venues in over 20 countries all over the world. It reminds of the network society, a phenomenon that was described by Manuel Castells. According to Castells, the world went through an information-technological revolution at the end of the 20th century. He suggests this to be one of those rare intervals that change the course of history. 'An interval characterized by the transformation of our "material culture" by the works of a new technological paradigm organized around information technologies' (Castells 1996:28). According to Castells, the effects of the new technologies penetrate all domains of human activity. The underlying logic is the logic of the network, which is based on flexibility: the network can continuously adapt, reset and expand. In other words, the network is fluid. Specific technologies converge in an integrated system, and so, the information technology paradigm is not a closed but an open system – a multi-sided and complex network that can expand in all directions (Castells 1996:70–76).

Obviously, this will have an impact on sacred place as we knew it. In this section, I will highlight several theological perspectives, in search of a theological framework that will help in evaluating the observations from my field research. Over the course of this section, I will take into consideration the notion that sacredness *happens*, as I have been arguing before. It happens inside church buildings – and just as well outside. For the sake of argument, I will take the reader with me on a theological excursus through several theological positions. The first position leaves little to no room for sacredness outside consecrated sacred buildings. Hence this position is far off from the sacredness that my respondents experienced in Park Frankendael, for example. Other theological positions can help to move from a rather static approach towards a more dynamic perspective.

Ratzinger: Sacrament

The Hofkerk is a stone's throw away from Park Frankendael. It is still in use as a Roman Catholic church, as a consecrated holy place, separated from its 'profane' surroundings by its thick stone walls. In the church – and not in the park – does the liturgy take place, which according to some theologians makes this structure an isolated sacred place, separated from its surroundings. This theological perspective was described extensively, for example, in a study by the Roman Catholic theologian Joseph Ratzinger (Pope Benedict XIV) on time and space. Ratzinger argues that in the liturgy humans can find an otherworldly reality. Humans cannot 'make' worship themselves. The eternal God must reveal himself to fill the space (Ratzinger 2014:A-I-1). In the Roman Catholic tradition, the Eucharist became the very core of this Divine revelation. 'It brings heaven into the community assembled on earth, or, rather, it takes that community beyond itself into the communion of saints of all times and places' (Ratzinger 2014:A-II-2). As the Divine self is present in the consecrated bread, the place in the church where this blessed sacrament is reserved can be viewed as the tent and the throne of God. Here his presence dwells among his people – 'in the humblest parish church no less than in the grandest cathedral' (Ratzinger 2014:A-II-4). For Ratzinger, sacred place has a lot to do with stones and bricks – with church architecture, with the proper arrangements of the interior of a church interior, whereby the presence of a tabernacle for reserving the blessed sacrament is an extremely important condition for a place to really become a sacred place. But what about the windows? Does our human experience also play a role in all of this? On a few occasions in his book, Ratzinger points at the role of human experience when it comes to the sacred. For example, when he describes what *happens* when the Eucharist is received by a believer during the liturgy (Ratzinger 2014):

> [T]he living Lord gives himself to me, enters into me, and invites me to surrender myself to him. [...] In the consecrated species *he* is there and remains there. When a man experiences this with every fiber of his heart and mind and senses, the consequence is inescapable. (n.p.)

The church will never become a lifeless space according to Ratzinger. It will always be filled with the presence of the Lord. 'What man has not experienced this? A church without the Eucharistic Presence is somehow dead, even when it invites people to pray' (Ratzinger 2014:A-II-4). Obviously, such a theological approach does not leave a lot of room for sacredness to happen outside of the brick walls of a consecrated and well-arranged church building. It begs the question whether it is possible to find ways out? For sacredness to break through these thick brick walls and find its way into the city?

Inge: Pilgrimage

An interesting voice over the last decades when it comes to a 'theology of place' has been John Inge, a bishop in the Church of England who published his *Christian Theology of Place* in 2003. Inge states that the incarnation – the living God entering in this world through Jesus Christ – is at the core of the New Testament witness and of the Christian faith. 'Places are the seat of relations or the place of meeting and activity in the interaction between God and the world'. Inge argues that 'place is therefore a fundamental category of human and spiritual experience' (Inge 2003:52). This relates to the Eucharist in consecrated churches, but Inge also pleads for a broader *sacramental approach* when it comes to sacred place. As a starting point for his thinking, he uses the work of William Temple (Inge 2003):

> [T]emple's sacramental approach to reality permeated all of his theology, for he believed that it is in the sacramental view of the universe, both of its material and of its spiritual elements, that there is to be found hope of making human both politics and economics, and of making effectual both faith and love. John Habgood makes a similar point when he writes: 'Indeed, the world itself only has meaning and value when seen as the sacrament of God's living presence. The secular vision of the world is a lie. It tells of emptiness and meaninglessness'. (p. 64)

One can think of the Eucharist as an important occasion in which this relationship is celebrated, whereby the church building becomes a sacred place. However, Inge also draws attention to the fact that there is 'a noble tradition of extending the notion of sacramentality from the Church's sacraments to Christ, the Church and the world' (Inge 2013:66). Even though this begs another important question. 'Are we simply to assert that the whole world is 'sacramental'? Do all material things, all places, speak equally of God?' (Inge 2003:66). According to Inge, the answer to this question is no (Inge 2003):

> [A]lthough God reveals himself in the world, sacramentality does not mean that the world itself is self-revelatory of God in a general and indiscriminate manner. Rather, it means that the world in all its diverse aspects can be the place of God's own self-revelation to us. (p. 67)

Inge argues that biblical stress on the importance of place is crucially interwoven with the experience of revelation. Think about the resurrection appearances and some of the crucial developments in the Church's history. Inge calls these sacramental events, and these events show that indeed 'places are the seat of relations and of meeting and activity between God and the world' (Inge 2003:68). And often, once such a Divine disclosure has *happened* in a particular location it remains associated with that place, evoking *pilgrimages* – and by doing so in fact breaking through the thick stone and brick walls of consecrated church buildings and introducing a dynamic network of sacredness in which people travel.

■ Bartholomew: Placemaking

A third perspective comes from the Reformed theologian Craig Bartholomew. In his study *Where Mortals Dwell*, Bartholomew points at the good creation of God, as one of the motivations for Christians to take place seriously, apart from other motivations such as the incarnation and redemptive work of Christ. Bartholomew – who's work shows influences from John Calvin, Abraham Kuyper and Herman Dooyeweerd – argues that the creator God is renewing its creation and will finally renew it at the end of the ages. The most fruitful way into a Christian view of place for today would be a trinitarian theology of place (Bartholomew 2011):

> [A]ny theology of place worth its salt must be Christocentric. As Newbigin asserts, Christ is the clue to all that is. Thus Inge is right to make the incarnation central to a theology of place. However, precisely because such a theology is Christocentric, it will be trinitarian. (p. 243)

Bartholomew points at the doctrine of creation as fundamental to a theology of place. This doctrine 'resists all dualisms which undermine the good materiality of our world and any attempt to privilege the soul or the "spiritual" over the material'. Proceeding along this line of reasoning, Bartholomew adds that a theology of place always requires a sense of *dynamism* of the created order. God's order is not static but provides for a development of history and culture (Bartholomew 2011:244-245). Bartholomew states that cultural development is fundamentally good, even though 'the fall' has opened up the possibility for the disastrous misdirection of cultural development. Nevertheless, it is the churches' duty to practice *placemaking*. And it is important to note that the church ought to do this in such a way, that it takes place along the grain of Gods order for creation. This indicates that placemaking should enhance the 'shalom' of all the creation (Bartholomew 2011):

> [A] biblical view of creation resists a nature-culture dichotomy which privileges wilderness over placemaking. Cultural development, including placemaking, is normative and fundamentally good. The fall opens up the possibility for the disastrous misdirection of cultural development and placemaking, the evidence of which is all around us. (p. 245)

Opposite to a Lutheran doctrine of two spheres, such a theology of place assumes that there is only one reality: God's reality of which the incarnation, life death and resurrection of Jesus are at the centre. Incarnation and resurrection are the ultimate affirmation of creation. What Christ's redemption is aiming at is the recovery of Gods purposes for the whole creation, leading it forward to the destiny God always has intended for it. Biblical eschatology, according to Bartholomew, is not about the destruction of the world but about its renewal to become the new heavens and the new earth (Bartholomew 2011:245-246).

Sheldrake: Connection

In the introduction to this chapter, we have seen how Philip Sheldrake argues that cities should be places that embrace the functional, ethical and spiritual dimensions of human life. Cities should reflect and affect the quality of human relationships, as human life is sacred rather than solely a biological phenomenon. 'We need human contexts that offer access to the sacred (however, we understand it) – or, better, relate us to life itself as sacred'. (Sheldrake 2014:13) According to Sheldrake (2014):

> [C]hristian theology, following St Augustine, affirms that there is no absolutely private identity. To be human embodies a common life and a common task. [...] It is important to note the intimate link between human identity and the Christian relational theology of God as 'Trinity'. The core of the Christian life – a paradigm of redeemed human existence overall – is to become united with God, in Jesus Christ, through a Spirit-led communion with one another. (p. 8)

According to Sheldrake, 'public life, city life, is the arena where diverse people attempt to establish some form of commonality'. He sees social interaction and active citizens as forms of spiritual practice. 'Living publicly implies real encounters with what is different and unfamiliar yet somehow establishing a common life' (Sheldrake 2014:9–10). And hence, the places that form the 'seat' of such relations, where people are brought into connection with each other, can be regarded as sacred places.

Reading Ratzinger, Inge, Bartholomew and Sheldrake one after the other, the focus shifts from a rather static and aesthetical approach towards a more dynamic and ethical perspective. Sacredness *happens*. It happens inside church buildings – but just as well outside, wherever and whenever people are brought into connection with each other and with the Divine. It happens 'ubi caritas et amor' – where charity and love are. From the perspective of the Christian church, one could argue that this thought assumes that the Divine is at work in our world and invites us to join, by making place for the sacred. Some theologians describe this as a Missio Dei. The Christian can be seen in church as an apostolic community that is called to participate in this sending mission of God, with the reign of God as the ultimate goal. 'The reign of God refers to the peaceful world where the loving and just rule of God is fully accomplished' (Youn 2018:226). According to this theological approach, it is a prime task for the Christian church to become a sign of the reign of God. The church must 'not conform to the pattern of this world but be transformed by the renewing of mind' (Rm 12:2) and therefore ought to become a community different from the world (Youn 2018:228). When it comes to recognising Christian sacred place in our contemporary city – indoors as well as outdoors – this theological perspective might be helpful and potentially directional. Imagine sacred places that are indeed like windows, telling the story of the 'ubi caritas et amor' and activating and inviting people to participate. In whatever form they appear.

■ Storied place

The cemetery De Nieuwe Ooster (Figure 6.3) is located in the Watergraafsmeer and opened its gates in 1894. At its 110th anniversary, a book was published about this cemetery titled: *A place of quietness and meditation* (Kruizinga 1995:1207). It was indeed in quietness and meditating, that I joined a funeral procession in January 2020. We had to bury a dear friend from Amsterdam-East. She was born on the island of Java in Indonesia, more than 60 years ago,

Source: Google Maps (n.d.b).
FIGURE 6.3: Aerial view De Nieuwe Ooster cemetery entrance area.

but moved to the Netherlands halfway across her life. Looking around I saw the sad faces of her relatives and acquaintances. I knew some of them personally. For a number of them, the stories of beautiful moments we had with our good friend immediately surfaced. It was a 10-min walk before we arrived at the place where she was to be buried. The path passed dozens of graves, beautifully embedded in a green landscape with trees and bushes. I read the names on the tombs, the years of birth and death, a single personal text on a stone sometimes. This observation is of course not unique. Each cemetery in the world is like a library, each grave like a brief biography. For those who know the person who is laid to rest here, the name alone speaks volumes. A cemetery has something sacred. It is a place of memories. A place of commemoration. A place with not just one story, but with thousands of stories. And cemeteries are not unique in that way. Every place has one or more stories to tell, related to personal experiences and relations.

Cities tell a story that is unfinished and always continuing. Places are always *storied places*: every place in the world has one or more stories to tell. The Swiss architect Peter Zumthor puts it this way: 'Almost everything that surrounds us [...] is full of history; we just have to see it. Everything has been made by someone' (Zumthor & Lending 2018:15). According to the architect and theologian Murray A. Rae architecture 'sets in stone, at least for a time, certain conceptions about the way the world is to be organized and human life is to be lived within it' (Rae 2017:18). 'The architectural definition of space and place contributes to the shaping of a people. It is a means for human orientation in and habitation of the world' (Rae 2017:19). One can think of places as texts, layered with meaning. Philip Sheldrake argues that it is indeed appropriate 'to think of places as texts, layered with meaning' (Sheldrake 2014:13). When it comes to Christian sacred place, what is the layer, the story that is added? Sheldrake (2014) puts us on an interesting track:

> [/]t is interesting that the Christian tradition suggests that God is often most powerfully experienced in places that are 'strange' to us, rather than safely protected. There, people who appear alien challenge our sense of familiarity and security. (p. 9)

According to Sheldrake, 'living publicly implies real encounters with what is different and unfamiliar yet somehow establishing a common life'. (Sheldrake 2014:9–10) He argues that social interaction can be seen as a form of spiritual practice. And while practicing this practice in the public area, new layers of meaning are added to the story of a place. Could it be that social interaction – as a form of 'ubi caritas et amor' – opens a way to experiencing and recognising sacredness?

Storied places play an important role in sacredness *happening*. As I have been arguing before (De Hek 2021) some places in our urban environment are richer than others, when it comes to the potential for sacredness to occur. They can be connected to a multitude of stories and to a variety of different functions that can trigger the experience of sacredness as perceived by its visitor. We might even say that the richness of a place determines the likelihood for sacredness to happen in that environment. Or, as the John Inge (2003) observes:

> [W]e should recover a sense of *storied* place. *Sacred* places will be those which have been associated with sacred stories, places linked with Divine disclosure. Surely the Lord is in this place; and I did not know it. (p. 47)

Searching for sacred place

The American religious scholar Thomas A. Tweed has argued that 'religions are confluences of organic-cultural flows that intensify joy and confront suffering by drawing on human and suprahuman forces to make homes and cross boundaries' (Tweed [2006] 2008:54). This concept gives some practical clues to explore our urban context in search for sacred place. To take the dynamic nature of religions into account, Tweed uses metaphors and frameworks that highlight movement and relation. The spatial metaphors he uses (dwelling and crossing) signal that religion is about finding place and moving across space, whereas his aquatic metaphors (confluences and flows) signal that religions are complex processes. Religions can be best imagined as a confluence of flows in which organic channels direct cultural currents. These confluences 'conjoin to create institutional networks that, in turn, prescribe, transmit, and transform tropes, beliefs, values, emotions' (Tweed [2006] 2008:69). They can also be imagined as artefacts and rituals that become visible as traces and trails in time and place. 'Religions are partial, tentative and continually redrawn sketches of where we are, where we've been, and where we're going'. (Tweed [2006] 2008:74) What has been described in the sections above – for example, what *happened* in Park Frankendael, in the Hofkerk or at the Nieuwe Ooster – can be seen as an interesting illustration to the theory of Tweed. Two phenomena or flows basically conjoined: on the one hand, the cultural flow of the stories that characterise the location and that are somehow materialised in the park, the church and at the cemetery – and on the other hand, the more emotive and devotional flow of the desires that a visitor brings to the place. In the merger of these two, we have seen how these places for the visitor became a sacred landscape – recalling what Tweed in his book calls a sacroscape (Tweed [2006] 2008:61).

But what about Christian sacred place? As I have touched on several times above, the *'ubi caritas et amor'* could function as an ethical framework to identify storied places where sacredness happens. It might be a place that is stored with religious phenomena, which according to the religious scholar Émile Durkheim belong to no constituted religion. Phenomena are no longer integrated into a religious system, but sometimes once were old, vague and, at first glance, perhaps unusable and dilapidated mirrors. As the original cult they were part of did not manage to survive and the whole to which they belonged has disappeared, these phenomena are the only surviving fragments from religious systems of the past (Durkheim [1912] 1995:39). But there still is this resemblance with the message it once broadcasted. In fact, what Tweed calls artefacts and rituals that become visible as traces and trails in time and place, fall in the same category. These are fragments of meaning, that often tell important stories about the context in which places are becoming. Stories about people that play a prominent role in the daily place-ballet of a certain location, about the distastes and desires they bring with them – and about their dedication to charity and love.

■ Conclusion

Strolling through Amsterdam in this chapter we have seen how sacredness happens – both inside traditional sacred places as well as outside. Sacredness can be seen as a dynamic layer that is added to a place and that tells a specific story. For example, it tells a story of *'ubi caritas et amor'*, shifting the focus of its visitors from the every-daily towards the otherworldly. The research material that I collected over the course of my research project – mostly pictures made by my respondents – showed how sacred place can be great or small, visible or hidden, vast or fluid. From a historical cathedral in the inner city to two people sitting at a bench. Our built environment is not merely about stones and bricks but rather about windows – and this seems to me a

Chapter 6

lesson we should take with us when thinking about the city of tomorrow. The spirituality of places can work with their economic, social or technological aspects by its potential to open up new perspectives and to invite for dialogue and action.

Take the Oude Kerk in the very centre of Amsterdam (Figure 6.4). It is a church that does exactly that for centuries. It is the endpoint of my stroll through town. It is almost 19:00 when I lock my bike at the square in front of this historical building. This church was built in the 14th century and was used as a Roman Catholic church until the Reformation in the 16th century. It is the oldest building and parish church in the city. The church was consecrated in 1306. Since the Reformation the church has been used as a protestant place of worship, currently by the Protestant Church in the Netherlands. Today the church is owned by a foundation, which has the official status of a museum and exposes high-profile art-expositions by well-known artists (Kruizinga 1995:799–802). When I park my bike in front of the church it is Saturday evening and tomorrow the Christian church will celebrate the Feast of Pentecost in the year 2017. That's why tonight a vigil has been organised in the church that I am about to attend.

When crossing the square to enter the building, I am struck by the impressions and stimuli that are everywhere around me. Youngsters hanging out on a bench in front of the church, smoking pot, a group of tourists listening

Source: Google Maps (n.d.d).
FIGURE 6.4: Areal view Oude Kerk and its surroundings.

to their guide telling them stories about the rich history of the city, some drunk young men part of a bachelor party, on their way to see a prostitute. The service in the Oude Kerk attracted my attention because of its invitation: 'We're celebrating the coming of the Spirit, which lets us experience unity within diversity. Crossing borders, we choose to meet each other in the things that inspire us'.[20] And because the vigil is organised in a period that I am doing research on sacred places and the soul of the city it actually is a must-go. Would I encounter sparkles of the soul of Amsterdam – here in this centuries-old sacred place in the heart of the city? And interestingly, that seems to be the case, when the pastor uses the motto of Amsterdam's Coat of Arms to structure her final prayer: 'May we be valiant, steadfast and compassionate when we leave this church and go out into the city'. When leaving this ages-old sacred place, this is the call I take with me into a dynamic and challenging world.

It is this world that the editors of this book project were thinking of, when inviting authors representing a diversity of disciplines to reflect on finding a way beyond modernity in rethinking our understanding of sustainability and development. Can we move beyond technology and science as the great equalisers that will necessarily wipe out all cultural diversity in the modern world? When it comes to architecture and urban planning as a discipline, the recognition of sacredness as a happening, a better understanding of sacred place as something fluid and dynamic and a revaluation of the potential of sacred place in our built urban environment surely opens possibilities to do so.

■ Acknowledgements

Some fragments in this chapter originate from my master's thesis in Practical Theology at the Protestant Theological University Amsterdam (De Hek 2017a). The author wishes to thank Marcel Barnard, Tjeerd de Boer, Hans Teerds, Sytse Strijbos and Attie S. van Niekerk for commenting on my master's thesis and/or earlier versions of this contribution.

20. https://oudekerk.amsterdam/nieuws/pinksterwake (viewed 11 December 2020).

PART 2

Approaches

Chapter 7

From isolation to relation: A trans-disciplinary analysis of an improved cookstove project in Molati, South Africa

Pierre Reyneke[a,b]
[a]The NOVA Institute, Pretoria, South Africa
[b]School of Geography, Archaeology and Environmental Sciences, Faculty of Humanities, University of the Witwatersrand, Johannesburg, South Africa

▪ Introduction

Scholars from various academic disciplines have attempted to address the complex challenges of socio-economic and environmental degradation of the present era. Such scholars have approached these challenges using methodologies unique but also limited to their own disciplinary idiosyncrasies. In attempts at overcoming this limiting factor researchers have formed study conglomerates that include individuals from numerous disciplines in order to form multi-, inter- or trans-disciplinary research groups. Such research

How to cite: Reyneke, P., 2021, 'From isolation to relation: A trans-disciplinary analysis of an improved cookstove project in Molati, South Africa', in A.S. Van Niekerk & S. Strijbos (eds.), *We cannot continue like this: Facing modernity in Africa and the West*, pp. 139–154, AOSIS, Cape Town. https://doi.org/10.4102/aosis.2021.BK283.07

endeavours might be considered as possible ways to avoid the pitfalls of getting caught up in one's own theoretical framework. However, this chapter considers the possibility that, at times, the failure of academic work to contribute towards sustainability might lie at a deeper ontological level.

In keeping with the theoretical themes and literary traditions the current book project seeks to build on, it seems fitting to mention some of the key works pre-empting it and how the current chapter fits within this dialogue. In its essence this discussion aims to deepen our understanding of the relationship between technological innovation and the everyday lived experiences and practices of people, with an aim to achieve the goal of sustainable communities. The economist Manfred Max-Neef finds an integral place within this discussion. Max-Neef (2005) developed a trans-disciplinary approach that aims to address the global challenges of the 21st century. He does this by introducing a unique epistemology that challenges linear logic by breaking away from a singular reality, one that aims to isolate the problem it seeks to address (Max-Neef 2005). Along a similar vein, the current chapter aims to develop an integrative approach to technology by introducing a non-linear epistemology, one that fosters an awareness of the multiplicity that constitutes technologies. Ingold (2000) and Hart (2016) accomplish this by emphasising *relationality* and *processes* in non-linear epistemologies, as opposed to emphasising categorisation and causal argumentation. Simply put, these approaches are less about 'ticking all the boxes' and more about showing how 'all the boxes' are interconnected.

Thereby, this chapter seeks to contribute to the academic body of work on Sustainable Communities by synthesising a novel methodological approach. The writer formulates the synthesis by placing two theoretical frameworks in conversation, namely, Ingold's (2000) relational-ecological-developmental approach and Hart's (2016) relational comparison method. In order to evaluate the possible contribution of the synthesis, it is applied as a processual analysis case study to an improved cookstove programme developed by NOVA Institute, a South African based non-profit organisation (NPO). Through this analysis, along with the emphasis on relationality, these approaches point to the historical relationship between church and community and how sustainable communities might emerge through the adoption of NOVA's 'Co-creation' approach. This aspect of the chapter contributes to the field of Practical Theology and situates the proposed synthesis within current debates in the discipline. In so doing, the chapter demonstrates the potential of theoretical frameworks to overcome problematic dichotomies existing between theory and practice, between technological innovation and social phenomena, between the natural sciences and human sciences and between the human and non-human world. It hereby attempts to develop a methodological approach that assists in the goal of establishing sustainable communities by emphasising the metabolic interconnectivity between humans and their environment.

■ Approaches to sustainable communities

To assist the reader in navigating the current chapter this section offers a brief definition of multi-, inter- and trans-disciplinary methods. This is followed by a thorough discussion of the methods suggested by Ingold and Hart in the section titled 'Innovative departures', with the aim to show how these approaches could offer new perspectives and possibilities for sustainable community establishment.

Multi-disciplinary

The term multi-disciplinary refers to a collaborative effort of a research team consisting of scientists from various fields of study who aim to examine a similar, broad research question. In this approach these individuals might come together for discussion, but in general each person approaches the problem from their own disciplinary lens, come to different conclusions and circulate their conclusions on their own. This is seen as a very modest attempt at collaboration (Schmalz, Janke & Payne 2019).

Interdisciplinary

Following an interdisciplinary approach entails researchers across different fields informing each other's perspectives and comparing their results. Key to this approach is the transference of knowledge across disciplines to possibly create a new field of study or discipline altogether. Although researchers are all contributing to the research, they remain grounded in their root disciplines (Schmalz et al. 2019).

Trans-disciplinary

Other than the previous two approaches mentioned, in trans-disciplinary studies researchers seek to deal with problems as experienced in practice in its entire complexity. This approach is thus moving away from purely theoretical knowledge production by incorporating the involvement of practitioners and local viewpoints on the practical problem situation (Schmalz et al. 2019).

In making a case for a trans-disciplinary approach Max-Neef makes the following point, 'An integrating synthesis is not achieved through the accumulation of different brains. It must occur inside each of the brains [...]' (Max-Neef 2005). He makes a useful distinction between 'Weak Transdisciplinarity' and 'Strong Transdisciplinarity'. 'Weak' being the kind of trans-disciplinary approach that entails coordination between hierarchical academic levels ranging from empirical level, towards a purposive or pragmatic level, continuing to a normative level and finishing at a value level (Max-Neef 2005:9). By 'Strong' he means to go beyond an approach that is overly influenced by *rationality* to one that emphasises *relationality*. Ingold and Hart share this dialectic theoretical thrust with Max-Neef as the following section illustrates.

▪ Innovative departures

This section comprises an explorative and comparative discussion of the two aforementioned theoretical works and their methodological implications. The works I will be discussing are: (1) Hart's (2016) *Relational comparison revisited: Marxist postcolonial geographies in practice*, and (2) Ingold's (2000) *The Perception of the Environment*.

Similar to Max-Neef, the approaches adopted by Ingold and Hart take a somewhat critical stance against modernist influences and aim to rid themselves of the positivist paradigm. They formulate innovative methodologies in understanding real-life processes, where social, material, technical, economic and spatial aspects are never seen as separate, isolated entities but are rather constantly forming part of 'new becomings' as the processes are interwoven and remain in constant flux. In this way both scholars are able to bring together the practices and thought processes of numerous disciplines. Both also incorporate critical ethnography as methodology, which allows for the formulation of theory and analysis that is in rhythm with people's actual lived experiences.

Hart (2016) analyses different fragments of socio-spatial processes through critical ethnography in order to understand how they stand in relation to one another through their specificities. These are then further linked to broader processes through conjunctural analysis. She argues that this sort of analysis enables one to open up the political significance of spatio-historical dialectics which extends beyond academic endeavours to the way that it effects the everyday lived experiences of people in the situation of focus. In this way she bridges the gap between theory and practice. For our purposes it is used to analyse the way a global process, the Clean Development Mechanism propagated by the United Nations, becomes entangled with a local cookstove programme and captures the socio-political significance thereof. This is an aspect often lacking in the sustainable community discourse.

My use of Ingold (2000) on the other hand, is to topple the authoritative prominence of the scientific method, to put it in its rightful place as one of many necessary paradigms needed to move towards a sustainable future. To even out the playing field so to speak. What follows is a brief introduction to the work of Ingold (2000) and Hart (2016). But first we navigate a brief historical account of the development of Western philosophy and the scientific method serving as the backdrop for the comparative discussion of the two theoretical works.

Theory and history

Scientific research as we have come to know, understand and apply it today was deeply influenced by the hylomorphic model (Ingold 2010). Although hylomorphism is a 19th-century term derived from the Greek words hyle (wood/matter) and morphe (form), it is used to refer to the metaphysical theories markedly explored by Plato and Aristotle, contending that reality consists of the coming together of form and matter. Their arguments developed along similar lines, but where Plato reasoned that form could be conceived of as separate from matter, Aristotle thought more dialectically focusing on the relationship between form and matter. He argued against the possibility of form perceived separate from matter.

A similar debate occurred earlier in the development of Western philosophy between the philosophers Parmenides and Heraclitus (Graeber 2001). The debate mainly revolved around opposing theories of change and permanence. Heraclitus argued for change as the only constant and any idea of permanence or the fixity of objects as illusions. He is famous for the statement that one cannot step into the same river twice, which aptly describes the basis of his argument. In contrast to this, Parmenides reasoned that change was an illusion and that objects could only be comprehended if they existed to a certain degree outside of time and change (Graeber 2001:50). Parmenides' theory gained wide acceptance greatly influencing Plato, Pythagoras and most thinkers in Western philosophy allowing for the conceptualisation of the workings or mechanics of physical and abstract reality. The allure of Parmenides' thoughts is quite reasonable as it opened up the potential for *a priori* truths to be discovered. Parmenides' thoughts inspired other rationalist thinkers to go in search of these truths thought to have been self-evident in reality (Russell 2011).

A definite line can be traced from these early Greek philosophers all the way to the development of the scientific method during the Enlightenment. Research conducted in this era weighed over to Parmenides and Plato's side of the debate focusing on that which can be applied universally regardless of time and context, leaving the dialectics of form and matter and 'change as constant' to be silenced in their wake. Intellectuals were interested in discovering grandiose universal truths not only of the physical world but also of human nature and society. In this period intellectuals like Locke, Voltaire and Rousseau produced ground-breaking work in their theories on society and its historical development, but it was the work of Auguste Comte that established a strong positivist influence in social sciences. Positivism has had a lasting influence on social scientific research especially given its potential to predict human behaviour and societal shifts. However, what were thought to have been great advances in research were also used to justify major social atrocities during the emergence and expansion of colonisation and industrialisation around the globe. At the time it set the stage for some of the most devastating ecological exploitations ever to be unleashed upon the natural environment. The climax of this could arguably said to be the United States' dropping of the first atomic bombs on Japan, bringing a definitive end to the world wars era. Humankind began to realise the extent of its destructive potential by controlling natural forces and phenomena. Because of this fact the second half of the 20th century was dominated by a critical reaction and a move away from positivist approaches to social phenomena in most of the social sciences (Russell 2011), so as to right the wrongs of our past.

■ Assemblage and relational comparison in conversation

Ingold

Anthropologist Ingold (2010) is critical of the hylomorphic model. He argues that the distinction between form and matter became unbalanced in its use throughout Western thought as humanity sought to wield its mastery over nature. It changed progressively to be seen as a human agent exercising form onto passive non-human matter. This perspective of reality has misguided social scientists from capturing what he calls *processes of formation* or *meshwork*. It is this very disjuncture between humanity and nature that Ingold finds to be at fault and what he aims to overcome in his formulation of a relational-ecological-developmental synthesis. For this synthesis, Ingold employs ecological psychology and developmental biology theories as both carry a strong relational emphasis. The approach gives preference to processes rather than objects and accentuates verbs rather than nouns. In a paper titled 'Bringing Things to Life' Ingold (2010) discusses his epistemological concept 'Environment Without Objects' whereby he suggests a view of the material world as constantly in flux and in movement, a world where things are constantly 'coming to life' through its entanglement with various simultaneous processes. It is through its outward surface that an object reveals itself to the perception, serving as an interface to more-or-less solid substances. The theory emphasises the permeability of surfaces and borders, arguing that it is the constant patterning of flow and flux that constitute surfaces and borders. By emphasising the flow of things between meshwork or nodes the approach carries a de-alienating characteristic, not just in the Marxist sense, in terms of capitalist production of commodities, but in all aspects of our everyday lives. Through this ontological shift he aims to eradicate the rift between the perceived human and non-human world, and thereby awaken a more sustainable awareness.

Hart

When looking at socio-material processes in a postcolonial context, as in any other contexts, questions around relationality are key, as no single process can thoroughly be understood in isolation from every other process that constitutes it. Hart's (2006, 2016) work, which applies a method of *Relational Comparison* to reveal power-laden practices in post-apartheid South Africa, renders actions of everyday life as essential to the analysis of larger processes. She explains that (Hart 2016):

> [T]he focus of relational comparison is on key processes in relation to one another through power-laden practices in the multiple, interconnected arenas of everyday life; and that clarifying these connections and mutual processes of constitution – as well as slippages, openings and contradictions – helps to generate new understandings of the possibilities for social change. (pp. 4–5)

Hart extends her relational comparison method to include conjunctural analysis in establishing a method for Marxist postcolonial geographic studies. In doing so she exposes a power-laden process that can now be recognised as resurgent imperialism within the neoliberal global context. However, for this current chapter the importance of her approach lies in its ability to show interconnectivity of power-laden processes on a local, regional and global level.

From the outset my intention in the use of these theories is to, in some sense, get back to Heraclitus' ontology that highlights change as constant, rather than an ontology which perceives reality as constituted by a set of universal truths or forms, existing independent of time and space, imposed upon a passive material world. We will now compare these two theories according to their resemblance of the Heraclitus tradition. Why? In order to take ourselves on a journey of self-reflection. In order to ask ourselves to what extent we might be reproducing an ontology guised in discursive practices that is at the same time reproducing the devastating socio-ecological ills of the past?

Hart's approach is grounded in a non-teleological conception of dialectics which she argues is what distinguishes Marx from most other dialectical theorists and allows for a philosophy of internal relations rather than seeing processes as part of an overarching whole. Hart and Ingold share this relational, non-teleological emphasis in their approach whereas conventional conceptions of capitalism and the market is understood to have an abstracting effect in the form of commodification, allowing 'things' to be seen as isolated from the processes that comprise it. In this sense both approaches carry a *demasking* property. However, Ingold's relational approach is more aligned to assemblage theory as he draws heavily on the work of Deleuze and Guattari (1987) and incorporates the concept of 'matter-flow' in his understanding of materials as processes, whereas Hart grounds her approach in Marxism. In summary Hart adopts dialectic materialism whereas Ingold falls within the new-materialist or assemblage school of thought. The main difference here being that assemblage theory completely rids itself of the prominence given to the human position, and dialectic materialism centres human action (labour) imposed onto a material world. In short, the former negates human agency, and the latter allows it. However, Marx did not view the material world as a passive receiver of human labour but rather argued that as humans transform nature, nature is also transforming humanity. Marx referred to this as the metabolic relationship between humans and nature (Wolf 1982). This brings us to the question of how assemblage theory relates to Marx's concept of metabolism?

Foster and Clark (2004) have written extensively on the historical process of ecological imperialism arguing that there has been a neglect of this aspect in Marx's work, '[...] understanding has also been impeded by the underdevelopment of an ecological materialist analysis of capitalism within Marxist theory as a whole' (Foster and Clark 2004:187). Foster and Clark (2004) further describe the workings of the capitalist process and its implications for the natural world:

> [C]apitalism had, as he [*Marx*] put it, created an 'irreparable rift' in the 'metabolic interaction' between human beings and the earth; a 'systematic restoration' of that necessary metabolic interaction as a 'regulative law of social production' was needed, but the growth under capitalism of large-scale industrial agriculture and long-distance trade intensified and extended the metabolic rift (and still does). (p. 188)

Whereas Marxism aims to uncover the processes that have caused the metabolic rift, Ingold argues that it is the very distinction made between humans and nature that has allowed for this metabolic rift to develop into the ecological catastrophe that we face today. Ingold's argument, therefore, traces it all the way back to the ontological driver.

In looking at the material world of our immediate environment through these theoretical lenses it is almost impossible to consider anything as an object with clearly defined borders or demarcations. For Ingold value is embedded in the constant flux and movement in processes of formation. Ingold's theory also carries spatial implications and for this he employs the concept of *meshwork* that views social processes as lines that relationally entangle to form nodes of symbolic and material value. To expand on the spatial implications of his theory Ingold formulates the *dwelling perspective* which he contrasts with the *building perspective*. In the former the organism–person immerse themselves into an environment where both entities are continually coming into being in a regular pattern of life activity (Ingold 2000:153). In the latter, people inhabit a world of sociocultural phenomena to which form and meaning has already been attached and is perceived through an essentialist epistemology as static entities. This comparison is especially useful in developing approaches to establish sustainable communities. Where often the developing entity or initiator is not necessarily resident in the target community or space.

In terms of spatial conceptualisations Hart's approach is valuable as it offers a spatialised understanding of Marx's method pivotal to the study of interventions geared towards establishing sustainable communities. For this

Hart refers to the work of Lefebvre (1974) which is known for its use of dialectic materialism specific to social production of space. She particularly applies Lefebvre's regressive–progressive method that refuses separation between space and time. The crux of this method lies in the point that space is socially produced; thus, it illustrates how human socialities form intersections of economic and cultural activity and that this is what truly produces and reproduces space. This perspective is especially useful when designing a project effectively, one needs to zoom out from the local sphere to the regional, national and global, to identify linkages essential to the shaping of local processes.

Hart's theory compliments Ingold's approach as she argues that questions of method are always questions of theory and always questions of politics. Theories are always political and always integral to the construction of knowledge. She, therefore, takes a critical stance on knowledge produced by exclusively applying methodologies grounded in the positivist paradigm which arrive at forms of generality based only on statistical representativeness. Hart chooses to use relational comparison as it focuses on illustrating the interconnections between the *arenas of everyday life*. As mentioned earlier her aim with this approach is to formulate new understandings which allows for conception of possibilities for social change (Hart 2016:4–5). Generalisations are formed on the basis of demonstrating interconnectivity. Simply put, she aims to move beyond the quantitative versus qualitative binary by applying her method of relational comparison. Keeping the demonstration of interconnectivity in focus, the following sections offer accounts of the historical processes that led to the establishment of NOVA as well as the formation of the relationship between NOVA and the Molati community. The ethnographic accounts serve as a prime example of how a sustainable solution is developed not simply through technological innovation but also through a complexity of socio-spatial processes together forming a meshwork of connections and relations.

■ NOVA Institute: A brief history

NOVA Institute was established in 1994; however, the idea and concept which it was to become was conceived a few years prior to the formal registration of the NPO. Nova was founded by Dr Attie S. van Niekerk and prior to this he taught practical theology in the Faculty of Theology, at the University of the North. Here he was offering theological training to the soon-to-be ministers of the Dutch Reformed Church in Africa (a brief history on the church further on). It was from his interaction and experience of living in a rural community, during the height of the apartheid era, that he developed a need to understand the relationship between Christianity and traditional African beliefs, a point that he deemed necessary to understand in order to make a meaningful impact on a poverty-stricken context.

Towards the end of the 1980s he formed an interdisciplinary group of researchers consisting of one architect, two engineers and himself, a theologian with well-accumulated contextual knowledge. The original idea behind the initiative was to bring together experts from outside the community and local residents of a selected low-income community to put their heads together and develop concrete solutions to face the most urgent challenges experienced by the community in question. It was during these initial research endeavours that the name NOVA was coined, an acronym derived from the Afrikaans title 'Navorsing en Ontwikkeling vir die Voorkoming van Armoede' – in English it translates to 'Research and Development for the Prevention of Poverty'. From the research deliberations between the local community members and the academic experts, Attie identified a gap between the technical innovations proposed and the realities of the given context, such as unique cultural practices. This gap was exactly where he envisioned NOVA as ideally positioned to make a meaningful contribution in improving experts' efficacy and thereby increasing the quality of life of low-income communities.

After South Africa's transition to a democratic state in 1994 the Faculty of Theology of the then University of the North (now named the University of Limpopo) closed down and soon after Attie and his family relocated to the country's capital Pretoria. Still intrigued by the concept of NOVA and the potential societal role it could fulfil, he decided to look for possible opportunities among his own network of industry experts, churches and academics. He eventually struck a chord with contacts working within industries such as Sasol and Eskom, two parastatal companies working in the energy sector of South Africa. Here they drew a connection between the quality of life of communities situated in proximity to industrial plants and the ambient air quality that they could relate to a Green House Gas off-set programme, funded by the same industry. From these interactions an interdisciplinary group was formed and began engaging with the community upholding a trans-disciplinary approach as ideal. By this it is meant that the input from community residents were regarded as carrying the same value as that of the technical experts. This process culminated in NOVA's flagship project known as Bassa Magogo, a top-down coal ignition method that was implemented in more than 80 000 low-income households.

It would be useful at this point to offer a brief summary of NOVA's approach to project development which evolved and became more articulated as the organisation grew. NOVA combines a trans-disciplinary and a phased approach[21] in their development of solutions with low-income households. Only the

---

21. Nova develops products and services by taking them through phases from a 'bright idea' to a full-fledged large-scale programme. All business units are involved in all phases, but in different ways. The Incubation business unit is mainly accountable for what is done in Phases 1–3, whereas the Implementation business unit is mainly accountable for what is done in Phases 4–6. http://www.nova.org.za/phased-approach

trans-disciplinary approach is of relevance for the purposes of this paper. By trans-disciplinary NOVA aims to bring together scientific rigor with the everyday lived experiential knowledge of the people within the situation that needs solving. NOVA uses two terms to describe this process, namely, 'together with households' and 'co-creation'. Hereby, it is meant that solution development emerges from the households through the guidance of experts and cannot be something that is given from the outside expert to the local residents. For the idea or solution to become a useful tool in a given context somebody must intuitively see this idea as a possibility for a specific context where people live every day. No *researcher* can see the final solution: *the people who live in that context every day must see it as a possibility for themselves.* It is a long process to come to that point and the researcher has an important role to play to help make that happen. Before the *people* in the context can 'see' it, a *researcher* may have to 'see' something. The researcher must visit the community, study the relevant technology, maybe visit similar projects that may have succeeded or failed, in the region and worldwide and come to a preliminary conclusion. It must come together *in the head* of one or more researchers. At this stage it is still theory, but it is something that can be discussed and thought about.[22] From the above description of NOVA's approach one could make correlations to Ingold's dwelling perspective where he describes the immersion of an organism into an environment and numerous entities are in continual transformation together in forming regular patterns of life activity.

■ The formation of NOVA and the Molati community relationship

It was during the formative years of the organisation that its activities crossed the radar of Maria Nyathi. At the time she served as minister in the Uniting Reformed Church in Southern Africa (URCSA) situated in Molati, a rural village in the Limpopo province, and it was through attending a public discussion facilitated by Attie S. van Niekerk that her first exposure to NOVA occurred. Historically, URCSA was formed through the independent mission work of the Dutch Reformed Church in South Africa in the early 20th century. In 1951, following the implementation of the apartheid regime a separate independent church was established for black church members called the Dutch Reformed Church in Africa. The apartheid era gradually began to unravel and in 1986 the Belhar Confession was formulated emphasising church unity, reconciliation and justice which lead to the unification of the Dutch Reformed Mission Church and the Dutch Reformed Church in Africa to form URCSA.[23]

---

22. From internal organizational document: *Guideline for developing solutions with households (programme development, unpublished).*

23. https://urcsa.net/history/.

This brief historical account shows potential for a relationship based on church denominational affinity between the historically black URCSA congregations and the historically white Afrikaans Dutch Reformed Church (DRC) congregations, especially after the transition to democracy. However, within the agricultural hinterland of the South African context it is not common for such relationships to exist. But, contrary to the norm, the URCSA congregation in Molati and the DRC congregation from the closest situated town Letsitele were on good terms with ongoing ministry activities and events being shared between them. Maria was eager to become more acquainted with the work that NOVA was doing and therefore contacted the minister of the DRC in Letsitele, Ds. Paul Grobler. This was in the late 1990s. Ds. Grobler in response made contact with Attie S. van Niekerk and after some discussion they agreed to look into possible ways of engaging with Maria and the community of Molati village.

The initial interaction between NOVA and Maria revolved around an assessment to identify the most pressing needs experienced within the community. This entailed conducting a survey with a large number of households and the gathered data showed a general lack of nutrition among the households of Molati. These findings coincided with the fact that numerous community members expressed a need to be given training in innovative agricultural methods. The research offered a clear indication of what the most contextually relevant next step should be and taking the process forward. NOVA deployed a project developer, Christiaan Pauw, to co-create an innovative farming method involving Maria and several interested community members. These actions culminated in the development and piloting of an infield rainwater harvesting method that proved to yield larger crop produce compared to the traditional methods practiced at the time.

In reflection of these historical events integral to the formation of the relationship between NOVA and the Molati community, we now turn to some current themes in Practical Theology. The philosopher and theologian Rollins (2011) shares an intriguing take on the comic book superhero character Batman, in his book titled *Insurrection*. Rollins points to the ironic duality embedded in the two lives that the character sustains. In the day he is Bruce Wayne the owner of a multi-national company at a time when the city Gotham faces severe economic inequality giving rise to an emerging criminal class. At night, Bruce Wayne takes on the role of the superhero Batman, who combats the activities of this criminal mob. Rollins, therefore, argues that Bruce Wayne produces the same criminal in the day that he combats at night. Rollins further suggests that it would be better for the character Bruce Wayne to use his wealth to create a city whose populace has access to opportunities leading to a good quality of life, which in effect would minimise the likelihood of producing criminals. Rollins views this as an analogy of the church today. He argues that the church is too focused on personal salvation and superficial charity work than creating a world where charity is no longer necessary.

Along a similar vein Schoeman (2020) discusses, in his paper titled, 'Re-imagining the congregation's calling – moving from isolation to involvement' that, 'As an open social system, a congregation is part not only of a local community, but also of the society and the global world' (Schoeman 2020:326). He urges congregations to reimagine the calling of the church to move from a position of isolation to one that is involved within their given context. This point reminds of Ingold and Hart's approaches, discussed earlier, which encourages viewing one's socio-political and material environment relationally and becoming aware of the processes that constitute it. To further flesh out the implications of these approaches we now move on to a brief case study of the Brickstar project mentioned earlier.

■ Brickstar stove project: Case study

Globally as well as in Southern Africa the level of domestic wood use has become unsustainable. The World Health Organisation estimates that 3 billion people around the world still make use of traditional cooking methods that require biomass for fuel (World Health Organisation 2018). The global rise of unsustainable energy practices and its effect on the environment garnered significant attention of the United Nations and states around the world, culminating in the formation of the Kyoto Protocol in 2005. Two noteworthy advances arose from the Kyoto Protocol which are important to mention here, namely, the Clean Development Mechanism (CDM) and the establishment of numerous clean cookstove programmes aimed at mitigating green house gas emissions and offering cleaner cooking to its end-users (UNFCCC 2014). It is important to mention here that NOVA's flagship success programme Basa Magogo, mentioned earlier, is registered on the voluntary carbon credits market and through this NOVA has generated and traded thousands of verified emission reductions. Further, given their initial success with this project they had every intention to repeat this in a newly developed project such as an improved cookstove programme that could potentially allow for it to be sustained over a period of 10 years.

Following in the wake of emerging global concerns about unsustainable wood use, NOVA initiated the process of developing an improved cookstove project in 2011. At the time, a longstanding relationship was already established between NOVA and the community of Molati, as was discussed earlier. The plan to co-create the improved cookstove project was, therefore, simply a continuation and extension of an existing commitment to improve the quality of life of Molati households. These households traditionally cook their meals on an open fire in separately built kitchens that are situated outside the house. Most of these outside kitchens have little or no ventilation, which means that the person cooking is exposed to open fire smoke inhalation. This situation is detrimental to any person present in the kitchen while cooking is in process, and even more alarming where children are present.

In response to this, the Brickstar stove was co-designed over a couple of years by NOVA and about 20 women residing in Molati. Currently, the stove is built by residents, with technical support from NOVA, tailor-made to suit their needs and requirements. Installation teams are locally trained and contracted, and they make use of materials that are readily available in the area, incorporating skills that community members already have, at no cost to the end-user. The integration of the Brickstar stove into household cooking practices allows for a 40% decrease in firewood consumption and almost completely eradicates the presence of harmful smoke, which the user and children at times were exposed to in the closed-off area of the kitchen. This improvement occurs because of a more efficient firewood combustion, which has the effect of significantly reducing the amount of smoke released.

However, it must be stated here that the local cultural practices mentioned were and are never viewed as a static traditional practice independent of time and change. It is rather viewed as a fluid process that transforms with each generation and individual who takes up the task and passes it on to the next generation. To be more specific, and in keeping with our theory under discussion, Ingold describes this process in the following way, 'Skills are not transmitted from generation to generation but rather regrown in each organism, through experience and training in the performance of tasks' (Ingold 2000:5). In relation to the Brickstar project, this process not only included local residents but also involved the NOVA staff members. It further entailed acknowledging the continued change and transformation of the project on every level, from the actual stove design to the way it is assimilated into local cooking practices by the end-user. The progression described in this section offers some ethnographic vignettes of what Ingold refers to as a meshwork or the coming together of numerous threads of life to form a project in constant flux. It also illustrates Hart's notion of relational comparison showing the interconnectivity of numerous processes and how it allowed for change towards a sustainable future in the example of the drafting of Kyoto Protocol, the establishment of the CDM and NOVA's eventual trading on the voluntary carbon credits market.

The rocket stove concept as innovative technology

In essence the Brickstar project entails an alternative method of cooking which employs the 'rocket stove' concept pioneered by Dr Larry Winiarski in 1982.[24] The rocket stove concept offers a more efficient energy utilisation compared to the traditional open-fire method still largely used by households around the globe. The concept is innovative in two ways: (1) more efficient

---

24. Dr Mark Bryden, Dean Still, Peter Scott, Geoff Hoffa, Damon Ogle, Rob Bailis, Ken Goyer. Design Principles for Wood Burning Cook Stoves. Aprovecho Research Center, Shell Foundation Partnership for Clean Indoor Air.

firewood combustion, (2) and heat insulation. These are the technical aspects of the project which draw 'purely' on scientific principles. However, it cannot on its own offer a viable solution to the problem it seeks to address. This is exactly where the co-creative approach that NOVA bases its work on fits in. Along with the local practices and knowledge, a new cooking culture, one that is geared towards creating sustainable communities, needs to emerge. As the NOVA staff members and community members come together, the rocket stove concept gets 'wrapped-up' in local cultural practices and freely available materials. Hereby, an iterative process of co-creation occurs where clay and cow dung are collected from a nearby kraal or open patch of land to form a new sustainable cooking alternative viable and accessible to the low-income communities. At this point, you might ask yourself whether the above description is describing the hylomorphic model, the exact paradigm the paper aims to critique. But what I am arguing for is not the complete discrediting of the scientific method all together; rather, the aim is to topple the authority it commands in matters that also necessitate a socio-spatial perspective. To see it as one of many perspectives. If we allow ourselves to view the same process through Ingold's lens of *Environment Without Objects*, we are reminded that the rocket stove concept, the age-old cultural practice of using clay and cow dung to make bricks, the cattle producing cow dung, the earth forming clay and even the presence of Nova staff members are all examples of processes coming together in a node that could be labelled as the *Brickstar-project-meshwork*. This allows for the form and matter distinction to dissipate and only processes and things to remain.

▢ The Green Economy Machine

As briefly discussed earlier, Nova was able to register the Basa Magogo project on the voluntary carbon credits market and generate a significant amount of Verified Emission Reductions (VER) over a period of 10 years. Although not directly linked the voluntary carbon market was an indirect initiative following the establishment of the CDM by the UNFCCC in 2006. Unfortunately, the carbon credit market sustained a significant collapse in 2013 and the British writer George Monbiot, known for his critical views on the effects of the global market on climate change, explained that this downfall in the carbon market was because of an oversupply of credits which was coordinated by the lobbying power of large businesses (Monbiot 2013). Monbiot argues that rather than creating a sustainable process of natural resource utilisation, it has had the effect of rationalising the polluting practices of the private sector (Monbiot 2013) (Reyneke 2017). This tumultuous period in the compliance carbon market also had a disastrous effect on the voluntary carbon market and Nova struggled to trade their VER's for the anticipated price. Be that as it may, to date the Brickstar project has generated a considerable amount of carbon credits and the problematic aspect of the CDM set aside, it can potentially assist in financially sustaining the project to a certain extent in the long run. There are, therefore, two global processes that have and continue to shape the cookstove programme: the first being the historical development and spread of the Protestant Church which led to the intersection between the Dutch Reformed Church and the Uniting Reformed Church, and the other being the establishment of the CDM initiative. These are some of the socio-spatial linkages that Hart's refers to which are constituted in relation to one another through power-laden practices that are also interconnected in the everyday life, here being the everyday cooking practices of a rural community in South Africa (Hart 2016).

■ Conclusion

Through the lens of *meshwork*, as Ingold suggests, we are able to witness how the presence of an urban based NPO within the rural Molati community became enmeshed and has formed in many households an innovative part of their everyday cooking practice. When one zooms out further on a regional, national and global scale, applying Hart's lens of relational comparison we are able to perceive how processes initiated by the United Nations in the form of the CDM become catalysts in transforming the layered relationship between NOVA and the Molati community, fostered over two decades. The approach, therefore, allows the researcher to become aware of the multi-layered process of the co-creation of a cookstove project that at face level seems to be much more simplistic than what the reality of the matter is. The hope is that the insights gained from the analysis of the Brickstar project, viewed through the lens of the discussed methodologies creates a greater awareness of the processes that constitute potential sustainable solutions other than purely focusing on technical innovation and scientific rigor in the modernist sense. Perhaps this might enable researchers, project developers and policymakers to formulate fresh approaches for the study and development of new programmes to achieve sustainable communities.

Chapter 8

Decolonising the engineering curriculum at the university

Willem van Niekerk
Department of Mechanical Engineering,
Faculty of Engineering, North-West University,
Potchefstroom, South Africa

Attie S. van Niekerk[a,b]
[a]The Nova Institute, Pretoria, South Africa
[b]Sustainable Communities Research Cluster, Centre for Faith and Community,
Faculty of Religion and Theology, University of Pretoria,
Pretoria, South Africa

■ Introduction

In reflecting on the role of universities, three tasks are often mentioned: teaching, research and community engagement. Besides the transfer and the production of knowledge as core tasks, universities are nowadays also increasingly aware of their responsibility towards society at large and the socio-political role they play.

The aim of this chapter is to contribute to the current debate on the decolonisation of universities, which is one of the socio-political issues of our time.

How to cite: Van Niekerk, W. & Van Niekerk, A.S., 2021, 'Decolonising the engineering curriculum at the university', in A.S. Van Niekerk & S. Strijbos (eds.), *We cannot continue like this: Facing modernity in Africa and the West*, pp. 155–166, AOSIS, Cape Town. https://doi.org/10.4102/aosis.2021.BK283.08

It is the result of reflections at the Faculty of Engineering at the North-West University (NWU) in South Africa regarding ways in which it can decolonise its teaching. The university has issued a declaration on decolonisation, which *inter alia* states (NWU 2018):

> It is thus acknowledged that every faculty should attempt to decolonize both the content of its academic programmes, and its approaches to, and methods of teaching, learning and assessment in its lecture halls, laboratories and other teaching venues in a differentiated manner. (n.p.)

Decolonisation refers to a process to end the hegemony of the West. One can either have a narrow or a broad perspective on decolonisation:

- The narrow perspective focuses on Western countries and their former colonies and strives to correct the events of the past. It has clear geographic demarcations: the Western countries are in Europe and the colonies in Africa, Asia or Latin America.
- The broad perspective refers to the hegemony of the West in the present. Some focus on the hegemony of the West in the economic sphere; others on identity, for example culture, language and/or religion. These two are sometimes combined, so that all spheres of life are included in the drive for decolonisation. Grosfoguel (2011), for example, refers to the 'broad entangled "package" called the European modern/colonial capitalist/patriarchal world-system', which is the object of decolonisation. This package includes the European Judeo-Christian patriarchy and European notions of sexuality, epistemology and spirituality. He refers to the 'modern/colonial Western-centric Christian-centric/capitalist/patriarchal world-system'. In this perspective, no geographic demarcations exist, and the oppressed races are also found in the Western countries and in the USA.

In the broad perspective, modern Western science and technology, and all that is produced by it, can be regarded by many as alien to their own cultural and religious traditions. However, this position is difficult to maintain consistently under all circumstances. It is then often found that science and technology is rather regarded as the heritage of all of humanity and not as something that is by its nature Western. The result is that an effort is then made to make use of Western science and technology and all that is produced by it, sometimes even to take ownership thereof and to combine it with, or assimilate it into one's own tradition.

Both the narrow and the broad perspectives can be employed by those who use the language of decolonisation merely to gain power or to benefit financially. In doing so, they may become guilty of what they accuse the colonisers of doing.

In discussions on the decolonisation at the Faculty of Engineering, one often encounters a point of view that science and technology have no relation to culture and religion. It is often argued that research which takes place in laboratories and in technological environments is 'objective and neutral', in other words, independent of the subjective views and values of the researcher. Engineering knowledge is, therefore, seen as valid in all contexts. A popular statement in this regard is that water boils at 100 °C at sea level, independent of politics or culture or race or any social movements or ideology. In debates about decolonisation it is often asked: 'How can you decolonize Newton's Laws?' The implication is that the debate about decolonisation in engineering is without meaning, as engineering is about objective and neutral facts that cannot be decolonised.

This approach has been dominant in many engineering faculties. This can be seen in the way that the third task of a university, community engagement, has traditionally been considered in such engineering faculties. In these faculties, community engagement is encouraged to ensure that academics stay in touch with the practice of engineering. Community engagement usually takes the form of specialist consulting work in the field of expertise of the academic. Except when it is part of the scope of the consulting work, it will not be necessary for the academic specialist to take cognisance of the wider socio-economic context of the project. Such community engagement, therefore, tends to have a narrow, technical focus.

From this point of view, it is understandable that many engineering faculties will find it difficult to see how decolonisation can be achieved in engineering education and research. However, calls for decolonisation remain strong – which is evident in the Black Lives Matter and the Fees Must Fall movements.

Attention to the decolonisation of engineering is not required merely because of pressure from outside the engineering field. In this article it is argued that the way in which technology functions within society and the environment, is intrinsic to engineering, and that a good understanding of the context in which the engineer applies knowledge, is essential in engineering education and research. It would also help in understanding the manner in which engineering, and education of engineers, can be decolonised.

Three elements are usually distinguished in education (Pellegrino 2006):

- Curriculum, which describes the content, scope, width and breadth of the knowledge and skills that teachers teach and students learn.
- Instruction, which refers to the teaching and learning activities used to help students master the objectives stated in the curriculum.
- Assessment, the means used to determine if, and to what extent, the students mastered required outcomes.

The curriculum has a central role in the overall process, because it determines to a significant degree the process of teaching and what will be evaluated and will be the focus of this chapter.

It is argued that the content and skills which are taught to engineering students are the result of human design, based on a certain mindset and certain social conditions and needs. Related to this, it is argued that it is possible to decolonise the engineering curriculum. An attempt will be made to provide pointers on how such decolonisation can be achieved.

In the African context, there is a discourse on the role that engineering and technology can play in African societies to deal with the past and present impact of the modern world and colonisation by the West. By proposing, in this chapter, a possible approach to the decolonisation of the engineering curriculum, we hope to contribute to this discourse.

■ The engineering curriculum

With regard to the curriculum, the Engineering Council of South Africa (ECSA) (2014) distinguishes five knowledge areas: Mathematics, Natural Sciences, Engineering Sciences, Design and Synthesis and Complimentary Studies. The latter covers all other disciplines that are relevant for the practice of engineering, including but not limited to management, engineering economics, the impact of technology on society, effective communication and the humanities.

Those who argue that engineering knowledge is objective and neutral, that is, independent of subjective views and values, would understand *Complementary Studies* as additional or secondary, not as intrinsic to engineering knowledge. The view is, however, being replaced, also in Europe and the United States of America (USA), by the recognition that engineering and technology are always practised and implemented in a certain context, so that the way in which technology functions within society and the environment is intrinsic to engineering knowledge (see Winner, *Do artefacts have politics?* in *The Social Shaping of Technology*, eds. MacKenzie & Wajcman [1999]).

The first two knowledge areas identified by ECSA are usually taught in the junior years and are the foundation on which the later years are built.

▪ Mathematics and natural sciences

Knowledge in Mathematics and the Natural Sciences strives to be independent of context and is usually abstract. This is an important reason why some engineers maintain that Engineering cannot be decolonised.

It seems that there is, to a large extent, agreement that the goal of decolonisation is not to reject established knowledge in mathematical and natural sciences (Winberg & Winberg 2017), but rather rethink how the subject matter is produced (Roy 2018), applied and taught (Fomunyam 2017). That implies that natural sciences and mathematics are important tools in engineering, but that a more fundamental question in engineering is how this knowledge is used within the engineering process. This opens the way for a debate.

Engineering sciences

The third ECSA knowledge area, Engineering Sciences, has a unique aim. Whereas the natural scientist strives for better understanding (in other words more scientific knowledge) – or according to Houkes (2009:312) 'the truth' – the engineer evaluates scientific knowledge based on its usefulness in the design process (Hansson 2007). A distinguishing characteristic is that Engineering Sciences deal with man-made artefacts, not natural phenomena. But one must consider even more: engineers and the artefacts they produce shape our human-social practices and the landscape that we live in. All over the world, there is a growing concern about the impact of engineering on the broader context of the natural and social–human environment.

Engineering scientists often have to develop their own theoretical and empirical knowledge. Engineering Science is thus not Applied Physics or Chemistry or Mathematics, it is a science in its own right, that has developed its own methodologies and generates its own data and theories. The development of Mechanical Engineering Thermodynamics as an engineering science was driven by the need to improve the efficiency and safety of the steam engines built by Newcomen and Watt. Another, more recent example of an engineering science is nuclear technology developed for power generation and military purposes, which was built on the research by physical scientists (Ziman 1994). The fear that Germany could have developed and used an atom bomb during the Second World War played an important role in ensuring that the Manhattan project, the development of the nuclear bombs to be dropped on Hiroshima and Nagasaki, continued to receive funding (Wyden 1984).

It is clear that context has played a determining role in the development of engineering sciences. A strong relationship has always existed between engineering faculties and industry. This relationship plays an important role in the determination of the content of the curriculum. To be accredited by the Engineering Council of South Africa (ECSA), faculties of engineering need to appoint an Industry Advisory Council, which must convene every second year. The accreditation team visits faculties every five years and has to have at least two members who are, at the time of the visit, active in industry or working professionally (ECSA 2017).

There is no doubt that engineering is closely linked with industry and must serve industry. However, engineering and industry are increasingly considering their key roles in the social and natural landscape which they help shape. Furthermore, the social and natural landscape differs from one situation to the other. This applies everywhere in the world, and the term decolonisation refers to a specific understanding of our African context that requires a relevant response, also from engineering. Engineering faculties and industries that find themselves in this context have to consider their role in the search to develop postcolonial engineering sciences that will enable them to solve postcolonial problems. As mentioned before, engineers evaluate scientific knowledge based on its usefulness in the design process.

Design

Design is a defining activity of engineering – it is the conceptualisation and quantification of the characteristics of an artefact (man-made object) that must meet a predetermined set of requirements or solve a problem.

The importance and content of design (as with engineering sciences) have changed with time and circumstances. Warren Seering, a professor in Mechanical Engineering at MIT, gave a talk on the history of design at the Massachusetts Institute of Technology (Seering 2016). Around 1870, MIT included mechanical engineering in its curriculum. Initially, the problems that had to be solved were relatively easy to define, for instance, designing and building a bridge. With the turn of the century, as the steam engine came into general use, designs became more complicated and engineers had to learn how to design integrated systems such as power stations, which contained several sub-systems and focused on meeting specific needs – such as electricity generation. The same happened with the building of roads and dams.

After the Second World War, the theoretical content of the engineering curriculum was expanded. The assumption was that, with enough theoretical knowledge, engineers would be able to meet the need for cost-effective designs for a variety of clients. Engineering studies did not respond to societal needs as before, but focused on theoretical knowledge that would enable the engineer to respond to narrowly-defined needs after completing his or her studies – and the approach generally worked well.

The focus on solving societal challenges was about to change again, as the need for engineers to solve specific social, economic and other problems became important again. One thing that changed was the needs of the market. Until 1980, the balance of payment in the USA was positive and stable and there was not much competition in the market. However, the late 20th century brought globalisation, and the context in which engineers had to function became more volatile and complicated. Producers in the USA now had to compete with producers from overseas.

The effect that technology had on the environment was also increasingly raising concerns. The Greenpeace movement was founded in 1971.

The result was that the design process became more important and in modern curricula, an increasing emphasis is placed on design (Froyd, Wankat &

Smith 2012). The design process also became more complicated. The modern engineer must take technical, economic, health and safety, legal, social and environmental constraints into account and incorporate them all in the design (ECSA 2012). Marc Steen (2012:72) in a paper on human-centred design states that innovation and design are often driven by technological considerations: 'This technology push approach brings a risk of creating products or services that people cannot or do not want to use'.

Since 1980, user needs have become a common topic in design textbooks. It, therefore, became increasingly important for engineers to also be taught non-technical skills (Nguyen 1998; Redish & Smith 2008). According to Jonassen, Strobel and Lee (2006) the type of problems modern engineers are likely to encounter in the workplace, will be ill-structured and complex with conflicting goals, more than one solution strategy and several possible problem representations.

Design and synthesis are listed by ECSA as a knowledge area but should perhaps be seen as a skill. Redish and Smith (2008) define a skill as the ability to apply factual knowledge in practice. Coaching and receiving feedback are important steps in skills development (Felder & Brent 2003; Whimbey, Lochhead & Narode 2013). Furthermore, the ability to determine which knowledge is appropriate for the given task, may require wisdom. The data–information–knowledge–wisdom hierarchy, referred to as the 'Knowledge Hierarchy', the 'Information Hierarchy' and the 'Knowledge Pyramid', is one of the fundamental, and widely recognised models in the information and knowledge literature.

In 2011 Engineers Without Borders (EWB) launched 'The Engineering for People Design Challenge' initiative. As the name implies, the focus is primarily on people, rather than on cost or profit. EWB argues that the traditional approach fails to satisfy the needs of 80% of the population and that it is critical to develop engineering skills and talent that considers the human and environmental aspects of design. This is considered important to meet the challenges of the 21st century: ecological crises, population growth, poverty, scarcity of food and water and urban densification.

The design process must, therefore, become a more open process. Which factors to include or exclude during design are the result of human choice and can, therefore, be tailored for a postcolonial era.

In this, decolonisation is part of a global development: in the West it is emphasised equally emphatically that the design of technology must be a more open process, which engages the end-user and takes the ecology into account.

The goal of education is often stated as imparting knowledge, developing skills and nurturing attitudes. We have discussed the knowledge areas defined by ECSA and discussed developing design skills. This brings us to the third goal of education: nurturing attitudes.

■ Attitudes

In the Introduction it was mentioned that there can be a conflict between science and technology, on the one hand, and cultural and religious traditions, on the other. During the COVID-19 pandemic, many placed their hope in medical technology and science. However, some did not display this attitude. For example, the former president of the USA, Donald Trump, explicitly rejected the advice of medical experts. Also, with regard to climate change, many people who accept the view that our lifestyle harms the environment, do not significantly change their lifestyle.

It may perhaps be safe to assume that in general, an engineering faculty has an axiomatic belief in the superiority of modern science and technology. It may, therefore, be illuminating to consider its origins.

Modern technology developed in Europe in the last 500 years although, at that time, Europe was not necessarily the best or highest developed in a scientific and technological sense. Two examples illustrate this. The Ottoman Empire reached its peak under Suleiman the Magnificent, who died in 1566. Science and Mathematics were regarded as important fields of study and were well-developed. They invented surgical instruments such as forceps, catheters and scalpels, which are still used today. Much of the knowledge developed in the Ottoman Empire is part of modern science.

In China, during the reign of the Ming Dynasty between 1406 AD and 1420 AD, the magnificent Forbidden City was built. In Figure 8.1, Zheng He's bigger flagship (1418) and Columbus' smaller flagship (1492) are compared. Zheng's fleet crossed the Indian Ocean and he visited several places, including Africa, but he had no desire to colonise them.

Modern science and technology, however, evolved in Europe over the past centuries through the interaction or the feedback loop between science, politics and economics, plus a certain mentality. A core element of this mentality is the belief in progress through human control over nature, including human nature. An important goal in the search for knowledge was to acquire new technologies and new powers (Harari 2014:275–279).

It was this attitude towards science and technology, namely, of gaining control and power, in the belief that this could lead to a better world that distinguished Europe from China in the 15th century – rather than superior science and technology, as the size of Columbus' ship illustrates. This mentality is one of the roots of the colonial drive. Eventually, much of the world embraced modern technology. Lesslie Newbigin already observed in 1961 that there is a

Source: Plougmann (2006).
FIGURE 8.1: A comparison between the flagships of Zheng He and Columbus.

widespread tendency to combine an emphasis on a non-Western identity with the use of modern technology (Newbigin 1961):

> The scientific technical culture that has developed in the West is now regarded as the world civilization of our time. It is regarded as something which is not specifically Western but universal, something in the sharing of which one shares in the civilization of our time… one can take Western science and technology in the biggest available doses without the risk of damaging one's Eastern digestion. The large and able body of Asian graduates [….] are sure that they are not in any way cutting themselves off from their own religion and culture. They are sure that this world of technology, while it has originated in the West, belongs to the whole world, and that the East can take them on its own terms and use it in their own way […]. (pp. 13–14)

An uncritical acceptance of modern technology, and the view that modern technology is universal, is also evident among some in South Africa.

Shortly after 1990, when the decision was taken by the white minority government to negotiate for a fully democratic government in South Africa, a team of leaders from liberal big business and academia proposed a change-of-gears or kick-start approach to introduce massive structural changes. They envisioned this through massive schemes to provide housing, electrification, education, health care and job creation to those who did not have it, in order to transform the country in one forceful effort towards modernisation, development, productivity and social stability (Morgan 1992:134–141; eds. Tucker & Scott 1992). The motive of this initiative was the assumption that, without quick and tangible improvements in the level of the daily lives of the masses, political efforts to become a democracy, would fail.

The Electrification Drive led to the electrification of millions of households in a short period of time. It was based on the assumption that there had to be a change of gears, done for the people, rather than an approach of enabling people to do things for themselves, or being involved in the process.

One can also call it a colonial/colonisation/coloniser mindset. Modern science and technology are regarded as the norm for everything else, and other forms of knowledge and problem-solving are not taken into account.

While the motive for this initiative – to improve the living conditions of people – cannot be faulted, the recipients were not part of the process and in that sense this initiative shows similarities with a colonising mindset. As the speed of implementation was deemed to be important, the initiative was implemented without engaging the end-user. Electrification was not tailor-made for the context in which it was implemented. Mass electrification has had a mixed result: it brought improvement to the lives of many people but has had a negative impact on the relations between Eskom, municipalities and residents. The debt of municipalities to Eskom presently amounts to ZAR46 billion (BusinessTech 2020).

The flipside of a colonial mindset is a colonised mindset characteristic of those who are colonised: the superiority complex of the coloniser often creates an inferiority complex in the colonised. Feelings of inferiority lead to a negative self-perception of own identity, history and culture (see the chapter by Luc Kabongo in this book).

In the decolonisation discourse and black conscious movement, there is a deliberate drive to overcome the colonised mindset. There is a call to 'decolonise the intellectual landscape of the country [...] and, ultimately, [to] decolonise the mind of the formerly colonized' (Oelofsen 2015:131).

Neither of these mindsets belong to the past, as is evident in the calls to decolonise university education and the (engineering) curriculum.

Engineering students must be aware of and understand this discourse between acceptance and rejection. It will be a pity if they merely accept the top-down approach followed during the Electrification Drive as correct. They must realise that the design approach should be open, that the people who are supposed to benefit, should also have a say in the design process. Students should be able to critically evaluate the approach followed by modern industry and be allowed to at least contemplate and suggest alternative approaches.

Experience has taught us that this is a daunting task. Many have argued that the policy of Black Economic Empowerment, which was introduced after the fall of apartheid and was supposed to benefit the wider black community, has only benefitted a small minority. Efforts to include local residents in construction projects have often led to violence and the postponement of work on important projects. It is also necessary to consider belief systems. A project to reduce rodent infestation in a black township by introducing owls, led to the killing and mutilation of the owls because many of the residents believed that the owls were inhabited by evil spirits (Samuels 2014).

The personnel of an engineering faculty should also identify their own attitude towards technology and engineering: Do they hold the belief that modern science and technology is independent of context and that it is sufficient to only provide a good technological design? We do think that in engineering sciences and the design process, there is scope and opportunity to co-create new knowledge and skills.

■ Decolonising the curriculum

According to Jonathan Jansen, 'those in power select what to learn and how to teach and therefore curriculum is inherently a political act with symbolic value' (Du Preez 2018:20). Engineering Faculties, therefore, have to realise that their approach towards the curriculum reflects a certain attitude. They can have a narrow or a broad perspective on the curriculum:

- The narrow perspective focuses on knowledge and skills as a given that must be transferred to the students.
- The broad perspective shows understanding that the curriculum functions in the economic, social and political context, as well as in the personal context of the lecturer and the student.

The first step would, therefore, be to formulate – to use engineering language – the design specifications. Muller (2018) laments the fact that we have not developed a vision of a decolonised future: 'The failure to date to articulate a clear vision of a decolonised future is unfortunate'. To formulate such a vision, it would be necessary to adopt the broad perspective and follow an inclusive, open process.

It will also be necessary to decide what the scope of this vision should be. While decolonisation has a determining role in our history, today there are other aspects to consider as well (Jansen 2018). There is considerable overlap between the decolonisation discourse and the sustainability discourse. Both Western colonisation and the modern human-built environment, that many increasingly regard as unsustainable, are products of modernism, specifically of a key tenet of modernism, namely, that human control will bring progress. The relationship between modernity, the sustainability issue and (de)colonisation should be better understood and investigated.

The engineering faculty is the custodian of the technology that the world needs. It would improve its contribution if it has a better understanding of the interaction between science and technology and the cultures and traditions that determine the way in which technology is used, and how the engineer can deal with it.

A third aspect is that we need to discover for ourselves (both faculty and students) what our attitude towards technology and engineering is. What you believe about what you teach and what you are learning, is obviously important.

In this chapter we, therefore, do not propose a vision or a roadmap, but a process. The first step is to develop a broader view and to engage with role players other than the industry also. The participants in this conversation can include the community surrounding the university, black consciousness movements, human rights activists and environmentalists.

■ Conclusion

In a globalised economy it is important for engineering faculties (and according to a survey, their students also [Winberg & Winberg 2017]), to be internationally recognised while striving to be locally relevant. Engineering Faculties in South Africa are all accredited by ECSA according to the Washington agreement. The accreditation guidelines leave enough space to allow universities to develop design methodologies (as well as engineering sciences that inform the design process) that will enable them to be also locally relevant. Important insights may be gained by engaging Engineering Faculties in the Global South and Latin America to determine to what extent they were able to engage role players other than industry and adapt their curriculum accordingly.

The second step is to develop a vision of a decolonised future. It can be a utopian vision: a world without poverty, or at least less poverty, where human dignity and cultural traditions are respected and cultivated, with a healthy ecology, where natural resources are not exploited beyond the capacity of the earth to replace it, and no more waste is produced than the earth can absorb. All of this may be technically achievable, but requires a specific mindset.

Chapter 9

Mobilising people to emerge as transformation agents for society building: A reflection on a missional team practice

Luc Kabongo[a,b]
[a]InnerCHANGE,
Pretoria, South Africa;
[b]Department of Religion Studies, Faculty of Theology and Religion,
University of Pretoria, Pretoria, South Africa

■ Introduction

African communities living in poverty long for an improved quality of life. The catalysing of inside out efforts could provide a sustainable solution to this longing. However, communities living in poverty are often passive recipients of top-down plans from powerful institutions such as the government, international non-profit organisations or the church. Although these plans are put together with the best intentions possible, they can be disempowering because they prevent ordinary people being part of the solution to the

How to cite: Kabongo, L., 2021, 'Mobilising people to emerge as transformation agents for society building: A reflection on a missional team practice', in A.S. Van Niekerk & S. Strijbos (eds.), *We cannot continue like this: Facing modernity in Africa and the West*, pp. 167–185 AOSIS, Cape Town. https://doi.org/10.4102/aosis.2021.BK283.09

problems they face. As mentioned earlier, the institutional church can sometimes be disempowering. However, it is acknowledged that faith and church can play a unique role in empowering ordinary people. The church could be proactive in mobilising ordinary people to emerge as transformation agents who are described as (Kabongo 2019):

> Individuals who generally observe principles of human dignity and worth, human rights, good social values, and socio-political transformation. They can recognise existing needs of individuals and a community, and engage them in a way that is solution-seeking. Their engagement usually leads to new insights into ways to heal or build a community through its residents. (p. 9)

Transformation agents are rare to find in communities of poverty. This research is an in-depth reflection on what InnerCHANGE[25] does to catalyse the development of transformation agents. It is learning to be intentional in catalysing the emergence of hope-filled society builders from below. Transformation agents are hope-filled people who are practically building the future they would like to see around them. Sacks (2018:2) states that it is critical for people living in communities of poverty 'to perfect the world, refusing to accept the inevitability of suffering and injustice' around them. Their main inspiration should be hope. Sacks (2018:3) sees hope as the willpower that makes it possible for human beings to 'overcome the difficulties of any given here and now' and to believe that the improvement of their quality of life is possible.

The church should participate in the emerging of transformation agents in taking into cognisance some historical factors that explain the scarcity of them in African grassroots communities. An important factor to take into consideration is the impact of colonisation and apartheid on Africans (this research uses the word African to refer to black Africans). They have nurtured colonised minds in Africans which impede transformation agency. A colonised mind is an imprisoned mind that feels disarmed to be an agent of the kind of society it would like to become. The colonised mindset disables people from participating in seeking solutions to their communal issues.

InnerCHANGE as a representative of the church serving in communities of poverty seeks to deconstruct a colonised mindset through practical ministry initiatives it is involved in. This chapter reflects on these practices guided by this question: How can the church creatively nurture society building agents through its efforts from below? InnerCHANGE attempts to answer this question through its training programs where it promotes the teaching of local history, experiential learning, networking and learning to engage societal disempowering structures.

---

25. See https://www.innerchange.org.

The knowledge of local history

History can be a critical tool to help understand the identity of a family, clan or people group. The author grew up in a context where the history of his lineage, clan, tribe and village where his parents originated from, were shared regularly by grandparents and other elderly in the community. These stories he heard are a knowledge capital in the understanding of his identity. History is so critical in the identity formation of a people that colonisation and apartheid worked hard at the 'usurpation' of African history (Maluleke 2019:179). The history the author learned at school as well as the one he sees children learning in Soshanguve prioritise other contexts at the expense of Africa. InnerCHANGE believes that the knowledge of the local history in places such as Soshanguve can empower ordinary people to emerge as transformation agents. Learning about local history may give people the power for renewal, reinvention and restoration. It may also be an empowering tool in how they interact with their current affairs and envision their future.

The knowledge of history could allow ordinary Africans to be aware of stories of pain and joy that surround them. It can challenge them to not repeat the shortcomings from the past and inspire them to prioritise the building of their society, starting from their local communities. In places like Soshanguve, InnerCHANGE encourages ordinary people to 'be exposed to black role models' from the past and present so that a 'can-do attitude' can be nurtured (Ramphele 2017:56). Such an attitude stands the chance to come to fruition when 'the history and intellectual accomplishments of [fellow] Africans' is taught to them (Diop 1964:47). From times immemorial, African societies did things that should not be repeated as well as things that should be emulated today. Transformation agents should hold dearly the things from the past that should be emulated today and seek creative ways to reinterpret them. Osafo-Kwaako and Robinson (2013:6), for instance, point out that many African pre-colonial societies had political systems that promoted the collective welfare' of villagers. They 'continually reinterpreted the lessons of the past in the context of the present' which sustained their livelihoods (Spear 2003:3).

A content on local history is a missing portion in the history curricula taught in Soshanguve from primary to high school. Learners are taught the history of the world, and biased content about their continent and country. They are left in the dark about their local communities. There is a need for curriculum transformation so that history could help learners deepen the understanding of their context. Such an understanding could deepen their agency to participate in building their local communities. We could be inspired by Europeans who seem to 'draw their strengths from their version of history' (Ramphele 2017:52). Africans could also strengthen their identity and rootedness to their continent by 'the feeling of historical continuity' (Diop 1964:54). A 'collective memory well-remembered' has the potential to cultivate a sense of confidence (Hayes 2006:236). Such a sense of confidence has the potential to equip ordinary Africans to learn to participate in building a future they would like to walk into. Such a future should guard itself against the self-sabotage we have become accustomed to seeing in communities such as Soshanguve. This self-sabotage plays out as inferiority complex, self-hatred and naivety.

Inferiority complex

In communities such as Soshanguve, there seems to be a common belief that Africans are inferior to white people. There is a well-known Sotho idiom that says *'sithari tsa Mosotho ki likhuwa'* (meaning for a black person to be professional, a white person must supervise him/her). The inferiority complex seems to permeate through the fabric of Africa as a continent and is seen to be prevalent among the elite as well. Such is the case of prominent figures such as Nelson Mandela and Desmond Tutu. One such example is the way the way Mandela (1995) expressed it in his book 'Long Walk to Freedom':

> We put down briefly in Khartoum, where we changed to an Ethiopian Airways flight to Addis. Here I experienced a rather strange sensation. As I was boarding the plane I saw that the pilot was black. I had never seen a black pilot before, and the instant I did I had to quell my panic. How could a black man fly an airplane? But a moment later I caught myself: I had fallen into the apartheid mindset thinking Africans were inferior and that flying was a white man's job. I sat back in my seat and chided myself for such thoughts. Once we were in the air, I lost my nervousness […]. (pp. 334–335)

Similarly, in his book 'No Future without Forgiveness', Tutu (1999:193–194) talks about a visit to Nigeria where on a trip to Northern Nigeria, the pilot was black. He reflects that coming from South Africa where blacks were not allowed in such professions, he was a proud black African. However, during the flight, there was some turbulence and he found himself doubting that the black pilot will get them out of trouble and a white pilot could have been a trustworthy rescuer.

These two stories demonstrate an acceptance of white supremacy even among the black African elite known for their promotion of race equality. This inferiority complex seems to be rooted in our subconscious as Africans. Our current generation should remember that 'many years of slavery and colonialism, followed by generations of economic exploitation, political oppression, racial discrimination and educational deprivation', have created in Africans feelings of inferiority, instability and total dependency (Perkins 2014:101). Therefore, 'freeing ourselves' from the remnants of this systemic oppression which leads to an inferiority complex, should be prioritised (Ramphele 2017:22–23). Many Africans have been told countless times that their place is at the bottom of the world and society. This has created a sense of collective low self-image and self-esteem in them. It is equally critical to free ourselves from self-hatred which is a paradox to society building.

Self-hatred

In local communities such as Soshanguve, black-on-black discrimination is common. This has been true throughout history. Pre-colonial Africa constituted rival kingdoms. Some of those kingdoms such as the Zulu, Ashanti and Congo became powerful at the expense of others. These kingdoms were regularly at war with others and expanded their territorial boundaries by shedding blood. It is been documented that many African kings contributed to the promotion of slavery by selling war prisoners and naughty citizens to slave traders (Maathai 2009). It seems like distinctiveness, which is an accident of history, has always been a reason for 'othering' fellow human beings. Such a mindset has led to violence related to nationalism, tribalism, xenophobia, homophobia, abuses against vulnerable people such as women, children and senior citizens. Donovan (2005:37–38) shares a pertinent story about 'othering' from one of his evangelist trips to 'Tanzanian villages'. One time after he finished evangelising, his audience gave him the feedback that the core message of the Bible is to love. However, the people felt like it was impossible for them to love their neighbours from their nearest villages because of some conflicts that had occurred in the past. Such a challenge to reconcile and live in harmony with others was a test for Christianity, according to Donavan. He wondered what could be the outcome of a suggestion to his audience about working together towards a common cause such as establishing a school, a community centre or a medical clinic. Such projects would have probably failed in that context.

In current Africa, self-hatred seems to be an epidemic. Maathai (2009:26) points out how 'many postcolonial African leaders treat their citizens cruelly, and why [...] many African countries still remain' poor and dysfunctional. These practices are a paradox to nation-building. InnerCHANGE is learning to point out these paradoxical practices to neighbours who are struggling 'to understand why the face of poverty remains black when the government of the day is predominantly black' (Ramphele 2017:58). InnerCHANGE points out, for example, the issue of corruption that South Africa and the rest of Africa face as a key paradox to nation-building. The current African political leaders inherited the systems of oppression such as colonialism, and have proven time and time again to be 'good students of oppressive, exploitative and corrupt colonial regimes' themselves (Chikane 2013:218). The majority of the African population is poorly served by their fellows who have political power.

Self-hatred is also seen in local communities such as Soshanguve through acts of destruction and violence in the name of protest actions. Chikane (2013:227) postulates that people 'have the right to protest' but should refrain from stoning innocent motorists, or looting shops, or destroying goods of ordinary street traders who have nothing to do with the things you are protesting about. During protest actions, sometimes people go to the extent of destroying schools where their children go to, clinics they need for health care, a library that could improve their ability to understand the world around them, a community hall they need for gatherings and service, a road infrastructure they need daily. It seems like destroying has become a modus operandi to demand an improvement in living conditions.

Self-hatred contrasts our aspiration to live in shalom communities. Linthicum (2003:38) describes the latter as 'an environment where socio-economic justice is available to all and the community's problems and their resolve is a concern for all'. Those communities are characterised by 'order and harmony, fruitfulness and abundance, wholeness, beauty, joy and well-being' (Linthicum 2003:38). Those communities are desirable. They are places where the quality of life is at its best. This is the kind of community the church is called to foster and catalyse. Aspiring transformation agents are meant to be catalysts of shalom communities and challenge self-hatred practices around them. They should be involved in these efforts in partnership with other stakeholders and should be aware of the issues of naivety around them.

Naivety

Some of the most trusted stakeholders in African societies are people who made a lot of sacrifices in fighting colonialism or apartheid. They are called revolutionaries or liberation movement heroes. Aspiring transformation agents need to be sober-minded in their embracing of these revolutionaries. Their ability to question conventional wisdom or commonly accepted truths is critical here. In the Congo, for example, a so-called liberation movement toppled a 32-year dictatorship. In the process of liberating the country, many innocent people who were meant to be liberated were killed. The so-called liberation movement took over power and established its dictatorship under the sponsorship of foreign powers. In the new system, 'the supposedly liberated have been the primary victims of political, social and economic oppression while the liberators have insulated themselves into an authoritarian and affluent class' (Lwamba 2017:78–79). The supposed liberators are in fact oppressors.

In the context of South Africa, Chikane (2013:144) points out that apartheid activists went into exile for 'different reasons'. Some went because of their commitment to justice; some others, because they were part of the dynasty of the movement but had no commitment to justice; some others, because they had committed a crime and were not prepared to go to jail; some others got involved simply because they hated being treated like a lesser being or were not allowed to participate fully in the economy because of the apartheid system; finally, others hated the racist apartheid system and wanted it gone. This diversity of intentions is seen in how political leadership is expressed in the country. Some politicians work wholeheartedly for the common good.

Whereas others are in the game for self-gain and self-promotion. Generally, though, political leadership is seen as anti-common good. In our local communities, it is common to see fellow neighbours who have been chosen in some leadership capacity, only to abuse the trust of the community by becoming self-centred, greedy, nepotistic and self-serving. We also see servants of God behave in this disappointing way that displays a lack of solidarity.

Not being critical of conventional wisdom could lead to an implicit cult of personality that many Africans are comfortable with. This makes it easy for a president to rule a country for many decades, a pastor to be the sole conduit of God's vision through the church and an academic to be the only celebrity in a certain field of knowledge or a father to be the sole voice of wisdom in a household. In our local communities, the cult of personality is huge. It makes it difficult for the voices of the youth and women to be heard. It frowns upon the democratic value of rotation of power and communal responsibility to participate in building a society. Aspiring transformation agents should stress that all 'human beings desire the same things: love, peace, justice and participation in the economic and social developments of their countries' (Iheanacho 2020:7). They should continually stress that the best thing to do is the pursuit of the common good. Such a posture would avoid practices such as the scandal of the COVID-19 corruption allegations around Personal Protective Equipment (PPE) South Africa has experienced. It looks like some politicians who are meant to be liberation heroes gave tenders to friends and families in total disregard of procurement processes that are meant to be fair to all citizens. A direct consequence of this unethical practice has been the shortage of supply of PPE at public hospitals and schools. Many more people than expected have gotten infected by COVID-19 at public hospitals and schools, as a result. Lives have also been lost. It is, therefore, important to be aware of who the true heroes in a society are. Such awareness could have depth and meaning if it is combined with the knowledge of local communities such as townships history and their heroes from the past.

Learning about the history of a local context

Townships were started as locations for non-white economic migrant labours who moved to urban areas. They were physically separated from the rest of the urban areas as a way of enforcing the policy of separation or apartheid in South Africa. This is why townships are seen as peri-urban areas. The latter is defined as 'areas immediately adjacent to a city or town' (Mangayi 2016). The author has noticed that when asked the question about where is your home? Many senior citizens and middle-agers who live in Soshanguve name a location outside of Soshanguve where they were born or their parents are from. However, for many young adults and teenagers, their home is Soshanguve. It could be strategic to help residents of a place such as Soshanguve to be rooted in their context if we hope for inside out transformation to happen. Brueggemann (2002:3–4) says that 'rootlessness and not meaninglessness' is the crisis of our postmodern era. The concept of rootedness could be taught as a short version of the history of Soshanguve. The latter became home for thousands of people, mainly from townships of Atteridgeville and Mamelodi, who were affected by the government's policy to limit the number of black people living in the city. The first people to settle in Soshanguve were from Wallmansthal (North East of Pretoria city centre). Soshanguve has received world acclaim, as it is also the site of the famous Tswaing Crater. The latter is the first eco-tourism site in South Africa, boasting a 220 000-year-old meteorite crater 1.4 km in diameter with a brine lake at the centre of the large crater (tshwane.org.za 2020).

The people of Soshanguve are made up of several different cultures, mainly Sotho, Shangaan, Nguni and Venda. The township is divided into blocks. In the original relocation, people were placed into blocks according to their ethnic groups: (block L [Venda], block H [Tsonga], block G [80% Nguni, 20% Tsonga], block F [Bapedi], block K [Sotho]). Soshanguve, like most townships throughout South Africa, was also affected by the 1976 uprisings. Although affected on a smaller scale because it was still in its infancy, Soshanguve's students became active in the freedom movement from 1985. Their contribution was invaluable to the struggle. Meetings were regularly held at the Charles Luanga Hall in the Roman Catholic Church. A group of like-minded community activists was formed. Its leaders were father Smangaliso Nkhatswa, Matimela, Pubelate and Hlatetwe. Some women were also part of this commitment, the most prominent one was Elisabeth Matsimela who had come from the nearby township of Garankuwa where she was kicked out by the Boputaswana government because of her activism against injustice and not being a Motshwana (an ethnic group). It is this group of activists that distributed the land to many citizens in need of it in the current block HH area where InnerCHANGE has its site.

Until recently, Soshanguve was administratively and infrastructurally dependant on Mabopane, a nearby township and formerly part of the Bophuthatswana Bantustan. The democratic government is gradually working towards restoring the dignity of Soshanguve inhabitants in building infrastructures in the township. The majority of Soshanguve workforce commutes using public transport to and from work. The vast majority of these commuters use the Metrorail train. The round trip of the latter takes an average of 4 h between the township and Pretoria city centre.

InnerCHANGE uses Joshua 18:3–7 to point out that God led the residents of Soshanguve to settle in that location, to build it up (Neh 2:17–18) and seek its peace and prosperity (Jr 29:7) so that a good and fulfilling quality of life can be enjoyed by all. The end in mind of this historical overview is to see all the residents of a peri-urban area such as Soshanguve 'learn to be in charge' of their community and their country through their acts of service similar to the activists above-mentioned. It points to a 'theology of participation that encourages active citizenship' (Swart et al. 2009). Active citizenship has the potential to restore in people a sense of dignity. The latter is described as a discovery of 'self-worth, self-acceptance and a sense of having something to contribute to the world and others' (Cloete 2019:520). It is also 'where people are able to make their own contribution to the life of the community, especially as participants in decisions which affect them' (Cloete 2019:520).

Learning about the history of the active citizenry in a local community is also critical for inspiration. The neighbourhood the InnerCHANGE office is in started in 1990 and was run by local leaders. Many of these leaders are still alive and the team has had the privilege to interact with them and learn practical wisdom about community building. These leaders were front liners in making sure basic services such as water, toilets, electricity, roads and public transport were accessible to all. They have taught the team to learn to pay attention to positive role models and to emulate their legacy. The team interaction with these leaders is also a way to sing a different tune to a famous Malian writer Amadou Ampateda who is known for saying: 'When elderly die, a whole library goes with them' (Amadou Ampateda, writer, exact date unspecified; author's own translation). We would hate to see the founders of our neighbourhood die and take with them all the wisdom they had accumulated for many years in trying to build our community. We want to engage them, learn from them, challenge them to transfer their wisdom to us so that we can dissimilate them into praxis that will improve the quality of life in our community. Interacting with these leaders has pointed to InnerCHANGE many opportunities intentional local leadership development brings to the building of society. Many of those opportunities are explored through experiential learning.

■ Learning from doing

This research believes that a tangible way to aspire to transformation agency is, being involved in society building initiatives. Such an approach improves learning as well as confidence. There is a Chinese proverb that says that 'when I do, I understand'. It is, therefore, important for people to grow in their understanding of their role in society by doing something that would propel them to such an understanding. InnerCHANGE runs a volunteer programme where ordinary people are equipped to serve others in practical ways. It aims to develop them as servants through practical initiatives such as education, sport, healthcare and mentoring which are platforms for 'creative engagement' with their community (De Beer 2020:3). These practical initiatives are a way to try to be part of the common good and be aligned with global initiatives such as the United Nations SDGs. They are also platforms for discipleship. The latter enables the team to nurture and equip hope-filled neighbours.

Such neighbours would confidently participate in community development. Green and Haines (2012:17) say that community development is about 'helping people to learn how to help themselves [...] [and] to participate in the solution of collective problems'. Such participation has the potential to be empowering because it will equip them to take ownership of what matters in their lives. Empowerment can be achieved by starting somewhere, no matter how small. Community development could also be seen as 'work of love, cooperation, collaboration, co-creation and accompanying' for the sake of the common good we all aspire to be beneficiaries of.

Through its volunteer program, InnerCHANGE is paying attention to a role the church could play in society as an active participant in the catalysing of society builders. Kraybill (1990:269–270) says that the church can 'create communities that cultivate a commitment to care for each other's spiritual, social, intellectual as well as economic needs'. This care should not be confined to one neighbourhood. It should spread and multiply. For it to happen, collaboration with different stakeholders will be critical. Van Niekerk (2015:6) points out that 'several communities have discovered that the answer to societal challenging issues lies in getting involved with each other'. Such involvement could be impactful if active listening, intentional contextual observation and attention to issues arising in a particular context are taken into consideration.

Active listening

This is a discipline InnerCHANGE follows to regularly do home visits. These visits aim to listen and learn from neighbours in order to be in tune with what is a relevant and meaningful way to serve. It is through these visits that the team has been challenged to get involved in issues of crime, unemployment, education, healthcare, addiction, parenting, teenage pregnancies, cohabitation, littering, gender-based violence, financial stewardship and creation care.

It is through this active listening discipline that the team once initiated a trans-disciplinary research aiming at minimising the high prevalence of school dropout in a community such as Soshanguve. This was a tangible act of solidarity with school dropouts, which are a marginalised section of the community. The trans-disciplinary project relied entirely on community members in the execution of its findings. Klein (2001:1) describes transdisciplinarity as the coming together of various academic disciplines and practitioners to focus on the resolving of 'a real-world problem'. The real problem here was a high rate of school dropout in the community. The team had been serving its neighbours through after-school tutoring. It had very mixed results in this effort. The majority of beneficiaries improved their academic performance, but there was still a concerning percentage of those who did not improve. Some of the latter ended up dropping out of school.

The team learned later that school dropout was a countrywide problem that is very prominent in South African communities of poverty. The DG Murray foundation, a South African organisation that focuses on the improvement of the quality of education points out that about 40% of learners drop out of the schooling system between Grade 1 and Grade 12. Most of these dropouts will most likely be living in conditions of poverty and may only qualify for low-paying jobs (dgmt.co.za. 2020). The educationalist John Volmint (702 Radio station [interview] pers. comm., 20 March 2020) stresses that 'every time a learner drops out of school, it impacts the fabric of our society'. It translates into another human being who will have difficulty making a meaningful contribution to issues that affect them or to fully tap into socio-economic opportunities around them. Therefore, creating an environment where school dropout is absent is about ensuring the creation of a just and equitable society. The involvement in minimising school dropout was, therefore, all about nation-building.

As stated above, school dropouts are marginalised in local communities such as Soshanguve. Part of the reason for this marginalisation is that our society believes that education is the only way out of poverty. Therefore, the lack of success in academia is equated to a lifelong poverty. The community sees many school dropouts ending up at street corners abusing drugs and alcohol, engaging in unsafe sex leading to sickness and unplanned child-rearing and being involved in crime. It, therefore, sees a school dropout as a liability. Families have seen many school dropouts remain dependant on their parents' income well into adulthood. They, therefore, frown upon family members who drop out of school.

InnerCHANGE started a reading club including 20 children who were at risk of dropping out of school. After a year of hard work with the children every week, we helped achieve an 80% improvement in their ability to read. Some of these children continue to come to InnerCHANGE reading clubs where the team continues to cultivate their appetite for reading. Such appetite is positively noticed at their schools and local churches. These children have become the primary referrals for the recruitment of new children every year. The team is learning a great deal about school dropouts from its involvement in the issue. Currently, two of its staff and five of its volunteers are high school dropouts. They are progressively learning to overcome the feeling of being marginalised and become society builders who care for the marginalised. One of the ways they express their agency in minimising school dropout is by becoming wounded healers. They have become 'living epistles' through their actions to see others succeed where they did not (Perkins 2014:9). Some of these high school dropouts are tutors in our reading club and they have been an asset in many creative things the reading club does which have been helpful for children. As they teach children and learn from workshops we hold to equip them, they have also nurtured a culture of learning. They have not necessarily gone back to mainstream schools, but they have ventured into alternatives models of skills development such as Early Childhood Development, Creative Arts, Fitness, catering and culinary schools. Many of them bring their acquired skills in the dynamics of our ministry initiatives. They have been very helpful in triggering the creative juice in many of the children and teenagers the team serves. Their input has also broadened the author's understanding of the contribution any person could make in the building of a society. Anybody could be an asset to their context of residence and society in general. Many people may not necessarily know how they could be an asset. The church could play the role of raising awareness in individuals about what they already have that could be an asset to others around them. Such a role could lead to the democratisation of community development efforts. This means that local community residents can all 'become part of the knowledge creation and mobilization process' of seeking solutions for the common good (James 2018:10). In this process, they will intentionally pursue their ideas about community building with a passion and commitment to reach the end they had in mind. The measure of such a commitment will be how well the contextual observation and analysis are done.

Intentionality in contextual observation and analysis

One of the ways InnerCHANGE has been learning to understand its context, is through observation and the analysis of what is observed. A method of observation it uses regularly is prayer walking. Weekly, its staff walks through the streets of the neighbourhoods they serve in and looks 'for signs of blessing as well as of trauma' (Kabongo 2020b:2). Through this exercise, it trains itself to see the neighbourhoods with new and fresh eyes after analysing what is observed. It has, for instance, noticed, many youths hanging out at street corners throughout the day. A reflection and analysis of this situation brought to the fore the issue of unemployment. Through its network, the team entered into 'partnership with local businesses' who have been able to recruit some youth of Soshanguve and surrounding townships for employment (Kabongo 2020a:6). To date, 122 youth have been employed. The team involvement with unemployed youth has also led it to participate in issues of crime prevention. It has learned that some of its neighbours who are involved in crime do so for survival because they are unemployed. The team connection with some businesses that can provide jobs has been a blessing to many of these youths. Another cause of people choosing crime as a means for survival is connected to the issue of instant gratification. This is a virus that seems to be present in the entire South African population. Many people want their need to be satisfied now. This mindset may explain why credit cards are popular as well as loan businesses. Some people such as some of the unemployed youth we interact with, resort to crime for instant gratification. This mindset taken to an extreme has led some friends to abandon their employment after receiving their first salary because of their inability to consume alcohol responsibly. The team is equipping itself to teach about the wisdom behind delayed gratification which comes with being frugal in spending money, saving a portion of an income and having fun in a measured and responsible manner. Delayed gratification is one of the wise ways to pave the way for a life of prosperity and a predictor of smooth generational wealth. Gratton and Scott (2016) believe that it assures material stability now and 'from one generation to the other'.

While walking in the streets of the neighbourhoods, the team observed many pupils hanging around their schools during class time. It further learned that many of those children did not like school for various reasons. Such knowledge led to the opening of after-school tutoring programs.

Walking in the streets of the neighbourhoods has also brought to the attention of the team how issues of women abuse have been normalised. It is very common to see and hear men sitting at a street corner or public transport drivers whistle at passing women. Tlhabi (2017:244) decries that habit as one of the ways our society still reinforces its patriarchal culture that is still accepting of 'rape, demands of sex in exchange for a job, a lift, or another favour'. She adds that it has become normal to find 'uncles who wink at young women when their parents are not looking' (Tlhabi 2017:244). Or for 'men to whistle and undress women with their eyes in public and private spaces' (Tlhabi 2017:244). The team started running programs with community members aiming to prevent abuses of any kind.

Walking in the streets of the neighbourhoods has also brought to the attention of the team how packed our streets are with children without supervision. Townships are renowned for child neglect. It would be simplistic to blame the parents and guardians for being irresponsible. However, wisdom could lie in understanding a township family comprehensively. One of the avenues of understanding is 'in light of the effects of colonialism, apartheid' with regard to migrant labourers and people working very far away from their homes (Rabe 2018:3). The ramifications of this system are still felt to this day when we still see many township residents 'removed from their families' by their employment (Rabe 2018:4). Many of them spend hours travelling to and from work and are mostly absent from many activities in their children's life because of the location of their employment. Statistics South Africa (2020) stresses that 'the deterioration of South African family structures' causes many children to grow up without close and consistent parental guidance. Another reason is the reality of teenage pregnancy. Many of these mothers are not yet mature enough to be responsible parents. There is also the issue of child-headed homes which is one of the remnants of the HIV and AIDS pandemic which saw many parents die and leave their children behind without adult supervision. There is also the issue of skip generation family (grandparents and grandchildren) where children are left with guardians who do not have the energy to take good care of them. A response to the reality of children playing in the street without adult supervision, which can be unsafe for their well-being, led the team to run after-school activities such as sport, tutoring, drama clubs which are connected to the African adage of 'it takes a village to raise a child'. The team sees itself as a village stakeholder that participates in raising its children.

Through the above-mentioned observations, analysis and actions are taken, InnerCHANGE aims to equip its staff and volunteers to conduct a contextual problem and solution analysis. It involves them in practical service projects so that they can be developed as servant leaders. It also challenges them to come up with suggestions of service projects that would be meaningful to their neighbours. They are taught to remain attuned to issues arising around them.

Attention to arising issues

An arising issue the team is grappling with is the Coronavirus pandemic and its effects on its neighbours. The novel COVID-19 is a global pandemic that has affected every human life in the world. It came as a disruption to normal life and forced the team to reflect on what it means to be a sign of the compassion of Christ during the crisis as it experienced it. On 27 March 2020, the government of South Africa locked down the country and all non-essential services had to close down as a consequence. The lockdown has meant that many of its neighbours went hungry as soon as it started because they survive daily through peace jobs. As a consequence, many of them needed immediate relief. Corbett and Fikkert (2009:104) define the latter as 'the urgent and temporary provision of emergency aid to reduce immediate suffering from a natural or man-made crisis [...] [and] the receiver is largely incapable of helping himself at that time'. The team responded to this food need by distributing food parcels to needy families.

The lockdown also meant that all the team activities had to close down. Many of the teenagers and children it works with, as well as their parents, were aggrieved by that and communicated to staff and volunteers whenever they met. Many of the children and teenagers normally navigate between three spaces daily: their home, school and at least one of the team programs. The imposition of the lockdown restricted their space to one – their home. They had lost, in essence, two of their most trusted safe spaces. When the lockdown restrictions were relaxed and a maximum of 50 people could gather, the team decided to re-open its doors. Before it did so, it initiated two things: contact all parents/or guardians and get their opinion about the decision to re-open and be involved with their child. It requested that parents sign an indemnity form permitting the team to be involved with their child and exonerate it from being guilty of any wrongdoing in case their child test positive for COVID-19. The team bought all the hygienic kit required by government regulations in order to minimise infection. The majority of the parents approved the team decision. Therefore, the team opened its doors in phases, starting with teenagers.

These two cases illustrate the team's attempt to be in solidarity with people from its context. It also believes that transformation agency should involve tangibly living in solidarity with others, especially the poor, neglected and marginalised. It encourages its neighbours to live in solidarity with one another. Jesus' incarnation in the world was a tangible sign of solidarity with the world. Bakole wa Ilunga (1978:32) stresses that 'our continent has a reputation for its value in solidarity. Yet, in this same Africa, we find misery, suffering, inequality cohabitating with egotistic opulence'.

We proclaim our value of life, yet children die every day of malnutrition and abortion has become a normal practice. Solidarity should be encouraged across fellow community residents or citizens. The Malian historian Joseph Ki Zerbo (2005:32) connects the general failure of African governments to improve the quality of life of citizens to 'a lack of solidarity' between countries as well as of leaders towards their fellow citizens. A heart of solidarity should propel aspiring transformation agents to network in order to be supported and surrounded by like-minded people and institutions.

■ Networking

Agency in community development can only be effective and sustainable if it is inclusive of as many stakeholders as possible. The church could play a critical role in involving others. In the South African context, there is a prospect of success in such an endeavour because the church is a well-trusted institution. The Global Value Survey shows that 'religious organisations remain among the most trusted institutions in South Africa' in contrast to the public and private sectors (Burchert & Winter 2015). InnerCHANGE is learning to take advantage of this reputation to engage the body of Christ in its diversity, like-minded organisations, potential partners located outside its community and political leaders.

■ Engaging the body of Christ in its diversity

The diversity of the body of Christ can be an asset to the world because each entity has a strength that could complement others. It can also be a liability when each entity works independent of one another and sees collaboration as a threat to its identity. In communities such as Soshanguve, many local churches do not collaborate. Many more do not see community development as a critical mandate of the church. Our missional team has been trying to engage local churches for collaboration in community development efforts. It has received positive responses from a few and negative from many others. It engages in these efforts with the belief that the church is called to be a tangible sign of the compassion of God. It exemplifies such a sign powerfully when working as a unit with one another in 'God's healing work in our world' (Huckins & Yackley 2012:7). This is also the case when it engages like-minded organisations.

Engaging like-minded organisations

They are also many organisations that are involved in initiatives similar to InnerCHANGE. The latter tries to engage them to the best of its ability for mutual learning and mutual resourcing. Engagement also extends outside its local contexts.

Engage potential partners located outside a local community

There are many organisations outside our context that value community development and are open to partnering with an organisation such as InnerCHANGE. We are learning to reach out to them for support and partnership. Some of these organisations require that we submit funding proposals to them. We have been learning to write proposals and attend meetings hosted to explain how funding is provided to organisations involved in community development.

The team engagement with people and organisations outside its context has also confronted it with the realities of inter-racial as well as different socio-economic interactions. In a country where classism is very prominent and seems to prefer a skin colour and a certain way of talking, the team has been learning to be both relevant to its neighbours as well as its network. There is still a lot of progress to be made in order to be rooted in the different worlds it has to navigate. The same could also be said about the team engagement of political governors.

Engaging governors

The team is learning to engage political governors. Community development is supposed to be their primary task. It can be helpful to know their plans and collaborate with them in serving a community. Many of the team neighbours are still troubled with the fact that Africans have political power in the country, yet their quality of life seems to be deteriorating. Political governors have very good policies that, if implemented, could improve the living conditions of a whole population. InnerCHANGE has found it helpful to engage and challenge governors so that existing policies can be implemented with integrity for the sake of the common good. It engages them as a stakeholder that seeks to 'form part of the movement for the transformation of the social, political and economic situation' of its society (Mbeki 2007:26). Such efforts also seek to interact with disempowering structures that impede good quality of life.

■ Learning to engage disempowering structures

Communities such as Soshanguve have well-established ways of living. Some of these ways can be disempowering. The author believes that 'questioning conventional wisdom' should be part of the intellectual enquiry of an aspiring transformation agent (Chikane 2013:261). Issues related to the hierarchical nature of the culture, patriarchy and violence have been normalised in our context. A transformation agent has the task to (de)constructively engage them.

Hierarchical nature of the culture

African communities have a hierarchical structure. As a consequence, experience seems to be equated to wisdom. The elderly are indeed the most experienced members of the community. In this society, they, unfortunately, tend to think that they are the only voice of wisdom. Codrington (2000:6) stresses that most of the elderly see 'the future as simply an extension of the past'. The majority of InnerCHANGE local leaders are young adults; it can be hard for them to be listened to by middle-aged and senior adults in the community. This is the age group of parents of the majority of teenagers, children and youth InnerCHANGE serves. The author, who is a middle-aged man, sometimes has to repeat a message that a young adult gives to an audience of parents for it to be accepted. As a team, we are learning to see this challenge as a resource to interact with our community persuasively. An interpretation of Mark 10:13–16 and 1 Timothy 4:12 has been helpful in this process. These two passages put children and the youth who are powerless in our communities at the centre of God's project to transform the world. InnerCHANGE is learning to challenge the norm of middle-aged and seniors to be the only leaders in the community, in equipping the youth to lead its initiatives and to be its face in the community. Baron (2017:7) believes that 'with their vigour and innovative ideas', the youth should be encouraged to take the agenda for society building starting from their local communities. Another disempowering force in Soshanguve in the patriarchal culture.

Patriarchy

African societies seem to be saturated with a patriarchal culture, including our township communities. Patriarchy is also a challenge when our female staff and volunteers minister to their community. They are not well-listened to by men and sometimes by fellow women. This is a challenge in a community in which the majority of involved parents are women. In this community, the majority of heads of households and local church members is also women. Sultana (2010) describes 'patriarchy as an ideology that gives power to men and legitimises the oppression of women in all sectors of society'. This ideology seems to be internalised by both the men and women in our community. In men, it is seen in how often they undermine opinions, suggestions and voices of wisdom coming from female, youth and children interlocutors. In females, it is seen in the lack of trust in their fellows and a constant seeking of assurance from men. In the youth and children, it can be seen in their emotional and physical distance towards father figures around them. The team is learning to remind its community members of the critical role women play in it and how listening to and respecting them is a wisdom capital of the building of our society. There are a lot more women role models in our community than men. Giving practical examples of such role models during our gatherings with neighbours has been a helpful way to debunk patriarchy in people. The debunking of patriarchy is generally still a work in progress along with the normalisation of violence in our community.

Violence as an expression of grievances

Violence has been normalised in communities such as Soshanguve. Aspiring transformation agents need to frown upon it and discourage such a practice. Communities such as Soshanguve are victims of a lot of unfulfilled promises about service delivery from the government. As a result, many ordinary people express their grievances by protesting. During their protest, however, they stone innocent motorists, burn schools, burn different communal infrastructures, loot shops, destroy goods of ordinary street traders who have nothing to do with the things they are protesting about. This culture of violence is increasingly prominent in schools where peers go to the extent of killing each other, or a learner killing an educator. Domestic violence has reached an epidemic level in the community and transformation agents are called to participate in halting this crisis by leading by example. A culture of peaceful resolution of conflicts is needed so that people can learn to still respect and care for one another even when they disagree about one thing or another.

Conclusion

This chapter was a reflection on InnerCHANGE practice intending to mobilise the emergence of transformation agents from below. Transformation agency was described as an ideal and the efforts of this missional team were to chase after this ideal. The chasing is done in using the knowledge of local history as a building block in inspiring confidence and a 'can-do' attitude in ordinary people. The history taught at schools does not include the history of the community as well as that of many local leaders who are participating and contributed to building it. The chasing is also done in involving ordinary people in practical ministries where they experientially learn to become servant leaders. It is also done in training ordinary people to network with the church in its diversity, political governors, other local organisations for mutual resourcing as well as other like-minded organisations from outside the geographic context. It is finally done in equipping ordinary people in the social activism of challenging disempowering structures such as the hierarchical culture, patriarchy and the normalisation of violence.

Chapter 10

The quest of sustainability in this present 'wicked world': How to overcome Enlightenment modernity?

Sytse Strijbos[a,b]
[a]IIDE-Europe,
Maarssen, Netherlands
[b]Centre for Faith and Community, Faculty of Theology and Religion,
University of Pretoria, Pretoria, South Africa

'Who […] might deliver us from this present evil world […]'

- Galatians 1: 4 (KJV)

■ Introduction

During the same period in which the discussion about sustainability came up, a fast-growing literature has also been developed concerning 'wicked problems'. This term has been adopted as a key notion in the sustainability debate about climate change and what is nowadays called the Anthropocene. 'Wicked problems' are portrayed as a new class of social problems because of the growing complexity of contemporary technological society (Australian Government 2018):

How to cite: Strijbos, S., 2021, 'The quest of sustainability in this present 'wicked world': How to overcome Enlightenment modernity?', in A.S. Van Niekerk & S. Strijbos (eds.), *We cannot continue like this: Facing modernity in Africa and the West*, pp. 187–207, AOSIS, Cape Town. https://doi.org/10.4102/aosis.2021.BK283.10

> The Australian Public Service (APS) is increasingly being tasked with solving very complex policy problems. Some of these policy issues are so complex they have been called 'wicked' problems. *The term 'wicked' in this context is used, not in the sense of evil, but rather as an issue highly resistant to resolution.*
>
> Successfully solving or at least managing these wicked policy problems requires a reassessment of some of the traditional ways of working and solving problems in the APS. They challenge our governance structures, our skills base and our organisational capacity.
>
> It is important, as a first step, that wicked problems be recognised as such. Successfully tackling wicked problems requires a broad recognition and understanding, including from governments and Ministers, that there are no quick fixes and simple solutions. (n.p.)

In this quote I have put in italics a line that has triggered my attention, in particular the words 'not in the sense of evil'. What exactly is meant there? What about evil in the age of the Anthropocene? Does one state there that wicked problems have nothing to do with evil and are problems without an ethical dimension? Or does it say that tackling these kinds of problems can be seen separately from the normative domain of human life? Be that as it may, the statement, 'not in the sense of evil', is not immediately clear to the reader and raises questions.

While I was writing this chapter, the Corona pandemic took us completely by surprise, and it should be no surprise that it has immediately been recognised by policy experts of the Antwerp Management School as another example of a wicked problem, a social system problem for which there are no quick technical fixes and simple solutions (Cambré, Marynissen & Van Hootegem 2020):

> If we look at the current crisis from a sociological perspective, we can describe the Corona pandemic as a 'wicked problem'. Literally translated, it is a tricky, thorny, common problem. It is a very complex problem, it is unique, the full extent nor the exact solution are known. Other wicked problems include poverty, the housing and care situation of our ageing population, social exclusion or climate change. Typical of the societal complexities associated with such a wicked problem are that each person involved can look at it differently, all with a little bit of value and a little bit of non-value. Do you have to go for group immunity or not, schools should open again or not, will there be a second wave that will be worse or not, are you allowed to joke or not [...]? All experts with an opinion on the subject are right and simultaneously wrong. (n.p.)

Most people do understand the complexities and uncertainties of the COVID-19 crisis and have accepted the constraints of the 'lock down' as necessary measures to protect public health. At the same time, it has made us highly aware of the vulnerability of the entire machinery of the modern global world. Moreover, many wonder today: what exactly went wrong in our society? Is there a way out; what can we do? It seems to me as if we hear far echoes in our present 'wicked world' of the old religious cry for deliverance from human misery. Of course, we should not neglect the differences between a religious understanding of the world and a technical-scientific discourse, but the question of a possible connection between these two is in my opinion too important to dismiss in advance. The main purpose of my argument is to investigate how biblical–theological notions can enrich the scholarly debate, can help to understand the specificity of modern technology and society and can take position in our present post-Enlightenment 'wicked world'.

In recent years, Jenkins (2013) and Conradie (2017) have made a much-needed theological contribution with regard to the big ecological issues that are troubling us today. I am very sympathetic to their attempt. What strikes me in their argument, however, is that although these authors correctly make a link to the debate in the policy sciences about 'wicked problems', they do not critically investigate this debate and its philosophical underpinnings. This implies that the concept of 'wicked problems' is uncritically taken as a given. Consciously or unconsciously they have accepted herewith a certain position in the problem of evil as raised above related to the APS document. In search of a normative approach for an ethics in the Anthropocene, Jenkins and Conradie argue that reducing structural problems of our society to moral wickedness would evade the most difficult questions, refusing the struggle to create social practices capable of answering those questions (Jenkins 2013):

> *Reducing a structurally wicked problem to a case of moral wickedness would evade the most difficult questions.* Wrong and ignorant actions certainly contribute to climate change, but its crisis lies in the difficulty of creating meaningful and adequate forms of responsibility. How might humanity collectively modify its influence within the world's atmospheric system? What commitments would allow a pluralist world to cooperate? How to allocate responsibilities across relations of justice and resentment, for multiple generations of humans, in respect for today's poor and the future of other species? If religious ethics avoids reckoning with those questions by supposing that the failures to this point are entirely attributable to evil, *it refuses the most difficult aspect of responsibility: the struggle to create social practices and political communities capable of answering those questions.* (p. 22; [author's added emphasis]; cf. Conradie 2017:xviii)

I agree with these authors that the ethics of a structurally wicked problem such as climate change and global warming cannot simply be reduced to a case of individual moral wickedness. I also recognise the need to create social practices with adequate forms of responsibility. In this, the policy sciences will play a leading role. However, I would like to emphasise the fact that in our science-based world these sciences are as much a part of the problem as they can be the solution. It is, therefore, of primary importance that theology contributes to the debate in this particular academic field (cf. Stackhouse 1998:166). The input of theology should not serve as an addition to defining the problem, but it must be present from the very beginning. The integration of theology and religious ethics later into a science-based management approach is doomed to fail, because then the horse has already bolted.

Against this background, the first challenge is to penetrate the religious roots of thinking in terms of 'wicked problems'. A critical evaluation of the scientific method also enables one to take a critical stance in the debate on the technological society. These are two sides of the same coin that will both be considered in the following sections. First, I will briefly discuss the search in the 1960s and 1970s for a scientific basis to tackle complex problems of design and management of human affairs, focusing on the positions of Horst Rittel (1930–1990) and C. West Churchman (1913–2004).[26] Both scientists clearly have an affinity with the Enlightenment and I hope to show the differences as they have worked through in their vision of the scientific method. Next, I will turn to the contemporary debate about the Anthropocene and investigate how Braden Allenby has incorporated the concept of 'wicked problems' or 'wicked complexity' into an analysis of technology and society and the search for sustainability. Finally, after a short 'Interim assessment', I will propose an alternative view on the problem of evil in our 'wicked world' entering into a conversation with a proponent of the Enlightenment, Susan Neiman.

■ Rittel and Churchman on the scientific method in design and social system problems

The characteristic of modern science-based technology is the turn of science towards practical problems. In contrast to traditional technology, design based on the scientific method has become a separate activity in modern technological practice (Van Riessen 1979). Usually, this activity is thought to be typical of engineers. However, following Herbert Simon, one could argue with good reason that it does not play a key role only in technology, but it is also encountered as a core activity in various other professions. In his fundamental study on design thinking, *The Sciences of the Artificial* (1996), he points out that engineers are not the only professional designers:

> Everyone designs who devises courses of action aimed at changing existing situations into preferred ones. The intellectual activity that produces material artifacts is no different fundamentally from the one that prescribes remedies for a sick patient or the one that devises a new sales plan for a company or a social welfare policy for a state. *Design, so construed, is the core of all professional training; it is the principal mark that distinguishes the professions from the sciences.* (p. 111; [*author's added emphasis*])

---

26. Rittel has been a leading representative in engineering design thinking and Churchman in management and systems thinking. For a broader historical and philosophical perspective on both related fields, cf. Buchanan (2009) and Strijbos (2017), respectively.

Chapter 10

The point that I want to make here is that Rittel and Churchman, representatives of different professions, both struggle with the scientific foundations of design thinking in their respective fields, architecture and business administration. Both have been associated with the University of California, Berkeley for a long time. In 1963, when Rittel, at the age of 33, moved from Germany to the architecture department of Berkeley, he became a colleague of Churchman, who was then a middle-aged man at the peak of his career and, since 1957, in charge of the School of Business Administration. Despite their difference in age they had in common the fact that Churchman, like Rittel, was at the beginning of a new phase in his career. To quote one of his students, 'In the sixties, Churchman took the step from operations research to the systems approach'. As with operations research before, he wanted the systems approach to be understood as an effort of applied philosophy (Ulrich 2002:7).

Given their overlapping interest in fundamental issues of design and planning, Rittel and Churchman could be expected to have had personal conversations with each other in Berkeley. Although it does not seem to have come to an intensive exchange of ideas, it can be concluded from their publications that they were well aware of each other's work and of the differences they had in respect of the scientific method in design thinking and problem-solving. In order to clarify my own position in this crucial matter, let us first have a look at their main points of difference and agreement.

In those years, since the 1950s, systems thinking came up as a booming interdisciplinary movement in which Churchman with his pioneering work in operations research and management science acquired a leading role (Strijbos 2017). When Rittel joined Berkeley as a young researcher, it clearly took some time before his ideas in the field of design studies were crystallised. During a seminar of his Department of Architecture in 1967, he introduced, probably for one of the first times, the term 'wicked problem' for a wider audience in which Churchman also participated. With reference to that event Churchman wrote a Guest editorial for the December issue of *Management Science* in the same year. The essence of his commentary is that the distinction made by Rittel between 'tame' and 'wicked' is not contrary to his own line of thinking, 'a continuous search for comprehensiveness [...] in the quest for a better management of human affairs' (Ulrich 2004:202). As I will explain in the following, this means that the management scientist has the moral obligation, according to Churchman, to focus on the problem situation as a whole. To put it in the words of Churchman's commentary, 'The moral problem is this: whoever attempts to tame a part of a wicked problem, but not the whole, is morally wrong'. (Churchman 1967:B142) Ethics is thus an intrinsic part of the scientific management approach and should be a 'whole-systems approach'. As far as I know, this is the only publication in which Churchman enters into a public discussion with Rittel.

After the aforementioned seminar in 1967, it took several years before Rittel began publishing his insights in the early seventies. In the current flood of publications on 'wicked problems' and related topics, his article of 1973 in the scientific journal, *Policy Sciences*, is usually referred to. However, two publications published the year before are most useful to get more clarity about the broader context of this concept and in which Rittel and Churchman agree and in which they differ from each other. One publication is an interview by Grant and Protzen in 1972 that has been republished in 1984; the other is a lecture prepared for a seminar at Karlsruhe on systems analysis. In both articles Rittel states that the apparent bloom of design methodology and systems thinking is in fact a sign of a crisis in these fields. In the interview he notes that he became interested in operations research because he felt that the methods developed in that area could also be of use for his field, 'but', says Rittel, 'I got into controversy with the proponents of these methods very soon – 1960 or so – because whenever I'd try to use them I'd run into trouble'.

To clarify this controversy, Rittel distinguishes between a first and second generation of system analysis and a first and second generation of design methods.[27] According to Rittel, the first-generation approaches are based on the 19th-century rational view of science, a rationalist belief in 'problem-solving' that ignores the limitations of rationality. However, the classical systems approach of operations research has not yielded what was expected of it. Why is that so? Rittel (1972b:395) argues, 'You cannot be rational in planning: the more you try, the less it helps'. This does not imply that one should just do whatever comes into one's mind, based on intuition. But there is no polarity, he argues, between what one might call an intuitive approach, on the one hand, and a controlled, rational approach on the other hand. 'The more control you want to exert and the better founded you want your judgment to be, the more intuitive you have to be' (Rittel 1972b).

Related to the distinction between first- and second-generation methods, one can distinguish between what Rittel calls 'tame' and 'wicked problems'. The classical systems approach addresses the first type of 'tame' or 'benign' problems, a type that scientists and engineers usually focus upon. Such a problem can be exhaustively formulated and can be solved next by a knowledgeable person without requiring any further information. By contrast, problems of planning and design are inherently 'wicked'. What usually happens is that these problems are reduced as if they could be addressed by a classical scientific approach. In this way, the real world is in fact bypassed. For 'wicked problems' we are in need, Rittel argues, of an approach of the second generation. He concludes his lecture for his audience at Karlsruhe in 1972 as follows (Rittel 1972b):

---

27. See Rittel's 1972 publications.

> Let me summarize. What I wanted to do first was to demonstrate that the systems approach of the first generation, which all of you know, is not suitable for attacking planning problems of your kind. The second point was to show that there are reasons for the failure of these procedures: *on the one side, the dilemmas of rationality, and on the other, the wicked nature of problems*. The final part demonstrated the characteristics of approaches of the second generation, the assumptions made and the foundations of the systems approach of the second generation. (p. 396; [*author's added emphasis*])

In the interview with Grant and Protzen, Rittel acknowledges the fact that Churchman and some others warned of the consequences of the belief in the first-generation approach and that they have taken some steps in the direction of a second-generation approach. In view of the positive appreciation of each other's work, one may wonder why it did not lead to greater cooperation between Rittel and Churchman. Of course, there may have been personal and/or institutional factors that have blocked the way. However, I guess that differences in appreciation of the Enlightenment tradition have played a major role at the background. Whereas Churchman, in my opinion, always remained a strong adherent of the ideals of the Enlightenment, Rittel seems to have been more aware of an intrinsic vulnerability of the proclaimed human rationality, 'The Enlightenment may be coming to full maturity in the late 20th century, or it may be on its deathbed' (Rittel & Webber 1973:158). In his Karlsruhe lecture he pointed out that the failures of the systems approach ultimately have to do with some deep-lying paradoxes of the concept of rationality. For the purpose of his argument he chooses the following definition (Rittel 1972b):

> [R]*ational behaviour means trying to anticipate the consequences of contemplated actions* [...] which means that you try to understand the problem as a whole, and to look at the consequences [...] if a person would not try to understand to be rational in this sense he would be irresponsible, not bothering about the consequences of his actions. (p. 391)

Let me clarify here the first of the four paradoxes that follow logically from this definition. Let us assume somebody, says Rittel, who seriously attempts to be rational in this way. Such a person would try to anticipate the consequences of his actions. However, he will quickly become aware that he has started a never-ending process, because anticipating the consequences is consequential by itself; that is to say, he should also trace the consequences of tracing the consequences, and so on. This leads Rittel to the conclusion, '*Therefore, there is no way to start to be rational*: one should always start a step earlier' (Rittel 1972b:392). In my opinion, this is a very important conclusion with far-reaching implications. Strictly speaking, this means the end of the supposed autonomy of human rationality. I will get back to this in the following text. For the moment this might suffice to make a link again to Churchman.

Although Rittel does not explicitly refer to Churchman's writings in the Karlsruhe lecture, it is obvious that he has in mind the basic problem of the systems approach as has been formulated by Churchman in the first pages of his book, *Challenge to Reason* (1968). Any rational intervention is meant to improve the problem situation. Therefore, the problem is, according to the latter, very simply the following: 'How can we design improvement in large systems without understanding the whole system, and if the answer is that we cannot, how is it possible to understand the whole system?' One can easily understand that Churchman's notion of 'the whole system' has similar consequences, as Rittel has noticed about the definition of rationality proposed by him. The definition of boundaries necessarily implies that something is not part of 'the whole system', as it is delineated. That is why the rational 'systems approach' for Churchman is, in principle, a never-ending process in a search of comprehensiveness.

Darek Haftor (formerly known as Darek Eriksson) nicely catches the basic problem of Churchman's philosophical life as 'the epistemo-ethical challenge'. Correctly, he notices that there is an inherent conflict between both sides of this challenge (Eriksson 2005):

> From an ethical viewpoint we have the imperative for comprehensive or holistic understanding […]. From an epistemological viewpoint, on the other hand, we have the challenge of the inevitable lack of comprehensive knowledge. (p. 69)

The two sides of the challenge seem to be related to two fundamental drives in Churchman's life. Being raised in his youth in the Quaker tradition of Christianity he was strongly devoted to leading an ethical life. As a scholar who followed the ideals of the Enlightenment, he believed in the idea of autonomous rationality as the source of light that illuminates our path in human life. However, both sides, the ethical and the epistemological, seem incompatible. If so, the question naturally arises: is there a way out?

Elsewhere I have commented on Churchman whether a necessary condition for responsible ethical action is to understand 'the whole system'. I have argued that that is not the case (cf. Strijbos n.d.). Similar comments can be made about Rittel's definition of rationality. Why is it necessary for responsible behaviour that one anticipates all the consequences of intended actions? Does that not result in an overstrained vision of human responsibility? Although Rittel acknowledges that rationality could also be defined in another way, he does not point out an alternative that overcomes its paradoxes. Looking back on how Churchman and Rittel as contemporaries have articulated their visions about 50 years ago, one could conclude that Churchman stays closer to the original ideals of the Enlightenment than Rittel. The considerations about the paradoxes of rationality, as Rittel has worded, fit the postmodern mindset that has arisen in later years. This could explain why his concept of 'wicked problem' has become so popular in recent years and in the meantime has become integrated as a new strand in the field of systems thinking (Cabrera & Cabrera 2015).

Let me conclude this section. In my view, it is positive that Rittel, in contrast to Churchman, seems to be more open to questioning the Enlightenment ideal of rationality critically. Rittel's analysis is astute, but it does not help us with an alternative. My point is: why should rationality be made dependent on goals that humans strive for in a search for a better world? Is this not precisely the obsession of the Enlightenment about human goals and progress? In discussing rationality, Rittel (1972b:392) concludes, as previously quoted, *'Therefore there is no way to start to be rational:* one should always start a step earlier'. Unfortunately, it is not clear what that 'step earlier' entails in Rittel's vision. It seems to me, however, that Rittel accepts here the fact that rationality is not a free-floating entity of human thought, but that rationality is necessarily rooted in a certain pre-theoretical understanding of reality in a view of man's place in his world. If so, why should it be rejected as non-rational to defend the fact that ultimately people cannot control the world and that they should take this into account when managing human affairs? Of course, the critical question then arises: how? Is there an alternative for the views that dominate current management thinking? I will return to this question later. But first, it is necessary to gain some insight into the situation of today's society and the contemporary debate about the Anthropocene.

■ Technology, society and our natural environment

My focus in the previous section was the scientific method as such, in particular the search for its renewal in the 1960s and 1970s and the proposal for a systems approach. I tried to identify the differences between Rittel and Churchman concerning their affinity with the rationality ideal of the Enlightenment. I argued that Rittel's doubts about rationality explain why his concept of 'wicked problems' has come to the foreground since the rise of a post-modernist climate of thinking. It is my aim here to investigate how this intellectual climate also plays a part in the current debate about technology and the Anthropocene.

At the word 'technology', most people usually think of material artefacts, such as a car, television, computer, mobile phone, etc. Speaking about technological society then refers to the fact that we use many of these artefacts every day and that we have also become dependent on them. I call this the naive conception of technology; naive, but not in a negative sense. The point is that such an understanding of technology does not fully grasp the phenomenon of technology in the modern world. One could indeed say that traditional technology consists of a world of tools and other artefacts, embedded in a specific cultural context. Even modern technology, in the earliest beginnings of the Industrial Revolution, still showed this character. In a later phase of development, however, it became more than obvious that modern technology is much more than the machine.[28]

So, what exactly happened? Here we touch the invisible factor X that gives our globalised technological world its special character; that is, along with technology at the level of artefacts and machines, organisational technologies entered into our lives. What first has occurred around the machine in the factory, namely, the organisation of human labour processes with a scientific method, has been transferred later to virtually any other domain of our society. In that way, a transformation took place from technology as a tool in the hands of man to technology as a completely new environment for humans and society. We became aware of that in the previous century.

This changed awareness of the scope of technology has aroused a new sense of ethical responsibility in some circles of engineers and policymakers. Sustainability, whatever this container concept may mean, then becomes the focus for the future.[29] In this sense, Karel Mulder, professor of Technology, Policy and Management at Delft University of Technology (the Netherlands), promotes the teaching of 'sustainable development for engineers'. Engineering means more than constructing artefacts for human use; in fact, engineers are builders of the society of the future (Mulder 2006):

> Engineers are future builders. They shape the world through their product and process designs, their management of technical systems and their innovations. It is the task of the engineer – in cooperation with other disciplines – to meet the needs of our society. (p. 9)

To meet the needs of society with technology is, however, not the same as 'we-deliver-on-request'. Therefore, engineers should oppose any attitude of docility by accepting a broad ethical responsibility for technology (Mulder 2004):

> Often, engineering deals with its responsibilities by defining three separate stages (society is responsible for the demand of technology, the engineers create it, and society is again responsible for its application). This self-proclaimed docility is empirically untenable and morally doubtful. (p. 237)

An influential spokesman from North America, Braden Allenby, professor of Civil and Environmental Engineering at Arizona University (North America), conceives the responsibility of the engineering profession in an even broader framework, based on the idea of the Anthropocene launched by Earth System scientists around the turn of the century, to capture a major shift in the relationship between humans and the global environment (Steffen et al. 2011):

---

28. Elsewhere I have elaborated with a more detailed analysis of this systems character of modern technology; cf., e.g. Strijbos and Basden (2006:ch. 6).

29. On conceptual problems with the term 'sustainability', I refer to Frodeman (2014:71–74).

> The term Anthropocene suggests: (1) that the Earth is now moving out of its current geological epoch, called the Holocene and (2) that human activity is largely responsible for this exit from the Holocene, that is, that humankind has become a global geological force in its own right. (p. 842)

In this new era of the Anthropocene in which the Earth System as a whole has become an object for technological manipulation, 'sustainable development' requires an engineering approach at a planetary scale, Allenby argues. In an ambitious attempt to pursue this vision, he proposes the concept of Earth Systems Engineering and Management (ESEM).

I do not want to give a detailed discussion here about ESEM's technical elaboration, but rather focus on the underlying idea of rationality. Time and again, Allenby emphasises in his publications that this type of engineering assumes 'that humanity is capable of *rational and ethical* design and engineering of earth systems' (Allenby 2005:187; [*author's added emphasis*]). There is something that stands out in Allenby's argument. He claims that ESEM is based on rational thinking, but at the same time he strongly attacks the Enlightenment and the driving ideal of rationality. The question arises: how do these two relate to each other? Is it possible to reconcile the emphasis on rationality on the one hand and the sharp criticism on the Enlightenment on the other hand? Another question is: how do the rational and the ethical side of the claimed human capability of ESEM relate to each other?

It seems to me that there are two key questions concerning Allenby's proposal that should be raised. Is he able to provide a satisfactory answer to them? What is his argument? In the context of this article, some publications in which Allenby wants to contribute to an interdisciplinary dialog and research between the sciences, religion, theology and philosophy deserve special attention. I refer to a lecture delivered at the Abraham Kuyper Institute for Public Theology at Princeton Theological Seminary on invitation of the late professor Max Stackhouse (1935-2016) in 2002 (Allenby 2003). In his invitation to the presenters the organiser asked them (DeWitt 2003):

> [T]o provide an overview of the contributions of their fields of study to understanding the responsibilities of technology toward the ecological order, and also to show the relevance of these contributions for understanding the character of Creation and human capacities for addressing related environmental issues that confront us. (p. 55)

Several years later, Allenby participated in a similar interdisciplinary event at Arizona State University with a Templeton Research lecture in 2007. Yet again, some years later, he published the book, *The Techno-Human Condition* (2013), which builds on his earlier work. In this book he expands his ideas considerably by using a three-layered systems model of 'technology and society' that he developed in collaboration with Daniel Sarewitz, a professor in Science and Society.

To briefly summarise the core idea of this model, you could say that Allenby is of the opinion that the original Enlightenment does not have the capacity to point the technological society in its current phase of development the way forward. This does not mean, however, to say farewell to Enlightenment thinking. Apparently inspired by a postmodern mentality, he argues that our global technological world requires a reinvention of the Enlightenment in which the contingent rationality of the European Enlightenment has to be expanded into a rationality that fits our global multicultural world (Allenby 2007):

> This, then, is our challenge: a new Enlightenment, one born not of a single culture or tradition; one that embeds uncertainty, dialog and change, not artificial stability; one that seeks not just authentic individuals, and authentic institutions, but an authentic world; one which, over the decades and centuries and millennia to come, reflects the best of human aspirations [...]. It is to raise the contingent rationality of the Eurocentric Enlightenment that is passing into the wisdom of a new global, multicultural Enlightenment. It is perhaps our most profound challenge as a species – but, if we meet it, if we can grow to create a truly authentic world, we will have validated our promise as sentient beings. (p. 17)

The challenge for a new Enlightenment has to do with the need for an extension of our rational capacities suited to the changing structure of technology and society and its related problems. To clarify this, Allenby makes use of the above-mentioned three-level systems model, distinguishing Level I, Level II and Level III technology. Level I consists of the material artefacts that we use for specific human purposes, such as an electrical device for making toast, a nuclear reactor for delivery of energy to industry and households, an automobile to enable social interactions, etc. At this level, one is dealing with a simple system. Technologies are, so to speak, cause–effect machines, in principle completely under the control of human will. Level II, however, is more complex. The automobile, for example, is a Level I technology, but operates in its use at Level II, consisting of a network of highway roads, traffic facilities, petroleum delivery infrastructure, etc. At this higher systems level we begin to experience a complexity that is often surprising and unpredictable, such as a traffic jam, but it is a complexity that we can understand. However, this is not the full story. The automobile did far more; 'it co-evolved with significant changes in environmental and resource systems; with mass-market consumer capitalism; (...)' (Allenby & Sarewitz 2013:39). Here we are confronted with Level III effects on Earth Systems that à la Rittel show a complexity of a 'wicked type' that are difficult to manage (Allenby 2012:178 *et seq*.; Allenby & Sarewitz 2013:109). In terms of this distinction between three levels of technology, one could diagnose the situation of our era as follows: we inhabit a Level III world with wicked problems, but we act as if we live on Level II, and we work with Level I rational tools that we have inherited from the Enlightenment (Allenby & Sarewitz 2013:161). Exactly here lies the challenge for what Allenby envisions in ESEM: no less than a concretisation of a new Enlightenment for the Level III world of the Anthropocene.

I agree with Allenby that for a good understanding of 'technology and society' it makes sense to distinguish between different levels of technology.[30] It is crucial in this regard how we explain the relationship of technology to ethics, values and normativity. This is the subject of the second key question that I have raised before: how do the rational and the ethical in ESEM relate to each other? Allenby argues that Level III technology in this sense differs radically from Levels II and I. When designing a Level I technology, take a toaster, the cultural environment in which it is used is of little or no importance to the design process. However, on the scale of ESEM at Level III one cannot limit oneself to such a traditional way of thinking; one must then explicitly delve into questions of culture, religion and morality. At Level III, the culturally religiously determined life-world of people is, namely, itself the object of intervention (Allenby 2002):

> While virtually all engineering activities to some extent reflect the cultures within which they are embedded, the cultural dimensions of traditional engineering are often not critical to the impacts of the engineering activity. Designing a toaster does indeed reflect some cultural dimensions, but understanding the roots of the Western technological discourse is hardly a necessary component of the activity (just as it is not for a design for environment analysis of a particular manufacturing technique, for example). But the scale and scope of ESEM, and the critical existential importance of the systems with which ESEM deals, means that one must comprehend not just the scientific and technological domains, but the social science domains – culture, religion, politics, institutional dynamics – as well. The human systems implicated in ESEM are extraordinarily powerful, with huge inertia and resistance to change built into them, and ESEM will fail as a response to the conditions of our modern world unless these are respected and understood. (p. 568)

A few lines further on the same page, Allenby (2002) continues his argument about another fundamental issue raised by ESEM on the role of values:

> *ESEM by its nature is a means to an end which can only be defined in ethical terms. Simply put, the question, 'To what end are humans engineering, or should humans engineer, the Earth?' is a moral and religious matter, not a technical one.* (p. 568; [author's added emphasis])

In this definition of ESEM, the ethical and technical are regarded as separate matters. As a means to an end, ESEM embodies a rational-technical instrument for human intervention in which normativity has to do with the choice of our ends. A proper definition of our ends, what we thus want to achieve with our instruments, confronts us with moral-religious issues on which we have to decide.

---

30. In successive publications I have elaborated a systems model of 'technology and society' that is fundamentally different. See for its latest version Strijbos (2014). This model is used as a conceptual framework for this book and briefly explained in the introductory chapter.

Here is clearly formulated the Enlightenment base underlying Allenby's programme. He argues that rationality that fits at Level I as a basis for action is of no help for Level III. The talk about 'problems' and 'solutions' at this level of complexity still reflects a Level I framework. Wicked problems cannot be managed successfully using the favoured child of the Enlightenment: applied reason. What we can do to face this type of problems is what he calls a process of 'muddling through'. This is not meant as something negative – not at all. 'Muddling through' is a skill and can be executed badly or quite well indeed. A seemingly inefficient and ineffective process is often the best that we can achieve, says Allenby (cited in Allenby & Sarewitz 2013):

> The problem is that the Enlightenment lens views this sort of incremental muddling as a strong indicator of failure and primitiveness and strives to overcome it, thus pushing action in the wrong direction. (p. 169)

However, at Level III we learn, through trial and error, through what works in particular situations, through incremental change that incorporates such learning, and through the difficult process of political compromise that allows people to take a next step. Examples are (Allenby & Sarewitz 2013):

> [P]roblems such as immigration, environmental degradation, healthcare-system dysfunction, the global drug trade, global poverty, corruption, and conflict in the Middle East don't get solved; at best they get managed, and at worst we lurch from crisis to crisis. (p. 93)

■ An interim assessment

First of all, I would like to express my appreciation for the broad vision that Allenby has developed on the evolution of 'technology and society' and for his diagnosis of the contemporary situation. In the conceptual elaboration of ESEM, intended as a 'rational and ethical approach' for the problems of the Anthropocene, he is keenly aware of the interdisciplinary nature of this endeavour and the complex moral and religious aspects involved. The critical question that has remained, however, is whether he has succeeded in developing a satisfactory vision with regard to the two key points of his argument that I have identified: (1) How to reconcile the criticism of the Enlightenment on the one hand and the plea for a New Enlightenment on the other? (2) How should the connection between the ethical and rational be considered?

In the foregoing text, it may have become clear that both points are not separate issues in Allenby's argument. Referring to his three-level model on technology and society, he argues that the favoured child of the Enlightenment, the scientific method, was successful at Level I as a guide for our acting in solving problems, but it falls short at Level III. From this, he concludes that the technological world that has emerged from Enlightenment thinking is confronted with problems that call for a new Enlightenment that should enable us to solve these complex problems of today. In this line of reasoning, Allenby has in fact accepted a problematic premise from the Enlightenment, separating the technical–rational and ethical–normative side of our actions. While the first concerns a morally neutral means–ends relationship, the second is about the normative questions of what goals we set.

Because the scientific method is the heart of our technological world, Allenby's uncritical acceptance of the Enlightenment is also reflected in his view on the three-layered systems model of 'technology and society' as he proposed in collaboration with Daniel Sarewitz. In about the same period in which Allenby developed these ideas, I have been involved in an interdisciplinary research with a comparable agenda (cf. Strijbos 2003). Besides other outcomes, this research resulted in two studies. The first book, *In Search of an Integrative Vision for Technology*, was published in 2006. A follow-up study, *From Technology Transfer to Intercultural Development*, was published a few years later in 2011. In these studies, I have attempted to overcome the goal-obsessions of the Enlightenment by introducing the notion of 'disclosure'. There this idea has been developed mainly in a critical conversation with the different streams of systems thinking. My purpose in what here follows is to clarify in more detail on how this idea relates to a biblical–theological understanding of our human condition, as opposed to the dominant Enlightenment vision of our culture.

■ The problem of evil in our 'wicked world'

In her book, *Evil in Modern Thought: An Alternative History of Philosophy* (2002, 2015), the German-American philosopher Susan Neiman presents an original view on the history of modern philosophy. She argues that this can be told as a history in which Western people have been trying to come to terms with the problem of evil. Looking back after a decade, she wrote an extended afterword for the 2015 Princeton Classics edition of the book, exploring the aspects that would have been written differently today (I will refer to that edition in the following). One of these aspects is the distinction between natural and moral evil that has been coined at the start of modernity in response to the much-discussed Lisbon earthquake in 1755. Susan Neiman (2015) argues that this Enlightenment distinction:

> [L]ooks increasingly unnatural, and impossible to maintain, in the face of the disasters the past decade has witnessed. Most have been not only deadlier than the Lisbon earthquake but, thanks to global media, more present. (p. 338)

Referring to the 2005 Katrina hurricane that hit New Orleans, among others, she notes that, as with Lisbon-1755, the discussion flared up again about this disaster as a 'deliberate act of God' a punishment for human sins.

While rejecting such interpretations of divine intervention and doom scenarios, Susan Neiman is touched by her youngest daughter's comment about the severity of the climate problem. The optimism of the Enlightenment's thinking of progress seems to be at least tempered. She concludes (Neiman 2015):

Climate change suggests that the difference between natural and moral evils no longer matters; what counts is taking moral responsibility for the natural disasters that our reckless use of nature provokes. Drawing distinctions between natural catastrophes and human evils makes increasingly little sense in a world where we have the power to call up natural forces that could be nature's undoing – whether intentionally, through the nuclear weapons whose use is less regulated than ever before, or thoughtlessly, through the looming environmental disasters that could make recent storms seem like a gentle warning. When human heedlessness stokes destruction, then leaves the world's poorest people at its mercy, it isn't merely tragic; it's evil. And nothing but the most banal of intentions is required for it to occur. *If the events of recent years make us realize that, they could provoke a change in our understanding as important as the one that occurred after the Lisbon earthquake.* (p. 342; [*author's added emphasis*])

This quote clearly shows that Susan Neiman recognises that today's climate problem and its consequences should be labelled as evil. However, the problem with this qualification is that the common distinction between moral and natural evil since the Enlightenment seems to have no meaning in the new era of the Anthropocene. If so, Neiman concludes, we may be at a new turning point in our thinking about evil that might extend at least as far as the turn that marks the beginning of the New Age. Of course, I am curious in which direction Susan Neiman's thinking is moving forward from this point. The Enlightenment originated from the tradition of Western Christianity and then followed its own path. But if we do indeed live at a turning point in history, is it conceivable that both tracks would meet again? Moreover, specifically with regard to the content of the Christian faith: can a renewed biblical understanding of the human condition and evil also shed new light on the future of our technological society with its 'wicked problems'? It is especially this question that I constantly had in mind while writing.

But let us go back to Susan Neiman first. How does she view our modern technological world? Regarding the Holocaust debate, Neiman firmly rejects the view that there is any connection between technology, the manifestation of evil in our modern world and Enlightenment rationality. It is wrongly assumed that there is a straight line from the Enlightenment to modern technology and then further to the Holocaust. There is no such direct link, according to Neiman. She, therefore, criticises two related claims: the notion that reason cannot be moral regarding technology development and the assumption that 'it has nothing to say about which ends are right or wrong, but only about the means to achieve them'. She further disputes that modern Enlightenment-based technology can be held responsible for the Holocaust. This is 'about as useful as holding airplanes responsible for 9/11, but unfortunately there are thinkers who seem to do both'.

With the latter, Neiman focuses the arrows of her criticism on British thinker John Gray, referring to his book, *Al Qaeda and What It Means to Be Modern* (2003). Gray opposes the much-held idea that Al Qaeda's fundamentalism would be a relic of a primitive past. He considers this view to be completely incorrect. Radical fundamentalist Islam is as modern as the ideologies of communism and Nazism, in which human history is seen as a prelude to a New World. All are convinced that they are capable of fundamentally revising the human condition. Therefore, according to Gray (2003):

> Al Qaeda is an essentially modern organization. It is modern not only in the fact that it uses satellite phones, laptop computers and encycled websites [...] The attack on the Twin Towers demonstrates that Al Qaeda understands that 21st century wars are spectacular encounters in which the dissemination of media images is a core strategy. (p. 78)

Responding to this, Neiman (2008) writes:

> They're supposed to use carrier pigeons? Operating with laptops and satellite phones makes Al Qaeda no more modern than the fact that when Bin Laden gets sick, he summons not a faith healer, but as good a physician he can get to pay a house call to a cave. *Contemporary technologies are as neutral as more primitive tools; the same hammer that built a frame can smash it.* (pp. 253–254; [*author's added emphasis*])

Making fun of someone's reasoning can, in addition to being witty, sometimes also provide clarification. Unfortunately, the latter is not the case here. The more often used 'argument-of-the-hammer' rests on a simplistic view of technology. Certainly, it is true that in technology one usually thinks directly of tools and other material artefacts, but with a little longer thought one soon realises that these are always interwoven into a certain cultural and socio-normative context. As I mentioned above about that context of our modern society – I spoke of 'the invisible factor X' – it is the scientific method that, together with the dominant Enlightenment thinking, underlies established practices of technical design, making of things and also their use in a man-designed environment. In this regard, Gray shows a better understanding of modern engineering than Neiman does. He rightly states that Al Qaeda has the character of a modern organisation based on rationality. The latter does not immediately make good or bad modern technology, I'd like to admit Susan Neiman. The decisive question is this: what is the normative landmark for our rationality?

The latter brings us back to what I have previously pointed out in the discussion between Rittel and Churchman: what determines the direction of rationality in our thinking, of a rational approach in tackling the 'wicked problems' which we stand for today? Although Susan Neiman does not address this question directly, I believe we can gain some insight into this point by following her critically in yet another rather voluminous follow-up study, *Moral Clarity* (2008), dealing with right and wrong in the 21st century. What particularly caught my attention was the fascination of Susan Neiman, in her defence of the Enlightenment, with the biblical figure Abraham, the father of all believers, and his intimate dealings with God. Let us take a closer look at this.

Susan Neiman takes two paradigmatic events in the life of Abraham as the starting point for her considerations: the story of Sodom and Gomorrah represents one paradigm; the other, God's command to Abraham to offer him his son Isaac. In Neiman's interpretation, Abraham can be described in the first case as a real Enlightenment hero. With great reverence, sure, he dares to ask God critical questions when he confides in Abraham about His purpose to destroy the cities of Sodom and Gomorrah because the sins there are unheard of. Abraham then refuses to accept this plan outrightly because, according to Neiman, there must be good reasons for what is happening in the world and people should be able to find it themselves (Neiman 2008):

> This is the fundamental law to which everyone, including God, must answer, and it leads us to seek not only justice but transparent justice. (p. 12)

In sharp contrast to this, according to Neiman, is Abraham's course of action at Mount Moriah. To speak with Kierkegaard, the Abraham who goes on his way to Mount Moriah with his son has left behind ethics and Enlightenment. He asks nothing at all (Neiman 2008):

> To do so, he thinks, would be an act of superstition, even violence. Does trust mean asking no questions? Does love mean never having to say you're sorry? This man of faith is certain: The demand to find reason after reason is at odds with a grateful acceptance of creation, and arrogant at that. (p. 12)

The passion and challenging tone echoed in the above shows that Neiman does not want to avoid the problem of evil intellectually; she wants to look it straight in the face. And rightly so, I believe. If there is no solution to the evils and 'bad problems' of our time, there is not much more to do than 'wander in the Anthropocene' in a postmodern spirit (Ten Bos 2017). We then lack a perspective of meaning on our existence. However, I would like to add as a comment: as with every problem, the rule applies here that finding the right problem is the beginning of a solution. I do not want to deny that the two stories about the life of Abraham to which Neiman refers show striking differences, but does this mean that we are forced to choose between Enlightenment logic on the one hand, or a form of slavish subjection of faith that disables intellectual thinking on the other hand? As a convinced defender of the Enlightenment, Neiman takes a sharp stand against all kinds of clichés that stick to the Enlightenment, for example, that religious faith should be regarded as an obsolete answer to the questions of the past. The Enlightenment, she notes, pointed her arrows not at faith but at idolatry and superstition.

I agree with Neiman on this point, but does her interpretation of Abraham not start from a dubious distinction between thinking and believing imposed on us by the Enlightenment?

The central issue, I believe, is this: where does our thinking about Abraham begin; where do we stand; what is the starting point? Or rather, where is Abraham standing himself, thinking and believing as 'father of all believers', when God puts him to the test and orders him to sacrifice Isaac? It is hard to imagine that Abraham is not dismayed at the assignment he is given. Not only is Isaac his only child, but does his death not also mean the end of the most precious thing that Abraham believed in all his life? With Isaac's death, the bottom seems to have been swept away from everything he had lived for so far? How is it possible that Abraham, apparently in peace of mind, sets out for Mount Moriah with little Isaac? Does he lack the boldness to argue with God now?

Over the centuries, Abraham's sacrifice of Isaac has drawn attention in the theological and philosophical discussion of the problem of evil. For your reference, I refer the reader to a study on *John Calvin's Ideas* (2006) by the British theologian and philosopher Paul Helm. In a short excursion on 'The Binding of Isaac' he clarifies Calvin's explanation. He shows that Calvin does not fit into one of the common interpretative traditions. After Kierkegaard's well-known book, *Fear and Trembling* (1843), it is usually stated that in his actions Abraham is confronted with a tension between two conflicting requirements; the ethical requirement not to sacrifice his son, on the one hand, and God's command to do just that, on the other. In this irreconcilable contrast between the poles of the religious and the ethical, Abraham decides to 'suspend the ethical', to become a 'Knight of Faith' (Helm 2006:355). This is the type of interpretation we also observe with Susan Neiman: Abraham chooses a servile faith that simply overrides the universal demands of ethics and mature reasonable thinking.

Paul Helm's point is that Calvin's thinking moves along other lines. Abraham's trial is another, as an enforced choice between ethics or faith. As Calvin explains, the most important thing for Abraham was not a moral crisis because of the command to give up his only son as a sacrifice, but that the loss of his son in obedience to such a command would imply the failure of the divine promise that through Isaac he would be the father of many nations (Helm 2006):

> So as Calvin sees it, *the conflict is produced by two conflicting words from God: the word of promise to Abraham, and the word of command* to him to sacrifice Isaac. (p. 355; [*author's added emphasis*])

The trial of Abraham concerns, according to Calvin, that the speaking of God has two sides: first, there is the promise and then the commandment. Also, how could Abraham keep these two together in his actions? Was the command not completely contrary to the promise? The core of Genesis 22 is not like some chapters earlier in the story of Sodom and Gomorrah, where Abraham asks God questions, but the son now asks the father a question: 'Father! [...] Where is the lamb for a burnt offering?' Abraham's answer reveals the secret of his faith. With a prophetic sharpness, pointing to Christ as the God-given sacrificial lamb for all the world, he then says: 'God himself will provide' (Gn 22):

> Isaac said to his father Abraham, 'Father!' And he said, 'Here I am, my son'. He said, 'The fire and the wood are here, but where is the lamb for a burnt offering?' Abraham said, 'God himself will provide the lamb for a burnt offering, my son'. So, the two of them walked on together. (vv. 7-8; [NRSV])

The greatness of Abraham's faith is that he kept putting God's promise first on his way to Moriah. There is no question, as Susan Neiman believes, of a slavish submission to a commandment that disables true humanity in thinking and believing. The secret of Abraham's life here is that in the misery of the trial, he holds fast to the promise of God. In this way he is able to walk a path that must be considered humanly impossible. As the father of all believers, Abraham's actions speak of someone who knows from a firm faith that God will do what He has promised under oath.

After this theological–philosophical elaboration on Abraham, we return to the question of what is the basis for the rationality of our thinking and acting? Does what we have said about the promise and commandment in Abraham's life also have significance for the contemporary debate about wicked problems and the crisis experiences of our time? Finally, a few remarks about this.

■ Conclusion

First of all, this. In the Bible as the book of God's promises and God's commandments, promise and command always go hand in hand. The believer does not have to doubt about God's promise, but often we stand with our hands in our hair when we ask ourselves the question: what does God want from us now; what should we do in this concrete situation? This applies not only to the life of Abraham; it applies no less to our time and us. To emphasise this biblical unity between promise and command, I would like to speak here of God's 'promise-command' for our existence and the history of man and world. This is the foundation of all our created reality and for its opening up to the future, up to the end of the world.

This understanding of 'promise and commandment' also constitutes, I believe, the possibility of a renewal of our thinking, if you will, for a renewed rationality. Then the focus of our thinking and acting is not determined by the goals we set and the power of science and technology to pursue them. We have to free ourselves from the Enlightenment obsession to control reality and focus ourselves (again) on God's 'promise-command' for a life in the Kingdom of God.

From here, a road opens up whose direction we know, but not its course. The future opens up in and with our actions, which is not yet the same as through our actions. Certainly, man matters, he is fully engaged as God's co-worker in the Kingdom of God, but the Builder is God himself. And, I would like to say, is not this just a liberating perspective for a rather overstrained technological activism in our postmodern world and its 'wicked problems'? Finally, to put the same thing in a different way, listening to the voice of Luther (1999) at the break of the Middle Ages and New Age in Western history, almost five centuries ago:

> The little birds fly about and warble, make nests, and hatch their young. That is their task. But they do not gain their living from it. Oxen plow, horses carry their riders and have a share in battle; sheep furnish wool, milk, cheese, etc. That is their task. But they do not gain their living from it. It is the earth which produces grass and nourishes them through God's blessing. [...]
>
> Similarly, man must necessarily work and busy himself at something. At the same time, however, he must know that it is something other than his labor which furnishes him sustenance; it is the divine blessing. Because God gives him nothing unless he works, it may seem as if it is his labor which sustains him; just as the little birds neither sow nor reap, but they would certainly die of hunger if they did not fly about to seek their food. The fact that they find food, however, is not due to their own labor, but to God's goodness. (p. 311)[31]

---

31. Cited from a classical text of Luther in 1524 on Psalm 127, as explained to the Christians in Riga in what is currently known as Latvia (Luther 1999).

References

Introduction

Frodeman, R. & Mitcham, C., 2007, 'New directions in interdisciplinarity: Broad, deep, and critical', *Bulletin of Science, Technology, and Society* 27(6), 506–514. https://doi.org/10.1177/0270467607308284

Hart, G., 2016, 'Relational comparison revisited: Marxist postcolonial geographies in practice', *Progress in Human Geography* 42(3), 371–394. https://doi.org/10.1177/0309132516681388

Ingold, T., 2000, *The perception of the environment: Essays on livelihood, dwelling and skill*, Routledge, London.

Mouw, R.J. & Griffioen, S., 1993, *Pluralisms and horizons: An essay in Christian public philosophy*, William B. Eerdmans, Grand Rapids, MI.

Pope Francis, 2015, *Encyclical letter Laudato Si' of the Holy Father Francis on care for our common home*, viewed n.d., from https://www.vatican.va/content/francesco/en/encyclicals/documents/papa-francesco_20150524_enciclica-laudato-si.html.

Rathbone, M., Von Schéele, F. & Strijbos, S. (eds.), 2014, 'Social change in our technology-based world', in *Proceedings of the 19th Annual Working Conference of the IIDE.*, Maarssen, Netherlands, May, 2014, n.p.

Strijbos, S., 1997, 'The paradox of uniformity and plurality in technological society', *Technology in Society* 19(2), 177–194. https://doi.org/10.1016/S0160-791X(96)00063-2

Van der Stoep, J. & Strijbos, S. (eds.), 2011, *From technology transfer to intercultural development*, Sun Media, Bloemfontein.

Van Niekerk, A., 2014, 'The cultural basis for a sustainable community in a South African township', in M. Rathbone, F. Von Schéele & S. Strijbos (eds.), *Social change in our technology-based world, Proceedings of the 19th Annual Working Conference of the IIDE*, Maarssen, Netherlands, May, 2014, pp. 50–64.

Chapter 1

Alkire, S., 2004, 'Culture poverty, and external intervention', in V. Rao (ed.), *Culture and public action*, pp. 185–209, Stanford University Press/World Bank, Stanford, CA.

Calderisi, R., 2006, *The trouble with Africa: Why foreign aid isn't working*, Yale University Press, New Haven, CT.

Chebvute, M.A., n.d., *A pernicious antidote: The role of the Southern African Development Community (SADC) in sustaining peace in Zimbabwe, 1980–2013*, viewed n.d., from https://www.academia.edu/35193680/A_Pernicious_Antidote_The_role_of_the_Southern_African_Development_Community_SADC_in_sustaining_peace_in_Zimbabwe_1980_2013.

Galbraith, J.K., 1980, *The nature of mass poverty*, Penguin, New York, NY.

Ijeoma, E.O.C. & Okafor, C., 2014, 'A review of South Africa's National Electrification Programme: The Buffalo City Municipality platform', *Journal of Public Administration* 49(1), 32–48.

Klitgaard, R., 1992, 'Taking culture into account: From "let's" to "how"', in I. Seragelden (ed.), *Culture and development in Africa. Environmentally sustainable development proceedings series no. 1*, pp. 75–120, World Bank, Washington, DC.

Kritzinger, J.J. (ed.), 1994, *On being witnesses*, Orion Publishers, Johannesburg.

Lamola, M.J., 2018, 'The de-Africanisation of the African National Congress, Afrophobia in South Africa and the Limpopo River fever', *Filosofia Theoretica: Journal of African Philosophy, Culture and Religions* 7(3), 72–93. https://doi.org/10.4314/ft.v7i3.6

References

Marnham, P., 1980, *Fantastic invasion: Dispatches from contemporary Africa*, Random House, New York, NY.

Mbeki, V. & Phago, K., 2014, 'Engagement of the Lephalale local municipality and its community on water services: A preliminary analysis', *Journal of Public Administration* 49(1), 206-216.

Mpehle, Z., 2014, 'Theoretical perspective on refugee movements and service delivery in South Africa', *Journal of Public Administration* 49(1), 217-228.

Moyo, D., 2009, *Dead aid. Why aid is not working and how there is a better way for Africa*, Farrar, Straus and Giroux, New York, NY.

Nathan, L., 2006, 'SADC's uncommon approach to common security, 1992-2003', *Journal of Southern African Studies* 32(3), 605-622. https://doi.org/10.1080/03057070600830755

Ndlovu-Gatsheni, S.J., 2009, 'Africa for Africans or Africa for "natives" only? "New nationalism" and nativism in Zimbabwe and South Africa', *Africa Spectrum* 1(1), 61-78. https://doi.org/10.1177/000203970904400105

Olutola, A.A., 2014, 'Crime rate in Africa: Time for African criminological theory', *Journal of Public Administration* 49(1), 314-329.

Quartz, 2013, 'Zimbabwean President Robert Mugabe received a standing ovation at Saturday's opening of the Southern Africa Development Community (SADC) Summit held in Malawi's capital Lilongwe', *The New Times*, 19 August, viewed 19 November 2021, from https://www.newtimes.co.rw/section/read/68474.

Roy, J.P., Tschakert, H., Waisman, S., Abdul Halim, P., Antwi-Agyei, P., Dasgupta, B. et al., 2018, 'Sustainable development, poverty eradication and reducing inequalities', in V.P. Masson-Delmotte, H.-O. Zhai, D. Pörtner, J. Roberts, P.R. Skea, A. Shukla et al. (eds.), *Global warming of 1.5°C. An IPCC special report on the impacts of global warming of 1.5°C above pre-industrial levels and related global greenhouse gas emission pathways*, s.n., s.l.

Sebola, M.P., 2014, 'The community policing philosophy and the right to public protest in South Africa: Are there positive developments after two decades of democracy?', *Journal of Public Administration* 49(1), 300-313.

Seitz, V., 2018, *Afrika wird arm regiert oder Wie man Afrika wirklich helfen kann*, dtv, Munich.

Sirota, B., 2004, 'Sovereignty and the Southern African development community', *Chicago Journal of International Law* 5(1), Article 24.

Soyinka, W., 1976. *Myth, literature and the African world*, Cambridge University Press, London.

Tsheola, J.P. & Lukhele, T., 2014, 'South Africa's twenty years of "civilizing missions" for Africa: Faded continental posture and agenda', *Journal of Public Administration* 49(1), 375.

UNESCO, 2018, *Culture in city reconstruction and recovery (CURE)*, UNESCO and the World Bank, Washington, DC.

Walls, A., 1994, 'David Livingstone 1813-1873. Awakening the Western World to Africa', viewed 18 November 2021, from https://dacb.org/stories/southafrica/legacy-livingstone/.

Whande, T., 2007, 'Joseph Southern Africa: SADC Applauds Mugabe for Destroying a Nation', *AllAfrica*, 31 August 2007, viewed n.d., from https://allafrica.com/stories/200709030042.html.

World Bank, 1999, *World Development Report 1999/2000: Entering the 21st Century*, Oxford University Press, New York, NY.

World Bank, 2016, *Africa's pulse volume 14. An analysis of issues shaping Africa's economic future*, World Bank Group, Washington, DC.

World Bank, 2018a, *Africa's pulse volume 17. An analysis of issues shaping Africa's economic future*, World Bank Group, Washington, DC.

World Bank, 2018b, *Africa's pulse volume 18. An analysis of issues shaping Africa's economic future*, World Bank Group, Washington, DC.

World Bank, 2019a, *Africa's pulse volume 19. An analysis of issues shaping Africa's economic future*, World Bank Group, Washington, DC.

World Bank, 2019b, *The sustainable development agenda and the World Bank group: Closing the DSGs financing gap*, viewed n.d., from https://pubdocs.worldbank.org/en/259801562965232326/2030Agenda-2019-final-web.pdf.

World Bank, 2019c, *Africa's pulse volume 20. An analysis of issues shaping Africa's economic future*, World Bank Group, Washington, DC.

World Bank, 2020, *Advance copy* of *Africa's pulse volume 22. An analysis of issues shaping Africa's economic future. Charting the road to recovery*, World Bank Group, Washington, DC.

World Faiths Development Dialogue, n.d., *History and Objectives of the World Faiths Development Dialogue*, viewed n.d., from https://berkleycenter.georgetown.edu/wfdd/about.

Chapter 2

Ashoka, n.d., *Social Entrepreneurship*, viewed n.d., from https://www.ashoka.org/en-za/focus/social-entrepreneurship.

Bornstein, D. & Davis, S., 2010, *Social entrepreneurship: What everyone needs to know*, Oxford University Press, Oxford.

Friedmann, J., 1973, *Retracting America: A theory of transactive planning*, Anchor Press, New York, NY.

Goudzwaard, B., [1976] 1997. *Capitalism and progress: A diagnosis of western society*, Paternoster Press, Carlisle.

Hart, S.L., [2007] 2010, *Capitalism at the crossroads: Next generation business strategies for a post-crisis world*, 3rd revised and expanded edition, Wharton School Publishing, Upper Saddle River, NY.

Mander, J. & Goldsmith, E. (eds.), 1996, *The case against the global economy: And for a turn toward the local,* Sierra Club Books, San Francisco, CA.

Nelson, J.A., 2011, 'The relational economy', in L. Zsolnai (ed.), *Ethical principles and economic transformation: A Buddhist approach*, pp. 21–34, Springer, Dordrecht.

Nicholls, A. (ed.), 2008, *Social entrepreneurship: New models of sustainable social change*, Oxford University Press, Oxford.

Norberg-Hodge, H., 1996a, 'The pressure to modernize and globalize', in J. Mander & E. Goldsmith (eds.), *The case against the global economy and for a turn towards localization*, pp. 33–46, Sierra Club Books, San Francisco, CA.

Norberg-Hodge, H., 1996b, 'Shifting direction: From global dependence to local interdependence', in J. Mander & E. Goldsmith (eds.), *The case against the global economy and for a turn towards localization*, pp. 393–406, Sierra Club Books, San Francisco, CA.

Norberg-Hodge, H., 2002, 'Buddhism in the global economy', in A.H. Badiner (ed.), *Mindfulness in the marketplace: Compassionate responses to consumerism,* pp. 15–27, Parallax Press, Berkeley, CA.

Polanyi, K., [1944] 2001, *The great transformation: The political and economic origins of our time*, Beacon Press, Boston, MA.

Prahalad, C.K., [2006] 2010, *The fortune at the bottom of the pyramid: Eradicating poverty through profits*, 5th revised and expanded edition, Wharton School Publishing, Upper Saddle River, NJ.

Prahalad, C.K. & Hart, S.L., 2002, 'The fortune at the bottom of the pyramid', *Strategy + Business* 26, 54–67.

Sachs, W., [1999] 2015, *Planet dialectics: Explorations in environment and development*, Zed Books, London.

Schumacher, E.F., [1973] 1993, *Small is beautiful: A study of economics as if people mattered*, Vintage Books, London.

Simanis, E. & Hart, S., 2009, 'Innovation from the inside out', *MIT Sloan Management Review* 50(4), 77–86.

References

Strijbos, S. & Haftor, D., 2011a, 'Re-integrating technology and economy in human life and society: The past, present and future of the IIDE-research', in L. Botes, R. Jongeneel & S. Strijbos (eds.), *Proceedings of the 17th Annual Working Conference of the IIDE, Volume I*, Maarssen, Netherlands, n.d., 2011, pp. 137–152.

Strijbos, S., 2011b, 'The problem of development: The decontextualization of technology in a global world', in J. Van der Stoep & S. Strijbos (eds.), *From technology transfer to intercultural development: Understanding technology and development in a globalizing world*, pp. 107–116, Rozenberg Publishers, Amsterdam.

Strijbos, S., 2011c, 'The inclusion of "culture and religion" in development: Beyond the technical-instrumental and participative-communicative approach', in J. Van der Stoep & S. Strijbos (eds.), *From technology transfer to intercultural development: Understanding technology and development in a globalizing world*, pp. 149–163, Rozenberg Publishers, Amsterdam.

Van der Kooy, T.P., 1953, *Op het grensgebied van economie en religie*, Kok, Kampen.

Yunus, M., 2007, *Creating a world without poverty: Social business and the future of capitalism*, Public Affairs, New York, NY.

Chapter 3

Adesina, J.A., Piketh, S.J., Qhekwana, M., Burger, R., Language, B. & Mkhatshwa, G., 2020, 'Contrasting indoor and ambient particulate matter concentrations and thermal comfort in coal and non-coal burning households at South Africa Highveld', *Science of The Total Environment* 699, 134403. https://doi.org/10.1016/j.scitotenv.2019.134403

Ayentimi, D.T. & Burgess, J., 2019, 'Is the fourth industrial revolution relevant to sub-Sahara Africa?', *Technology Analysis and Strategic Management* 31(6), 641–652. https://doi.org/10.1080/09537325.2018.1542129

Balmer, M., 2007, 'Household coal use in an urban township in South Africa', *Journal of Energy in Southern Africa* 18(3), 27–32. https://doi.org/10.17159/2413-3051/2007/v18i3a3382

Barnes, B., Mathee, A., Thomas, E. & Bruce, N., 2009, 'Household energy, indoor air pollution and child respiratory health in South Africa', *Journal of Energy in Southern Africa* 20(1), 4–13. https://doi.org/10.17159/2413-3051/2009/v20i1a3296

Bruce, N., Pope, D., Rehfuess, E., Balakrishnan, K., Adair-Rohani, H. & Dora, C., 2015, 'WHO indoor air quality guidelines on household fuel combustion: Strategy implications of new evidence on interventions and exposure-risk functions', *Atmospheric Environment* 106, 451–457. https://doi.org/10.1016/j.atmosenv.2014.08.064

Cilliers, J., Oosthuizen, M., Kwasi, S., Alexander, K., Pooe, T.K., Yeboua, K. & Moyer, J.D., 2020, *The poor lose again: Impact of COVID-19 on Africa*, in ISS Africa, viewed 07 April 2020, from https://issafrica.org/iss-today/the-poor-lose-again-impact-of-covid-19-on-africa.

Department of Energy, 2016, *South African coal sector report*, Department of Energy, Pretoria.

Eskom, 2019, *Eskom Integrated Report 31 March 2019*, Eskom Holdings SOC Limited, Sunninghill.

Feig, G., Garland, R.M., Naidoo, S., Maluleke, A. & Der Merwe, M.V., 2019, 'Assessment of changes in concentrations of selected criteria pollutants in the Vaal and Highveld Priority Areas', *Clean Air Journal* 29(2), 75–87. https://doi.org/10.17159/caj/2019/29/2.7464

Govender, K. & Sivakumar, V., 2019, 'A decadal analysis of particulate matter ($PM_{2.5}$) and surface ozone (O_3) over Vaal Priority Area, South Africa', *Clean Air Journal* 29(2), 65–74. https://doi.org/10.17159/caj/2019/29/2.7578

Hendryx, M., Zullig, K.J. & Luo, J., 2020, 'Impacts of coal use on health', *Annual Review of Public Health* 41, 397–415. https://doi.org/10.1146/annurev-publhealth-040119-094104

Hersey, S.P., Garland, R.M., Crosbie, E., Shingler, T., Sorooshian, A., Piketh, S. et al., 2015, 'An overview of regional and local characteristics of aerosols in South Africa using satellite, ground, and modelling data', *Atmospheric Chemistry and Physics* 15(8), 4259–4278. https://doi.org/10.5194/acp-15-4259-2015

Hofstede, G., 1984, 'The cultural relativity of the quality of life concept', *Academy of Management Review* 9(3), 389–398. https://doi.org/10.5465/amr.1984.4279653

IARC, 2010, *Household use of solid fuels and high-temperature frying, IARC monographs on the evaluation of carcinogenic risks to humans*, vol. 95, International Agency for Research on Cancer, Lyon.

Israel-Akinbo, S.O., Snowball, J. & Fraser, G., 2018, 'The energy transition patterns of low-income households in South Africa: An evaluation of energy programme and policy', *Journal of Energy in Southern Africa* 29(3), 75–85. https://doi.org/10.17159/2413-3051/2018/v29i3a3310

Kerimray, A., Rojas-Solórzano, L., Amouei Torkmahalleh, M., Hopke, P.K. & Ó Gallachóir, B.P., 2017, 'Coal use for residential heating: Patterns, health implications and lessons learned', *Energy for Sustainable Development* 40, 19–30. https://doi.org/10.1016/j.esd.2017.05.005

Maslow, A.H., 1943, 'A theory of human motivation', *Psychological Review* 50(4), 370–396. https://doi.org/10.1037/h0054346

Mathee, A. & Wright, C., 2014, 'Environmental health in South Africa', in A. Padarath & R. English (eds.), *South African health review 2013/2014*, pp. 105–116, Health Systems Trust, Durban.

Max-Neef, M.A., 1991, *Human scale development: Conception, application and further reflections*, The Apex Press, New York, NY.

MIT Energy Initiative, 2016, *Utility of the future*, viewed 07 April 2020, from http://energy.mit.edu/wp-content/uploads/2016/12/Utility-of-the-Future-Full-Report.pdf.

Naidoo, S., Piketh, S. & Curtis, C., 2014, 'Quantification of emissions generated from domestic burning activities from townships in Johannesburg', *Clean Air Journal* 24(1), 34–41. https://doi.org/10.17159/caj/2014/24/1.7047

Niele, F., 2005, *Energy, engine of evolution*, Shell Global Solutions, Elsevier, Amsterdam.

Pope, C.A., III, Turner, M.C., Burnett, R.T., Jerrett, M., Gapstur, S.M., Diver, W.R. et al., 2014, 'Relationships between fine particulate air pollution, cardiometabolic disorders, and cardiovascular mortality', *Circulation Research* 116(1), 108–115. https://doi.org/10.1161/CIRCRESAHA.116.305060

Rollin, H., 2017, 'Evidence for health effects of early life exposure to indoor air pollutants: What we know and what can be done', *Clean Air Journal* 27(1), 2–3. https://doi.org/10.17159/2410-972X/2017/v27n1a1

Smith, K.R., Bruce, N., Balakrishnan, K., Adair-Rohani, H., Balmes, J., Chafe, Z. et al., 2014, 'Millions dead: How do we know and what does it mean? Methods used in the comparative risk assessment of household air pollution', *Annual Review of Public Health* 35, 185–206. https://doi.org/10.1146/annurev-publhealth-032013-182356

Statistics South Africa, 2015, *Census 2011: Migration dynamics in South Africa (No. 03-01-79)*, Statistics South Africa, Pretoria.

Statistics South Africa, 2018, *Electricity, gas and water supply industry, 2016 (No. 41-01-02)*, Statistics South Africa, Pretoria.

Statistics South Africa, 2019, *General household survey 2018 (statistical release no. P0318)*, Statistics South Africa, Pretoria.

United Nations, 2019, *The sustainable development goals report 2019*, United Nations, New York, NY.

Wenig, M., Spichtinger, N., Stohl, A., Held, G., Beirle, S., Wagner, T. et al., 2003, 'Intercontinental transport of nitrogen oxide pollution plumes', *Atmospheric Chemistry and Physics* 3, 387–393. https://doi.org/10.5194/acp-3-387-2003

Wernecke, B., Language, B., Piketh, S.J. & Burger, R.P., 2015, 'Indoor and outdoor particulate matter concentrations on the Mpumalanga highveld – A case study', *Clean Air Journal* 25(2), 12–16. https://doi.org/10.17159/2410-972X/2015/v25n2a1

World Health Organization (WHO) (ed.), 2014, *WHO guidelines for indoor air quality: Household fuel combustion*, World Health Organization, Geneva.

World Health Organization (WHO), 2015, *Residential heating with wood and coal: Health impacts and policy options in Europe and North America*, World Health Organization, Regional Office for Europe, København.

Wright, C. & Diab, R., 2011, 'Air pollution and vulnerability: Solving the puzzle of prioritization', *Journal of Environmental Health* 73(6), 56–64.

Chapter 4

Al-Lahham, O., El Assi, N.M. & Fayyad, M., 2003, 'Impact of treated wastewater irrigation on quality attributes and contamination of tomato fruit', *Agricultural Water Management* 61(1), 51–62. https://doi.org/10.1016/S0378-3774(02)00173-7

Altieri, M.A., 2008, *Small farms as a planetary ecological asset: Five key reasons why we should support the revitalisation of small farms in the global south*, Malaysia Citeseer, Penang.

Ascott, M., Gooddy, D., Wang, L., Stuart, M., Lewis, M., Ward, R. et al., 2017, 'Global patterns of nitrate storage in the vadose zone', *Nature Communications* 8(1), 1–7. https://doi.org/10.1038/s41467-017-01321-w

Bezner-Kerr, R., Mcguire, K.L., Nigh, R., Rocheleau, D., Soluri, J. & Perfecto, I., 2012, 'Effects of industrial agriculture on climate change and the mitigation potential of small-scale agro-ecological farms', *Animal Science Reviews* 2011, 69.

Binns, J., Illgner, P. & Nel, E., 2001, 'Water shortage, deforestation and development: South Africa's working for water programme', *Land Degradation & Development* 12(4), 341–355. https://doi.org/10.1002/ldr.455

Blom-Zandstra, M., 1989, 'Nitrate accumulation in vegetables and its relationship to quality', *Annals of Applied Biology* 115(3), 553–561. https://doi.org/10.1111/j.1744-7348.1989.tb06577.x

Boyce, J.K., 2006, 'A future for small farms? Biodiversity and sustainable agriculture', in *Human development in the era of globalization: Essays in honor of Keith B. Griffin*, pp. 83–104, Edward Elgar Publishing, London.

Brklacich, M., Bryant, C.R. & Smit, B., 1991, 'Review and appraisal of concept of sustainable food production systems', *Environmental Management* 15(1), 1–14. https://doi.org/10.1007/BF02393834

Capdevila-Cortada, M., 2019, 'Electrifying the Haber–Bosch', *Nature Catalysis* 2(12), 1055–1055. https://doi.org/10.1038/s41929-019-0414-4

Chale-Matsau, J., 2005, 'Persistence of human pathogens in a crop grown from sewage sludge treated soil', PhD thesis, University of Pretoria.

Chowdhury, A. & Das, A., 2015, 'Nitrate accumulation and vegetable quality', *International Journal of Science and Research* 4(12), 1668–1672. https://doi.org/10.21275/v4i12.NOV152366

Connor, D.J., 2013, 'Organically grown crops do not a cropping system make and nor can organic agriculture nearly feed the world', *Field Crops Research* 144(20), 145–147. https://doi.org/10.1016/j.fcr.2012.12.013

Department of Environmental Affairs, 2012, *Second South Africa environment outlook*, A report on the state of the environment, p. 328, Department of Environmental Affairs, Pretoria.

Van Rooyen, J.A. & Versfeld, D.B., 2011, *Integrated water resource planning for South Africa: A situation analysis*, Department of Water Affairs, Pretoria.

Department of Water Affairs, 2012, *National water resource strategy 2*, Department of Water Affairs, Pretoria.

Department of Water Affairs and Forestry, 1996, *South African water quality guidelines. Edition 2; Volume 7: Aquatic ecosystems*, Department of Water Affairs, Pretoria.

Food and Agriculture Organisation, 2006, *Policy brief – Food security*, viewed 06 June 2020, from http://www.fao.org/fileadmin/templates/faoitaly/documents/pdf/pdf_Food_Security_Cocept_Note.pdf.

Food and Agriculture Organisation, 2012, *Smallholders and family farmers. Sustainable pathways*, viewed 01 March 2020, from http://www.fao.org/fileadmin/templates/nr/sustainability_pathways/docs/Factsheet_SMALLHOLDERS.pdf.

Food and Agriculture Organisation, 2017, *The future of food and agriculture – Trends and challenges*, viewed 10 June 2020, from http://www.fao.org/3/a-i6583e.pdf.

Global Carbon Project, 2020, *Global carbon budget 2020*, viewed 08 January 2021, from https://www.globalcarbonproject.org/global/images/carbonbudget/Infographic_Emissions2020.pdf.

Gunderson, L.H. & Holling, C.S., 2002, *Panarchy: Understanding transformations in human and natural systems*, Island Press, s.l.

Hansen, J.W., 1996, 'Is agricultural sustainability a useful concept?', *Agricultural Systems* 50(2), 117–143. https://doi.org/10.1016/0308-521X(95)00011-S

Helmecke, M., Fries, E. & Schulte, C., 2020, 'Regulating water reuse for agricultural irrigation: Risks related to organic micro-contaminants', *Environmental Sciences Europe* 32(1), 4. https://doi.org/10.1186/s12302-019-0283-0

ISO 14046, 2014, *Environmental management water footprint – Principles, requirements and guidelines*, International Standards Organisation, Geneva.

Kirchmann, H. & Ryan, M.H., 2004, 'Nutrients in organic farming – Are there advantages from the exclusive use of organic manures and untreated minerals', *New directions for a diverse planet. Proceedings of the 4th International Crop Science Congress*, Brisbane, Australia, September 26–01 October, 2004, n.p.

Kruger, E., 2020, *Personal communication*, Agricultural Scientist, Mahlathini Development Foundation. Pietermaritzburg.

Kumaraswamy, S. & Kunte, K., 2013, 'Integrating biodiversity and conservation with modern agricultural landscapes', *Biodiversity and Conservation* 22(12), 2735–2750. https://doi.org/10.1007/s10531-013-0562-9

Le Roux, B., Hay, R., Van Der Laan, M., Dlamini, Z. & Walker, S., 2021, *Evaluation of the management and impact of water quantity and quality for Agri-parks in Gauteng Province, South Africa*, Water Research Commission, Pretoria.

Le Roux, B, Van Der Laan, M., Vahrmeijer, T., Annandale, J. & Bristow, K., 2018, 'Water footprints of vegetable crop wastage along the supply chain in Gauteng, South Africa', *Water* 10(5), 539. https://doi.org/10.3390/w10050539

Maynard, D., Barker, A., Minotti, P. & Peck, N., 1976, 'Nitrate accumulation in vegetables', *Advances in agronomy*, Elsevier 28, 71–118,. https://doi.org/10.1016/S0065-2113(08)60553-2

Mazoyer, M. & Roudart, L., 2006, *A history of world agriculture: From the neolithic age to the current crisis*, NYU Press. New York, NY.

Mcpherson, I. & Zhang, J., 2020, 'Can electrification of ammonia synthesis decrease its carbon footprint?', *Joule* 4(1), 12–14. https://doi.org/10.1016/j.joule.2019.12.013

Musazura, W., Odindo, A.O., Bame, I.B. & Tesfamariam, E.H., 2015, 'Effect of irrigation with anaerobic baffled reactor effluent on Swiss chard (Beta vulgaris cicla.) yield, nutrient uptake and leaching', *Journal of Water Reuse and Desalination* 5(4), 592–609. https://doi.org/10.2166/wrd.2015.011

Nærstad, A., 2007, *Africa can feed itself*, The Development Fund, Oslo.

Nowak, B., Nesme, T., David, C. & Pellerin, S., 2013, 'To what extent does organic farming rely on nutrient inflows from conventional farming?', *Environmental Research Letters* 8(4), 044045. https://doi.org/10.1088/1748-9326/8/4/044045

Ogbazghi, Z.M., Tesfamariam, E.H., Annandale, J.G. & De Jager, P.C., 2015, 'Mobility and uptake of zinc, cadmium, nickel, and lead in sludge-amended soils planted to dryland maize and irrigated maize–oat rotation', *Journal of Environmental Quality* 44(2), 655–667. https://doi.org/10.2134/jeq2014.06.0261

Phalan, B., Balmford, A., Green, R.E. & Scharlemann, J.P., 2011, 'Minimising the harm to biodiversity of producing more food globally', *Food Policy* 36, S62–S71. https://doi.org/10.1016/j.foodpol.2010.11.008

Postel, S., 1999, *Pillar of sand: Can the irrigation miracle last?*, W.W. Norton & Company, New York, NY.

Pretty, J., 2008, 'Agricultural sustainability: Concepts, principles and evidence', *Philosophical Transactions of the Royal Society B: Biological Sciences* 363(1491), 447–465. https://doi.org/10.1098/rstb.2007.2163

References

Qiu, W., Wang, Z., Huang, C., Chen, B. & Yang, R., 2014, 'Nitrate accumulation in leafy vegetables and its relationship with water', *Journal of Soil Science and Plant Nutrition* 14(4), 761–768. https://doi.org/10.4067/S0718-95162014005000061

Reganold, J.P., Elliott, L.F. & Unger, Y.L., 1987, 'Long-term effects of organic and conventional farming on soil erosion', *Nature* 330(6146), 370–372. https://doi.org/10.1038/330370a0

Roodt, D., 2021, 'Goeie nuus, net waar jy kyk', in *Netwerk 24: Ekonomie*, viewed 03 May 2021, from https://www.netwerk24.com/netwerk24/sake/ekonomie/dawie-roodt-goeie-nuus-net-waar-jy-kyk-20210430

Scialabba, N.E., 2007, 'Organic agriculture and food security in Africa', in *Proceedings: Can Africa Feed Itself*, Oslo, Norway, June 06–08, 2007, pp. 1–13.

Silva, G., 2018, 'Feeding the world in 2050 and beyond – Part 1: Productivity challenges', viewed 06 June 2020, from https://www.canr.msu.edu/news/feeding-the-world-in-2050-and-beyond-part-1.

Smith, P., Martino, D., Cai, Z., Gwary, D., Janzen, H., Kumar, P. et al., 2007, 'Agriculture', in B. Metz, O.R. Davidson, P.R. Bosch, R. Dave & L.A. Meyer (eds.), *Climate change 2007: Mitigation. Contribution of Working Group III to the Fourth Assessment Report of the Intergovernmental Panel on Climate Change*, Cambridge University Press, Cambridge.

Stam, J.M. & Dixon, B.L., 2004, *Farmer bankruptcies and farm exits in the United States, 1899–2002*. Agricultural Information Bulletins 33689, United States Department of Agriculture, Economic Research Service, s.l.

Stanton, T.L. & Whittier, J., 2006, *Nitrate poisoning*, viewed 19 May 2020, from https://extension.colostate.edu/topic-areas/agriculture/nitrate-poisoning-1-610/

StatsSA, 2013, *Census 2011: Agricultural households*, Statistics South Africa, Pretoria.

Stirzaker, R., Mbakwe, I. & Mziray, N.R., 2017, 'A soil water and solute learning system for small-scale irrigators in Africa', *International Journal of Water Resources Development* 33(5), 788–803. https://doi.org/10.1080/07900627.2017.1320981

Stirzaker, R.J., 2010, *Out of the scientist's garden: A story of water and food*, Australia CSIRO Publishing, Collingwood.

Stirzaker, R.J., 2014, 'A traffic light soil water sensor for resource poor farmers: Proof of concept', viewed 25 July 2017, from http://aciar.gov.au/files/aciar_traffic_light_final_report_sept_14_2_2.pdf.

Stokstad, E., 2019, 'Nitrogen crisis threatens Dutch environment – And economy', *SCIENCE* 366(6470), 1180–1181. https://doi.org/10.1126/science.366.6470.1180

Tsegay, Y., Rusare, M. & Mistry, R., 2014, *Hidden hunger in South Africa*, viewed 01 July 2021, from https://ciaotest.cc.columbia.edu/wps/oxfam/0032673/f_0032673_26567.pdf

Van Der Walt, S., 2020, 'Gemengde gevoelens oor ramphulp-aankondiging', *Netwerk 24*, viewed 06 June 2020, from https://www.netwerk24.com/Sake/Landbou/gemengde-gevoelens-oor-ramphulp-aankondiging-20200605.

Van Niekerk, A.S., 1992, *Sáám in Afrika*, Tafelberg, Cape Town.

Van Niekerk, C.E., 2008, *The vegetation and land use of a South African township in Hammanskraal*, University of Pretoria, Pretoria.

World Economic Forum, 2020, *The global risks report 2020*, viewed 16 June 2020, from http://www3.weforum.org/docs/WEF_Global_Risk_Report_2020.pdf.

World Wildlife Fund, 2016, *Water: Facts and futures. Rethinking South Africa's water future*, viewed 16 September 2020, from https://www.wwf.org.za/?25181/Water-Facts-and-Futures.

Chapter 5

Austin, J., Stevenson, H. & Wei-Skillern, J., 2006, 'Social and commercial entrepreneurship: Same, different, or both?', *Entrepreneurship Theory and Practice* 30(1), 1–22. https://doi.org/10.1111/j.1540-6520.2006.00107.x

Biennial Report of the Centre for Development Support (CDS), 2009/10, *Centre for Development Support, University of the Free State*, viewed 22 August 2021, from www.ufs.ac.za/cdsknowledgecentre.

Bloom, P.N., 2009, 'Overcoming consumption constraints through social entrepreneurship', *Journal of Public Policy and Marketing* 28(1), 128–134. https://doi.org/10.1509/jppm.28.1.128

Botes, L. & Abrahams, D., 2008, 'Noka e Tlatswa ke Dinokana – A river swells from little streams: Responsive partnership building approaches to development', in S. De Gruchy, N. Koopman & S. Strijbos (eds.), *From our side. Emerging perspectives on development and ethics*, Rozenberg Publishers, Amsterdam.

Bull, M., 2018, 'Reconceptualising social enterprise in the UK through an appreciation of legal entities', *International Journal of Entrepreneurial Behavior and Research* 24(3), 587–605. https://doi.org/10.1108/IJEBR-11-2017-0470

Bull, M. & Crompton, H., 2005, 'Business practices in social enterprises', *Social Enterprise Journal* 2(1), 42–60. https://doi.org/10.1108/17508610680000712

Business Trust and Department of Provincial and Local Government, 2007, *Nodal Economic Profiling Project – Maluti-a-Phofung*, Free State, Phuthadijhaba.

Choi, Y., Chang, S., Choi, J. & Seong, Y., 2018, 'The partnership network scopes of social enterprises and their social value creation', *International Journal of Entrepreneurship* 22(1), 1–21.

Corner, P.D. & Ho, M., 2010, 'How opportunities develop in social entrepreneurship', *Entrepreneurship Theory and Practice* 34(3), 636–659. https://doi.org/10.1111/j.1540-6520.2010.00382.x

Curtis, T., Herbst, J. & Gumkovska, M., 2010, 'The social economy of trust: Social entrepreneurship experiences in Poland', *Social Enterprise Journal* 6(3), 194–209. https://doi.org/10.1108/17508611011088805

Dacin, P.A., Dacin, M.T. & Matear, M., 2010, 'Social entrepreneurship: Why we don't need a new theory and how we move forward from here', *Academy of Management Perspectives* 24(3), 37–57. https://doi.org/10.5465/AMP.2010.52842950

Dees, J., 1998, 'Enterprising nonprofits', *Harvard Business Review* 76(1), 55–67.

Defourny, J. & Nyssens, M., 2010, 'Conceptions of social enterprise and social entrepreneurship in Europe and the United States: Convergences and divergences', *Journal of Social Entrepreneurship* 1(1), 32–53. https://doi.org/10.1080/19420670903442053

Doherty, B., Foster, G., Mason, C., Meehan, J., Rotheroe, N. & Royce, M., 2009, *Management of social enterprise*, Sage, London.

Edmondson, A., 2011, 'Strategies for learning from failure', *Harvard Business Review* 89(4), 48–55.

Fox, C., Inter-American Development Bank, Brakarz, J. & Cruz Fano, A., 2005, *Tripartite partnerships: Recognizing the third sector*, Inter-American Development Bank, Washington, DC.

Free State's Regional Steering Committee, 2010, 'Free state, self evaluation report', in *OECD reviews of higher education in regional and city development*, viewed 22 August 2021, from http://www.oecd.org/edu/imhe/regionaldevelopment.

Galera, G. & Borzaga, C., 2009, 'Social enterprise. An international overview of its conceptual evolution and legal implementation', *Social Enterprise Journal* 5(3), 210–228. https://doi.org/10.1108/17508610911004313

Googins, B.K. & Rochlin, S.A., 2000, 'Creating the partnership society: Understanding the rhetoric and reality of cross-sectoral partnerships', *Business and Society Review* 105(1), 127–144. https://doi.org/10.1111/0045-3609.00068

International Institute for Development and Ethics (IIDE), 2011, *Annual Report*, International Institute for Development and Ethics, Bloemfontein.

International Institute for Development and Ethics (IIDE), 2012, *Annual Report*, International Institute for Development and Ethics, Bloemfontein.

International Institute for Development and Ethics (IIDE), 2013, *Annual Report*, International Institute for Development and Ethics, Bloemfontein.

References

Isidiho, A.O., 2016, 'Evaluating the top-bottom and bottom-up community development approaches: Mixed method approach as alternative for rural un-educated communities in developing countries', *Mediterranean Journal of Social Sciences* 7(4), 266–273. https://doi.org/10.5901/mjss.2016.v7n4p266

Laksov, K.B. & McGrath, C., 2020, 'Failure as a catalyst for learning: Towards deliberate reflection in academic development work', *International Journal for Academic Development* 25(1), 1–4. https://doi.org/10.1080/1360144X.2020.1717783

Light, P.C., 2009, 'Social entrepreneurship revisited: Not just anyone, anywhere, in any organization can make breakthrough change', *Stanford Social Innovation Review* 21–22, viewed on 15 November 2021, from https://ssir.org/articles/entry/social_entrepreneurship_revisited.

Lister, S., 2000, 'Power in partnership? An analysis of an NGO's relationships with its partners', *Journal of International Development* 12(2), 227–239. https://doi.org/10.1002/(SICI)1099-1328(200003)12:2%3C227::AID-JID637%3E3.0.CO;2-U

Littlewood, D. & Holt, D., 2018, 'How social enterprises can contribute to the sustainable development goals (SDGs) – A conceptual framework. In Apostolopoulos, N., Al-Dajani, H., Holt, D., Jones, P. & Newbery, R.,(eds.). 2018. Entrepreneurship and the sustainable development goals', *Contemporary Issues in Entrepreneurship Research* 8, 33–46. https://doi.org/10.1108/S2040-724620180000008007

London, T. & Rondinelli, D., 2003, 'Partnerships for learning: Managing tensions in non-profit organisation' alliances with corporations', *Stanford Social Innovation Revue*, viewed on 15 November 2021, from https://ssir.org/articles/entry/partnerships_for_learning#.

Maase, S.J.F.M. & Bossink, B.A.G., 2010, 'Factors that inhibit partnering for social start-up enterprises', *Journal of Enterprising Communities: People and Places in the Global Economy* 4(1), 68–84. https://doi.org/10.1108/17506201011029519

Mair, J. & Marti, I., 2006, 'Social entrepreneurship research: A source of explanation, prediction, and delight', *Journal of World Business* 41(1), 36–44. https://doi.org/10.1016/j.jwb.2005.09.002

Mair, J. & Marti, I., 2009, 'Entrepreneurship in and around institutional voids: A case study from Bangladesh', *Journal of Business Venturing* 24(5), 419–435. https://doi.org/10.1016/j.jbusvent.2008.04.006

Maluti-a-Phofung local Municipality, 2010, *Integrated development plan 2010–2011*, Maluti-a-Phofung Local Municipality, Bethlehem.

Martin, R.L. & Osberg, S., 2007, 'Social entrepreneurship: The case for definition', *Stanford Social Innovation Review* 29–39, viewed 15 November 2021, from https://ssir.org/articles/entry/social_entrepreneurship_the_case_for_definition.

Massetti, B.L., 2008, 'The social entrepreneurship matrix as a "tipping point" for economic change', *Emergence: Complexity and Organization* 10(3), 1–8.

Mayer, R.C., Davis, J. & Schoorman, D., 1995, 'An integrative model of organisational trust', *Academy of Management Science* 20(3), 709–734. https://doi.org/10.5465/amr.1995.9508080335

Moahisane Development Fund (MDF), 2008a, *MDF funding agreement*, University of the Free State, Bloemfontein.

Moahisane Development Fund (MDF), 2008b, *Minutes of a meeting of the Moahisane Development Fund (MDF) supervisory board held on 5 August 2008 at Room 171*, Flippie Groenewoud Building, University of the Free State, Bloemfontein.

Moahisane Development Fund (MDF), 2009, *Moahisane Development Fund: Annual report, 1 January 2009 – 31 December 2009*, Unit for Entrepreneurship, University of the Free State, Bloemfontein.

Moahisane Development Fund (MDF), 2010, *Moahisane Development Fund: Annual report, 1 January 2010 – 31 December 2010*, Unit for Entrepreneurship, University of the Free State, Bloemfontein.

Moahisane Development Fund (MDF), 2011a, *Moahisane Development Fund and the future vision of the IIDE – March 2011*, International Institute for Ethics and Development (IIDE), Bloemfontein.

Moahisane Development Fund (MDF), 2011b, *Self-evaluation and lessons learnt. 15 July 2011*, Unit for Entrepreneurship, University of the Free State, Bloemfontein.

Moahisane Development Fund (MDF), 2011c, *Minutes of the Supervisory Board of the Moahisane Development Fund (MDF) meeting held on 10 March 2011, from 10:00 – 12:00 Room 362*, Flippie Groenewoud Building, University of the Free State, Bloemfontein.

Mohanan, M., 2017, 'The real development failure would be not knowing regret', in *Future development*, The Brookings Institute, Washington, DC.

Mohr, J. & Spekman, R., 1994, 'Characteristics of partnerships: partnership attributes, communication behaviour and conflict resolution techniques', *Strategic Management Journal* 15(2), 135–152. https://doi.org/10.1002/smj.4250150205

Morse, S. & McNamara, N., 2006, 'Analysing institutional partnerships in development: A contract between equals or a loaded process?', *Progress in Development Studies* 6(4), 321–336. https://doi.org/10.1191/1464993406ps146oa

Nicholls, A., 2010, 'The legitimacy of social entrepreneurship: Reflexive isomorphism in a pre-paradigmatic field', *Entrepreneurship Theory and Practice* 34(4), 611–633. https://doi.org/10.1111/j.1540-6520.2010.00397.x

Park, J., Hwang, K. & Kim, S., 2018, 'We are forming a social partnership between a small enterprise and a large corporation: A case of the joint platform, H-JUMP', *Sustainability* 10(10), 3612. https://doi.org/10.3390/su10103612

Peredo, A.M. & McLean, M., 2006, 'Social entrepreneurship: A critical review of the concept', *Journal of World Business* 41(1), 56–65. https://doi.org/10.1016/j.jwb.2005.10.007

Persaud, R., Dixon, J. & Thorlby, K., 2017, *Exploring: Social entrepreneurs and failure*, viewed n.d., from https://www.unltd.org.uk/our-work/research/exploring-social-entrepreneurs-and-failure.

Republic of South Africa (RSA), 2005, *National Credit Act, No. 34 of 2005*, Government Printers, Pretoria.

Republic of South Africa (RSA), 2008, *Consumer Protection Act, No. 68 of 2008*, Government Printers, Pretoria.

Saebi, T., Foss, N.J. & Linder, S., 2018, 'Social entrepreneurship research: Past achievements and future promises', *Journal of Management* 45(1), 70–95. https://doi.org/10.1177/0149206318793196

Sako, M., 1992, *Prices quality and trust: Buyer-supplier relationships in Britain and Japan*, Cambridge University Press, Cambridge.

Seitanidi, M.M. & Crane, A., 2009, 'Implementing CSR through partnerships: Understanding the selection, design and institutionalization of non-profit-business partnerships', *Journal of Business Ethics* 85(2), 413–429. https://doi.org/10.1007/s10551-008-9743-y

Short, J.C., Moss, T.W. & Lumpkin, G.T., 2009, 'Research in social entrepreneurship: Past contributions and future opportunities', *Strategic Entrepreneurship Journal* 3(2), 161–194. https://doi.org/10.1002/sej.69

Social Innovation eXchange (SIX), 2020, *Co-creation guide realising social innovation together*, viewed 15 November 2021, from https://socialinnovationexchange.org/sites/default/files/uploads/co-creation_guide.pdf.

Sonenshine, J., 2018, 'Partnership in social enterprise: How to find the right partners and further your impact', *Social Enterprise Alliance*, viewed on 15 November 2021, from https://medium.com/social-enterprise-alliance/partnership-in-social-enterprise-how-to-find-the-right-partners-and-further-your-impact-f7a68c04d282.

Stibbe, D., & Prescott, D., 2020, 'The SDG partnership Guidebook. A practical guide to building high impact multi-stakeholder partnerships for Sustainable Development Goals', viewed 12 November 2021, from https://www.thepartneringinitiative.org/wp-content/uploads/2020/07/SDG-Partnership-Guidebook-1.0.pdf.

Strijbos, S., 2012, 'The inclusion of "culture and religion" in development: Beyond the technical-instrumental and participative-communicative approach', in J. Van der Stoep & S. Strijbos (eds.), *From technology . transfer to intercultural development: Understanding technology and development in a globalizing world*, pp. 143–155, Rozenberg Publishers, Amsterdam.

References

Sud, M., Sandt, C.V. & Baugous, A.M., 2009, 'Social entrepreneurship: The role of institutions', *Journal of Business Ethics* 85(1), 201–216. https://doi.org/10.1007/s10551-008-9939-1

Thabo Mofutsanyane District Municipality, 2010, *Integrated development plan 2010–2011*, Thabo Mofutsanyane District Municipality, Harrismith.

United States Agency for International Development (USAID), 1997, *Partnering with USAID: A guide for companies*, viewed on 15 November 2021, from https://www.usaid.gov/sites/default/files/documents/1880/Partnering_Guide_Updated2012.pdf.

The Global Goals for Sustainable Development, 2021, *17 Partnerships for the goals. Encourage effective partnerships*, viewed on 15 November 2021, from https://www.globalgoals.org/17-partnerships-for-the-goals.

University of the Free State, 2006, *Community service policy of the University of the Free State*, viewed 15 November 2021, from https://www.ufs.ac.za/docs/default-source/all-documents/community-service-policy-107-eng.pdf?sfvrsn=e23e421_0.

University of the Free State, 2020, *Engaged scholarship*, viewed 15 November 2021, from https://www.ufs.ac.za/supportservices/departments/community-engagement-home/community-engagement-at-the-ufs/engaged-scholarship.

Urban, B., 2008, 'Social entrepreneurship in South Africa. Delineating the construct with associated skills', *International Journal of Entrepreneurial Behaviour and Research* 14(5), 346–364. https://doi.org/10.1108/13552550810897696

Vujasinović, P., Lipenkova, S. & Orlando, E., 2019, 'The role of social entrepreneurship as a key driver of the Agenda 2030', viewed 15 November 2021 from http://www.ra-un.org/uploads/4/7/5/4/47544571/6_unido_the_role_of_social_entrepreneurship_as_a_key_driver_of_the_agenda_2030.pdf

Waddock, S.A., 1989, 'Understanding social partnerships: An evolutionary model of partnership organizations', *Administration Society* 21(1), 78–100. https://doi.org/10.1177/009539978902100105

Wangsirilrt, C. & Simon, L., 2017, 'How large-scale companies and social enterprises improve the sustainability of their partnership? The case study of IKEA and Doi Tung Social Enterprise in Thailand', Master's thesis, KTH Industrial Engineering and Management Industrial Management, Stockholm.

World Bank, 2015, *The millennium development goals*, viewed on 15 November2021, from https://www5.worldbank.org/mdgs/global_partnership.html.

Zahra, S.A., Rawhouser, H.N., Bhawe, N., Neubaum, D.O. & Hayton, J.C., 2008, 'Globalization of social entrepreneurship opportunities', *Strategic Entrepreneurship Journal* 2(2), 117–131. https://doi.org/10.1002/sej.43

Zahra, S.A. & Wright, M., 2016, 'Understanding the social role of entrepreneurship', *Journal of Management Studies* 53(4), 610–629. https://doi.org/10.1111/joms.12149

Zahra, S.E., Gedajlovic, E., Neubaum, D.O. & Shulman, J.M., 2009, 'A typology of social entrepreneurs: Motives, search processes and ethical challenges', *Journal of Business Venturing* 24(5), 519–532. https://doi.org/10.1016/j.jbusvent.2008.04.007

Chapter 6

Bartholomew, C.G., 2011, *Where mortals dwell. A Christian view of place for today*, Baker Academic, Grand Rapids, MI.

Bridge, G. & Watson, S., 2011, *The New Blackwell companion to the city*, Wiley-Blackwell, Malden, MA.

Castells, M., 1996, *The rise of the network society*, Blackwell Publishing Ltd, Malden, MA.

De Hek, W.J., 2017a, 'Strolling through Mokum: The dynamics of place, sacredness and souls of Amsterdam', Master's thesis, Protestant Theological University Amsterdam.

De Hek, W.J., 2017b, 'Place-making in Mokum. Searching for the Souls of Amsterdam', presentation at World Congress International Union of Architects, Seoul, South Korea, 05 September.

De Hek, W.J., 2021, 'Holy Mokum. A case study: The dynamics of sacred place at Kastanjeplein, Amsterdam', in P.B. Hartog, S. Laderman, V. Tohar & A.L.H.M. Van Wieringen (eds.), *Jerusalem and other holy places as Foci of multireligious and ideological confrontation*, vol. 37, Jewish and Christian Perspectives Series, Brill, Leiden.

Durkheim, É., [1912] 1995, *The elementary forms of religious life*, transl. K.E. Fields, The Free Press, New York, NY.

Graham, E. & Lowe, S., 2009, *What makes a good city? Public theology and the urban church*, Darton, Longman and Todd Ltd., London.

Google Maps, n.d.a, *Park Frankendael*, viewed n.d., from https://www.google.co.za/maps/place/Park+Frankendael/@52.3511869,4.9297105,287m/data=!3m2!1e3!4b1!4m5!3m4!1s0x47c6097b401785b3:0x8608fe3c45219b6e!8m2!3d52.3511853!4d4.9308048.

Google Maps, n.d.b, *Hofkerk*, viewed n.d., from https://www.google.co.za/maps/place/Hofkerk+Amsterdam/@52.3530673,4.9314742,575m/data=!3m2!1e3!4b1!4m5!3m4!1s0x47c6096549f98155:0x841cf5df9be21c16!8m2!3d52.3530897!4d4.9336631.

Google Maps, n.d.c, *De Nieuwe Ooster*, viewed n.d., from https://www.google.co.za/maps/place/De+Nieuwe+Ooster/@52.3456599,4.9366513,575m/data=!3m2!1e3!4b1!4m5!3m4!1s0x47c6096198dae171:0x1ca4112db40d29f5!8m2!3d52.3456566!4d4.93884.

Google Maps, n.d.d, *Oude Kerk*, viewed n.d., from https://www.google.co.za/maps/place/The+Oude+Church/@52.3743704,4.896018,575m/data=!3m2!1e3!4b1!4m5!3m4!1s0x47c609b8f3e17d2f:0x5e5932b26345ed22!8m2!3d52.3743671!4d4.8982067.

Hill, A., 2011, 'The city, the psyche, and the visibility of religious spaces', in G. Bridge & S. Watson (eds.), *The New Blackwell companion to the city*, pp. 367–375, Wiley-Blackwell, Malden, MA.

Inge, J., 2003, *A Christian theology of place*, Ashgate Publishing Limited, Surrey.

Kotkin, J., 2006, *The city: A global history*, Random House, New York, NY.

Kruizinga, J., 1995, *Het XYZ van Amsterdam*, Amsterdam Publishers, Amsterdam.

Rae, M.A., 2017, *Architecture and theology. The art of place*, Baylor University Press, Waco, TX.

Ratzinger, J., 2014, *Theology of the liturgy. Collected works*, Vol. II, Ignatius Press, San Francisco, CA.

Sheldrake, P., 2014, *The spiritual city: Theology, spirituality, and the urban*, Wiley Blackwell, Chichester, West Sussex.

Tweed, T., [2006] 2008, *Crossing and dwelling. A theory of religion*, paperback edn., First Harvard University Press, Cambridge, MA.

Youn, C.-H., 2018, 'Missio Dei Trinitatis and Missio Ecclesiae: A public theological perspective', *International Review of Mission* 107(1), 225–239. https://doi.org/10.1111/irom.12219

Zumthor, P. & Lending, M., 2018, *A feeling of history*, Scheidegger & Spies, Zurich.

Chapter 7

Deleuze, G. & Guattari, F., 1987, *A thousand plateaus: Capitalism and Schizophrenia*, University of Minnesota Press, Minneapolis, MN.

Foster, J.B. & Clark, B., 2004, 'Ecological imperialism: The curse of capitalism', *Socialist Register* 40(40), 186–201.

Graeber, D., 2001, *Toward an anthropological theory of value*, Palgrave, New York, NY.

Hart, G., 2016, 'Relational comparison revisited: Marxist postcolonial geographies in practice', *Progress in Human Geography* 42(3), 371–394. https://doi.org/10.1177/0309132516681388

Hart, G., 2006, 'Denaturalizing Dispossession: Critical Ethnography in the Age of Resurgent Imperialism', *Antipode* n.v., 977–1004.

Ingold, T., 2000, *The perception of the environment: Essays on livelihood, dwelling and skill*, Routledge, London.

Ingold, T., 2010, 'Bringing things to life: Creative entanglements in a world of materials', *Realities* 15, 1–14.

Lefebvre, H., 1974, *The production of space*, Wiley-Blackwell, London.

Max-Neef, M., 2005, 'Foundations of transdisciplinarity', *Ecological Economics* 53(1), 5–16. https://doi.org/10.1016/j.ecolecon.2005.01.014

Monbiot, G., 2013, *The Market is no friend to Nature*, viewed n.d., from https://mg.co.za/article/2013-04-26-the-market-is-no-friend-to-nature.

Reyneke, P., 2017, 'Dumpsite Bricolage: The responses of the urban waste precariat to the formalisation and privatisation of waste management in the City of Tshwane', Unpublished Master's Thesis, University of Pretoria.

Rollins, P.C., 2011, *Insurrection: The believe is human, to doubt, devine*, Howard Books, New York, NY.

Russell, B., 2011, *Research methods in anthropology: Qualitative and quantitative approaches*, 5th edn., AltaMira Press, Blue Ridge Summit, PA.

Schmalz, D.L., Janke, M.C. & Payne, L.L., 2019, 'Multi-, inter-, and transdisciplinary research: Leisure studies past, present, and future', *Journal of Leisure Research* 50(5), 389–393. https://doi.org/10.1080/00222216.2019.1647751

Schoeman, W., 2020, 'Re-imagining the congregation's calling – Moving from isolation to involvement', *Acta Theologica* 40(2), 321–341. https://doi.org/10.18820/23099089/actat.v40i2.17

UNFCCC, 2014, *Kyoto protocol: Mechanisms: Clean development mechanism*, viewed 12 September 2016, from http://unfccc.int/kyoto_protocol/mechanisms/clean_development_mechanism/items/2718.php.

Wolf, E., 1982, *Europe and the people without history*, 2nd edn., University of California Press, Berkley, CA.

World Health Organisation, 2018, *Household air pollution and health*, viewed 15 October 2020, from https://www.who.int/news-room/fact-sheets/detail/household-air-pollution-and-health.

Chapter 8

BusinessTech, 2020, *Municipalities owe Eskom R46.1 billion as Gordhan lists worst offenders*, viewed 16 November 2021 from https://businesstech.co.za/news/energy/446130/municipalities-owe-eskom-r46-1-billion-as-gordhan-lists-worst-offenders.

Du Preez, P., 2018, 'On decolonization and internationalisation of university curricula: What can we learn from Rosi Braidotti?', *Journal of Education* 74, 19–31. https://doi.org/10.17159/2520-9868/i74a02

ECSA, 2012, *E-01-P. Background to accreditation of engineering education programmes*, rev. 2nd edn., Engineering Council of South Africa, Johannesburg.

ECSA, 2014, *E-02_P. Qualification standard for Bachelor of Science in Engineering*, Engineering Council of South Africa, Johannesburg.

ECSA, 2017, *E-10_P. Policy on the accreditation of engineering programmes meeting stage 1 Requirements*, Engineering Council of South Africa, Johannesburg.

EWB, n.d., *Engineering for people design challenge*, viewed 16 November 2021 from https://www.ewb-uk.org/upskill/design-challenges/engineering-for-people-design-challenge.

Felder, R.M. & Brent, R., 2003, 'Learning by doing', *Chemical Engineering Education* 37(4), 282–283.

Fomunyam, K.G., 2017, 'Decolonising teaching and learning in engineering education in a South African university', *International Journal of Applied Engineering Research* 12(23), 13349–13358.

Froyd, J.E., Wankat, P.C. & Smith, K.A., 2012, 'Five major shifts in 100 years of engineering education', *Proceedings of the IEEE* 100(Special Centennial Issue), 1344–1360. https://doi.org/10.1109/jproc.2012.2190167

Grosfoguel, R., 2011, 'Decolonizing post-colonial studies and paradigms of political-economy: Transmodernity, decolonial thinking, and global coloniality', *Transmodernity: Journal of*

Peripheral Cultural Production of the Luso-Hispanic World 1(1), 10–38. https://doi.org/10.5070/T411000004

Hansson, S.O., 2007, 'What is technological science?', *Studies In History and Philosophy of Science Part A* 38(3), 523–527. https://doi.org/10.1016/j.shpsa.2007.06.003

Harari, Y.N., 2014, 'Sapiens: A brief history of humankind', Signal/McClelland & Steward, Toronto.

Houkes, W., 2009, 'The nature of technological knowledge', in A. Meijers (ed.), *Handbook of the philosophy of science: Philosophy of technology and engineering sciences*, vol. 9, Elsevier, Amsterdam.

Jansen, J., 2018, *The problem with decolonization*, viewed n.d., from https://www.youtube.com/watch?v=BFZdQAb80Ww.

Jonassen, D., Strobel, J. & Lee, C.B., 2006, 'Everyday problem solving in engineering: Lessons for engineering educators', *Journal of Engineering Education* 95(2), 139–151. https://doi.org/10.1002/j.2168-9830.2006.tb00885.x

MacKenzie, D. & Wajcman, J. (eds.), 1999, *The social shaping of technology*, 2nd edn., Open University Press, Philadelphia, PA.

Morgan, A.J., 1992, 'The importance of the electrification drive', paper presented at the Electricity for Development Research Forum, Midrand, South Africa, May.

Muller, M., 2018, 'Decolonising engineering in South Africa – Experience to date and some emerging challenges', *South African Journal of Science* 114(5/6), 1–6. https://doi.org/10.17159/sajs.2018/

Newbigin, L., 1961, *A faith for this one world?*, SCM Press, London.

Nguyen, D.Q., 1998, 'The essential skills and attributes of an engineer: A comparative study of academics, industry personnel and engineering students', *Global Journal of Engineering Education* 2(1), 65–75.

North-West University (NWU), 2018, *North-West University's declaration on the decolonisation of university education: The imperative to transform teaching and learning, the research agenda and community engagement*, North-West University, Potchefstroom.

Oelofsen, R., 2015, 'Decolonization of the African mind and intellectual landscape', *Pronimon* 16(2), 130–146. https://doi.org/10.25159/2413-3086/3822

Pellegrino, J.W., 2006, 'Rethinking and redesigning curriculum instruction and assessment: What contemporary research and theory suggests', *National Center on Education and the Economy*, Washington, DC.

Plougmann, L., 2006, *Zheng He's ship compared to Columbus's*, viewed 16 November 2021, from https://www.flickr.com/photos/criminalintent/361639903.

Redish, F.E. & Smith, K.A., 2008, 'Looking beyond content: Skill development for engineers', *Journal of Engineering Education* 97(3), 295–307. https://doi.org/10.1002/j.2168-9830.2008.tb00980.x

Roy, D.B., 2018, 'Time to decolonise science – Time to end another imperial era', *The Conversation*, 05 April 2018.

Samuels, S., 2014, 'Owld project under scrutiny', *Sandton Chronicle*, 14 October 2014, viewed 16 November 2021, from https://sandtonchronicle.co.za/103695/owl-project-under-scrutiny/.

Seering, W., 2016, *Design science – Seminar series* viewed n.d., from https://www.youtube.com/watch?v=_CNLBbtPmBc.

Steen, M., 2012, 'Human-centered design as a fragile encounter', *Design Issues* 28(1), 72–80. https://doi.org/10.1162/DESI_a_00125

Tucker, B. & Scott, B.R. (eds.), 1992, *South Africa: Prospects for successful transition*, Juta, Cape Town.

Whimbey, A., Lochhead, J. & Narode, R., 2013, *Problem solving and comprehension*, 7th edn., Routledge, New York, NY.

Winberg, S. & Winberg, C., 2017, 'Using a social justice approach to decolonize an engineering curriculum', paper presented at the IEEE Global Engineering Education Conference, Athens, Greece, 25–28 April.

References

Wyden, P.H., 1984, *Day one: Before Hiroshima and after*, Simon and Schuster, New York, NY.

Ziman, J., 1994, *An introduction to science studies*, Cambridge University Press, New York, NY.

Chapter 9

Bakole wa Ilunga, 1978, *Le chemin de liberation*, Archidiocese de Kananga, Kananga.

Baron, E., 2017, 'The role of church youth in the transformation agenda of South African cities', *HTS Teologiese Studies/Theological Studies* 73(3), a4771. https://doi.org/10.4102/hts.v73i3.4771

Burchert, L.T. & Winter, S., 2015, *Value change in post-apartheid South Africa*, viewed 08 August 2020, from www.kas.de/suedafrika/en/.

Brueggemann, W., 2002, *The land: Place as gift, promise, and challenge in biblical faith*, 2nd edn., Fortress Press, Minneapolis, MN.

Chikane, F., 2013, *The things that could not be said. From Aids to Zimbabwe*, Picador Africa, Johannesburg.

Codrington, G.T., 2000, 'Multi-generational ministries in the context of the local church', Unpublished Master's Dissertation, University of South Africa.

Corbett, S. & Fikkert, B., 2009, *When helping hurts: How to alleviate poverty without hurting the poor... and yourself*, Moody Publishers, Chicago, IL.

Cloete, A., 2019, 'Youth unemployment in South Africa. A theological reflection through the lens of human dignity', *Missionalia* 43(3), 513–525.

De Beer, S.F., 2020, *Urban Africa 2050: Imagining theological education/formation for flourishing African cities*, Unpublished draft, s.n., s.l.

DG Murray Foundation, 2020, *An education system in crisis*, viewed 23 April 2020, from www.dgmt.co.za.

Diop, C.A., 1964, 'Evolution of the Negro world', *Présence Africaine* 23(51), 5–15. https://doi.org/10.3917/presa.051.0097

Donovan, V.J., 2005, *Christianity rediscovered*, 25th Anniversary edn., Orbis Books, New York, NY.

Green, G.P. & Haines, A., 2012, *Asset building & community development*, 3rd edn., Sage, Los Angeles, CA.

Gratton, L. & Scott, A., 2016, *The 100-year life: Living and working in an age of longevity*, Bloomsbury Publishing, London.

Hayes, J.B., 2006, *Sub-merge. Living deep in a shallow world: Service, justice and contemplation among the world's poor*, Ventura, Regal.

Huckins, J. & Yackley, R., 2012, *Thin Places. 6 Postures for creating & practising missional community*, The House Studio, Kansas City.

Iheanacho, V.U., 2020, 'Oscar Romero (1917–1980): A model of pastoral leadership for church leaders in Africa', *HTS Teologiese Studies/Theological Studies* 76(2), a5849. https://doi.org/10.4102/hts.v76i2.5849

James, G., 2018, 'Releasing higher education from its elitist captivity: The change agency of Unisa's Chance 2 Advance programme', *HTS Teologiese Studies/Theological Studies* 74(3), a5045. https://doi.org/10.4102/hts.v74i3.5045

Kabongo, K.T.L., 2019, 'From victimhood to hubs of (trans)formation and local agency: Re-imagining poor urban communities', *Verbum et Ecclesia* 40(1), a1998. https://doi.org/10.4102/ve.v40i1.1998

Kabongo, K.T.L., 2020a, 'A partnership for prosperity agency: A case study of InnerCHANGE South Africa', *Theologia Viatorum* 44(1), a48. https://doi.org/10.4102/TV.v44i1.48

Kabongo, K.T.L., 2020b, 'Africanisation of theological education: An exploration of a hybrid epistemology', *HTS Teologiese Studies/Theological Studies* 76(4), a5911. https://doi.org/10.4102/hts.v76i4.591

Ki Zerbo, J., 2005, *A quando l'Africa*, EMI, Bologne.

Klein, J.T., 2001, 'The discourse of transdisciplinarity: An expanding global field', in Haberli, R. et al. (eds.), *Transdisciplinarity: Joint problem solving among science, technology and society*, pp. 35–44, Basel, Birkhauser.

Kraybill, D.B., 1990, *The upside-down kingdom*, rev. edn., Herald Press, Scottdale, PA.

Linthicum, R.C., 2003, *Transforming power: Biblical strategies for making a difference in your community*, Intervarsity Press, Downers Grove, IL.

Lwamba, L.F., 2017, *La pensee du philosophe Ka Mana. Redynamiser l'imaginaire African*, L'Harmattan, Paris.

Maluleke, T., 2019, 'Tutu in memory, Tutu on Memory. Strategies on remembering', *Missionalia* 47(2), 177–192.

Mandela, N.R., 1995, *Long walk to freedom*, Backbay Books, Boston, MA.

Mangayi, L.C., 2018, 'Township churches of Tshwane as potential change agents for local economic development: An empirical missiological study', *HTS Teologiese Studies/Theological Studies* 74(3), 4964. https://doi.org/10.4102/hts.v74i3.4964

Maathai, W., 2009, *The challenge for Africa. A new vision*, William Heinemann, London.

Mbeki, T., 2007, 'Steve Biko: 30 years after', in C. Van Wyk (ed.), *We write what we like. Celebrating Steve Biko*, pp. 21–40, Wits University Press, Johannesburg.

Osafo-Kwaako, P. & Robinson, J.A., 2013, 'Political centralization in pre-colonial Africa', *Journal of Comparative Economics* 41(1), 6–21. https://doi.org/10.1016/j.jce.2013.01.003

Perkins, J.M., 2014, *Let Justice roll down*, BakerBooks, Grand Rapids, MI.

Rabe, M., 2018, 'A care deficit? The roles of families and faith-based organisations in the lives of youth at the margins in Pretoria Central', *HTS Teologiese Studies/Theological Studies* 74(3), 5005. https://doi.org/10.4102/hts.v74i3.5005

Ramphele, M., 2017, *Dreams, betrayal and hope*, Penguin, Cape Town.

Sacks, J., 2018, *'The birth of hope'. In covenant and conversation*, 3rd edn., The Maurice Wohl Charitable Foundation, London.

Spear, T., 2003, 'Neo-traditionalism and the limits of invention in British colonial Africa', *The Journal of African History* 44(1), 3–27. https://doi.org/10.1017/S0021853702008320

Statistics South Africa, 2020, *Men, women and children. Findings of the living conditions survey, 2014/15*, viewed 11 July 2020, from http://www.statssa.gov.za/publications/.

Swart, J., Hagley, S., Ogren, J. & Love, M., 2009, 'Toward a missional theology of participation: Ecumenical reflections on contributions to Trinity, mission, and church', *Missiology* 37(1), 75–87. https://doi.org/10.1177/009182960903700109

Sultana, A., 2010, 'Patriarchy and women's gender identity: A sociocultural perspective', *Journal of Social Science* 6(1), 123–126. https://doi.org/10.3844/jssp.2010.123.126

Tlhabi, R., 2017, *Khwezi. The remarkable story of Fezekile Ntsukela Kuzwayo*, Jonathan Ball Publishers, Johannesburg.

Tutu, D.M., 1999, *No future without forgiveness*, Doubleday, New York, NY.

Tshwane Municipality, 2020, *Soshanguve*, viewed 09 January 2020, from www.Tshwane.org.za.

Van Niekerk, A.S., 2015, *Guidelines for visits to households GSW 310 and 314*, Unpublished paper, University of Pretoria, Pretoria.

Chapter 10

Allenby, B.R., 2002, 'Earth systems engineering and management', in R.U. Ayres & L.W. Ayres (eds.), *A handbook of industrial ecology,* pp. 566–571, Edward Elgar, Cheltenham.

Allenby, B.R., 2003, 'The anthropogenic earth: Integrating and reifying technology, environmentalism, and religion', *The Princeton Seminary Bulletin* 24(1), 104–121.

Allenby, B.R., 2005, *Reconstructing earth: Technology and environment in the age of humans*, Island Press, Washington, Covelo, London.

References

Allenby, B.R., 2007, 'From human to transhuman: Technology and the reconstruction of the world', Templeton Research Lecture, Arizona State University, Tempe, AZ, 22 October.

Allenby, B.R., 2012, *The theory and practice of sustainable engineering*, Prentice Hall, Pearson Education, Essex.

Allenby, B.R. & Sarewitz, D., 2013, *The techno-human condition*, The MIT Press, Cambridge, MA.

Australian Government, 2018, 'Tackling wicked problems : A public policy perspective', viewed n.d., from https://legacy.apsc.gov.au/tackling-wicked-problems-public-policy-perspective.

Buchanan, R., 2009, 'Thinking about design: A historical perspective', in A. Meyers (ed.), *Philosophy of technology and engineering sciences,* vol. 9, pp. 409–453, Elsevier, Boston, MA.

Cabrera, D. & Cabrera, L., 2015, *Systems thinking made simple: New hope for solving wicked problems*, Odyssean Press, Ithaca, NY.

Cambré, B., Marynissen, H., Van Hootegem, G. *Corona is mean. It's a wicked problem*, viewed n.d., from https://blog.antwerpmanagementschool.be/en/corona-is-a-wicked-problem.

Churchman, C.W., 1967, 'Wicked problems', *Management Science* 14(4), B141–B142.

Churchman, C.W., 1968, *Challenge to reason*, Mc Graw-Hill, New York, NY.

Churchman, C.W., Protzen, J.-P. & Webber, M.M., 2007, 'In Memoriam: Horst W.J. Rittel', *Design Issues* 23(4), 89–91.

Conradie, E.M., 2017, *Redeeming sin? Social diagnostics amid ecological destruction,* Lexington Books, Lanham, MD.

DeWitt, C.B., 2003, 'Science, theology and technological responsible praxis within the ecological order', *The Princeton Seminary Bulletin* 24(1), 55–83.

Eriksson, D., 2005, 'The epistemo-ethical challenge of systems thinking', in A. Helberg, J. Van der Stoep & S. Strijbos (eds.), *Towards humane leadership*, Proceedings of the 11th Annual Working Conference of CPTS, CPTS, Maarssen, Netherlands, April, 05–08, 2005, pp. 67–74.

Frodeman, R., 2014, *Sustainable knowledge: A theory of interdisciplinarity*, Palgrave Macmillan, New York, NY.

Gray, J., 2003, *Al Quada and what it means to be modern*, Faber and Faber, London.

Helm, P., 2006, *John Calvin's ideas*, Oxford University Press, Oxford.

Jenkins, W., 2013, *The future of ethics: Sustainability, social justice, and religious creativity*, Georgetown University Press, Washington, DC.

Luther, M., 1999, *Luther's works, vol. 45: The Christian in society II*, in J.J. Pelikan, H.C. Oswald & H.T. Lehmann (eds.), vol. 45, p. 311, Fortress Press, Philadelphia, PA.

Mulder, K., 2004, 'Guest editorial', *International Journal of Sustainability in Higher Education* 5(3), 237–238. https://doi.org/10.1108/ijshe.2004.24905caa.001

Mulder, K. (ed.), 2006, *Sustainable development for engineers: A handbook and resource guide*, Greenleaf, Sheffield.

Neiman, S., 2002/2015, *Evil in modern thought: An alternative history of philosophy*, Princeton University Press, Princeton, NJ.

Neiman, S., 2008, *Moral clarity: A guide for grown-up idealists*, Harcourt Inc., Orlando, FL.

Rittel, H., [1972] 1984, 'Second-generation design methods', in N. Cross (ed.), *Developments in design methodology*, pp. 317–327, John Wiley & Sons, Chicester.

Rittel, H., 1972b, 'On the planning crisis: Systems analysis of the "first and second generations"', *Bedriftsøkonomen* 8, 390–396.

Rittel, H. & Webber, M., 1973, 'Dilemmas in a general theory of planning', *Policy Sciences* 4(2), 155–169. https://doi.org/10.1007/BF01405730

Simon, H.A., 1996, *The sciences of the artificial*, 3rd edn., The MIT Press, Cambridge, MA.

Stackhouse, M.L., 1998, 'Public theology and ethical judgment', *Theology Today* 54(2), 165–179. https://doi.org/10.1177/004057369705400203

Steffen, W., Grinevald, J., Crutzen, P. & McNeill, J., 2011, 'The anthropocene: Conceptual and historical perspectives', *Philosophical Transactions of the Royal Society A* 369, 842-867. https://doi.org/10.1098/rsta.2010.0327

Strijbos, S., n.d., *Can we really improve the world? Some thoughts on bible, science, and technology*, Three unpublished lectures.

Strijbos, S., 2003, 'Systems thinking and the disclosure of a technological society: Some philosophical reflections', *Systems Research and Behavioral Science* 20(s), 119-131. https://doi.org/10.1002/sres.534

Strijbos, S., 2014, 'Introduction', in M. Rathbone, F. Von Schéele & S. Strijbos (eds.), *Social change in our technology-based world*, Proceedings of the 19th Annual Working Conference of the IIDE, Rozenberg, Amsterdam, May 06-09, 2014, pp. 5-11.

Strijbos, S., 2017, 'Systems thinking', in R. Frodeman, J. Thompson & C.S. Pacheco (eds.), *The Oxford handbook of interdisciplinarity*, Revised 2nd edn., pp. 291-302, Oxford University Press, Oxford, UK.

Strijbos, S. & Basden, A. (eds.), 2006, *In search of an integrative vision for technology: Interdisciplinary studies in information systems*, Springer, New York, NY.

Strijbos, S. & Van der Stoep, J. (eds.), 2011, *From technology transfer to intercultural development: Understanding technology and development in a globalizing world*, Rozenberg, Amsterdam.

Ten Bos, R., 2017, Dwalen in het anthropoceen, Boom, Amsterdam.

Ulrich, W., 2002, 'An appreciation of C. West Churchman', viewed n.d., from http://geocities.com/csh_home/cwc_appreciation.html.

Ulrich, W., 2004, 'In memory of C. West Churchman (1913-2004): Reminiscences, retrospectives, and reflections', Journal of Organisational Transformation and Social Change 1(2-3), 199-219. https://doi.org/10.1386/jots.1.2.199/0

Van Riessen, H., 1979, 'The structure of technology [1961], Translated by Herbert Donald Morton', in P.T. Durbin & C. Mitcham (eds.), Research in philosophy and technology, vol. 2, pp. 296-313, JAI Press, Greenwich, CT.

Index

A

academic performance, 176
accountability, 48, 95, 113
Accounting, 75, 106
Africa, 13-35, 51-58, 60-62, 64, 66, 68-70, 72-73, 78, 80-85, 87, 91, 93-95, 98-100, 102, 104, 108, 112, 119, 139, 145, 147-149, 151, 154-156, 158-159, 162-163, 166-167, 169-174, 179-181, 187
African communities, 167, 177, 183
African, 14-16, 18, 21-29, 31-33, 54, 56, 58-59, 69, 72, 76, 82, 84-85, 87-88, 90, 99-100, 108, 140, 147, 150, 158, 160, 167-172, 177-181, 183
Africanisation, 27
Afrocentric, 28
Amsterdam, 39, 46, 119-124, 127, 134-136
anthropocene, 187-190, 195-197, 199-200, 202, 204
architecture, 119, 121-122, 128, 132, 136, 191
authenticity, 125

B

benefits, 77, 86, 88, 95-96, 115
Bible, 171, 206
business, 17, 23, 36, 40-47, 93-94, 96-102, 104-105, 107-108, 112, 115, 148, 163, 191

C

capitalism, 40-41, 44-45, 47, 145-146, 198
Christianity, 14-15, 30, 147, 171, 194, 202
circular economies, 77, 86
coal use practices, 51-54, 56, 58, 60, 62, 64, 66, 68, 70, 72
co-creation, 140, 149, 153-154, 176
collective, 169-170, 176
colonial mindset, 164
colonisation, 143, 158, 164-166, 168-169
communication, 43, 96, 158
community, 13-15, 18, 20, 28-29, 31-32, 35, 38, 43, 48, 58, 66-68, 73, 90, 99, 101-102, 104-105, 107, 111-113, 115-116, 119-121, 123, 125, 128, 131, 140-142, 146-155, 157, 165-166, 168-169, 171-179, 181-185, 187
concept, 23, 37, 45, 67, 75-76, 80, 88, 90, 94, 101, 110-112, 114, 118, 133, 144-148, 152-153, 174, 189-190, 192-197
connection, 18, 28, 130-131, 148, 178, 189, 200, 202
context, 17-19, 26, 29, 32-33, 66, 70, 95, 120-121, 133-134, 143-145, 147-151, 157-160, 164-165, 169, 171-174, 176, 178, 181-183, 185, 188, 192, 195, 197, 203
contexts, 14, 17-18, 32-33, 56, 121, 130, 144, 157, 169, 182
contextualisation, 32
conversation, 35, 121, 140, 144, 166, 190, 201
corruption, 14, 23, 33, 171, 173, 200
cultural changes, 74, 88

D

data, 19, 43, 58, 77, 80, 122, 124, 150, 159, 161
decolonisation, 24, 27, 155-159, 161, 164-165
decolonising, 155-156, 158, 160, 162, 164-166
deliberate reflection, 118
design, 18, 53, 90, 116, 119, 152, 158-162, 164-166, 190-192, 194, 197, 199, 203
developing countries, 42-43, 73, 80
disclosure of society, 35-36, 38, 40, 42, 44, 46, 48

E

economic growth, 16-18, 30, 78
economy, 15-20, 22, 35-38, 40-44, 46-48, 69, 77, 82-83, 85, 153, 166, 172
energy transition, 51-52, 54, 56, 58, 60, 62, 64, 66, 68-70, 72
enlightenment, 143, 187, 189-190, 193-195, 197-206
environment, 15, 17-18, 37-38, 42, 44, 48, 52-53, 67, 69-70, 74-76, 82, 84-86, 101, 104, 106-108, 114-116, 120-123, 133-134, 136, 140, 142, 144, 146, 149, 151, 153, 157-160, 162, 165, 172, 177, 195-196, 199, 203
epistemology, 29, 140, 146, 156
ethical development, 101, 104, 106, 108
Eurocentric, 28, 198
evaluation, 91, 109, 116, 190

F

failure, 28, 95, 98, 116-118, 140, 165, 181, 193, 200, 205
family, 19, 23-25, 29, 33, 36, 68, 119, 148, 169, 177, 179
Fourth Industrial Revolution, 69
framework, 15, 17, 25, 27, 30-31, 34, 37, 47, 67, 74, 121-122, 127, 134, 140, 196, 199-200
Free State, 35, 54, 56-60, 70, 93, 99-102, 104, 112
future, 16, 33-34, 37, 41, 44-45, 47, 74, 76, 78-80, 84, 86, 89-90, 94, 101, 105,

Index

107, 114, 117-118, 120, 142, 152, 165-166, 168-170, 183, 189, 196, 202, 206-207

G
global south, 112, 166

H
holy place, 121, 126-127
housing, 53-55, 65, 67-72, 124, 126, 163, 188
human capital, 16, 18
hylomorphism, 143

I
identity, 24, 26-28, 67-68, 105, 119, 131, 156, 163-164, 169, 181
ideologies, 203
ideology, 75, 157, 184
impact, 16-18, 22, 32, 39, 44, 70-71, 76, 82, 84-87, 91, 93, 97, 101-102, 104, 109-110, 116, 124, 127, 147, 158-159, 164, 168
indigenisation, 32
Indigenous Knowledge, 42
indigenous, 29, 32, 39, 42-43, 99, 116
inferiority, 164, 170

L
leadership, 40, 172-173, 175
learning, 38, 48, 102, 111-113, 115, 117-118, 156-157, 166, 168-169, 171, 173, 175, 177-178, 181-184, 200
local knowledge, 42
local, 17-20, 26, 28-29, 31, 33, 35-42, 53, 56, 58-59, 66, 69-70, 81, 84, 90, 94, 97, 99-100, 105, 107, 116, 141-142, 145, 147-149, 151-153, 165, 168-169, 171, 173, 175, 177-178, 181-185

M
management, 25, 27, 31, 51, 78, 82, 84, 87, 91, 93, 102-104, 107-109, 113, 158, 188-191, 195-197
mandate, 181
mapping, 41
marginalisation, 177
marriage, 19
materialism, 145, 147
mathematics, 158-159, 162
meaning, 32, 67-68, 71, 84, 121-123, 129, 133-134, 146, 157, 170, 173, 202, 204
media, 93-94, 201, 203
medium, 43
meeting, 21, 30, 55, 67, 123, 128-129, 160
member, 20-21, 32, 110
memory, 122, 169
mental, 47
mentoring, 103, 105, 110, 175

meshwork, 144, 146-147, 152, 154
message, 13-15, 32-33, 36, 38, 41, 45, 47, 134, 171, 183
method, 59-60, 70, 77, 81-82, 116, 122, 140, 142-143, 145-148, 150, 152-153, 178, 190-191, 195-196, 200-201, 203
methodologies, 118, 139, 142, 147, 154, 159, 166
methodology, 122, 142, 192
migrants, 55
mission, 13-14, 16, 18, 20, 22, 24, 26-28, 30, 32-33, 45, 94, 98, 131, 149
mistakes, 117
mobilise, 26, 41, 184
model, 38, 52, 90, 101, 143-144, 153, 197-201
modern, 13-18, 20, 24-26, 32-33, 36-39, 42, 52, 68, 88, 136, 156, 158, 160-165, 188-190, 195-196, 199, 201-203
modernization, 27
money, 19, 42, 53, 63, 112, 115, 179
monitoring and evaluation, 116
moral, 14, 189, 191, 199-202, 204-205
morality, 27, 199
motivation, 41
movement, 24, 27, 38, 45, 47, 133, 144, 146, 160, 164, 172, 174, 183, 191
Muslim, 19
myths, 125

N
narrative, 122
narratives, 18, 125
nation, 22, 26, 52, 171
nation-building, 171
need, 17-18, 25, 31, 33, 39-41, 44-46, 48, 52, 54, 56, 67-69, 71, 74, 79, 81-82, 89-90, 95, 111, 114-115, 121, 125, 130, 147, 150, 159-160, 166, 169, 172, 174, 178, 180, 184, 189, 192, 198
needs, 15, 20, 30-31, 40, 42, 45, 47, 52-53, 67-69, 71-72, 77, 90, 101, 103, 106-107, 114-115, 117, 147, 149-150, 152-153, 158, 160-161, 166, 168, 176, 196
negative, 18, 39, 44, 52-53, 64, 71, 74, 76, 78-79, 82, 117, 164, 182, 195, 200
network, 19, 69, 96, 110, 127, 129, 148, 178, 181-182, 185, 198
networks, 96, 101, 133
nexus, 29
number, 20, 23, 25-27, 58-59, 61-62, 65, 72, 74-76, 80, 87, 96, 104, 122, 132, 150, 174
nurture, 168, 175

O
objective, 27, 45, 157-158
objectives, 20, 27, 53, 97, 157
obligation, 191

230

observe, 90, 168, 205
obstacles, 25, 33
offer, 44, 97, 121, 130, 141, 147-148, 153, 204
office, 97, 99, 102, 104, 175
ontology, 145
open, 41, 43, 47, 66, 96-97, 116, 125, 127, 135, 142, 151-153, 161, 164-165, 180, 182, 188, 195
openness, 48
operates, 23, 76, 198
operational, 97, 101, 104, 107-108, 111, 113
operations, 95, 113, 191-192
opportunities, 16, 26, 40, 55, 69, 74, 86, 94, 115, 148, 150, 175, 177
order, 20, 31, 53, 67, 71, 76, 78, 81, 90, 130, 139-140, 142, 145, 147, 164, 172, 176, 181-182, 191, 197
organised, 135-136
orientation, 46, 133
origin, 102
outcome, 29, 95, 115, 171
outsider, 110
ownership, 32, 106, 116, 156, 176

P

paradigm, 17, 37, 39, 44, 74, 127, 131, 142, 147, 153, 204
parents, 19, 82, 169, 173, 177, 179-181, 183-184
partial, 134
participation, 14, 29-30, 67-68, 104, 111, 115-117, 173, 175-176
parties, 20, 29, 44, 95-96, 103, 110, 114-115
partners, 96-99, 101-104, 108-117, 181-182
partnership, 26, 95-99, 103, 108-111, 114-117, 152, 172, 178, 182
patriarchy, 156, 183-185
pattern, 54, 61, 67-68, 71, 131, 146
perceptions, 65-68, 95
periods, 67, 80
persistence, 53, 69
personality, 23, 68, 173
personnel, 165
perspective, 18, 41, 75, 83, 88, 95, 120, 126-129, 131, 144, 146-147, 149, 153, 156, 165, 188, 190, 204, 207
phenomenon, 19, 28, 75, 94, 121, 127, 130, 195
philosophy, 28, 39, 80, 142-143, 145, 191, 197, 201
physical, 15, 68, 71, 76, 96, 124-125, 143, 159, 184
pilgrimage, 128
pivotal, 146
place, 15-16, 18, 25, 32, 56, 66, 68, 109, 119-136, 140, 142, 156, 170, 173, 195-196
place-making, 122
policy, 16, 27, 30, 32, 115, 165, 173-174, 188-190, 192, 196

political, 20, 22-23, 25, 28, 32, 70, 142, 147, 151, 155, 164-165, 168-173, 181-183, 185, 189, 200
politicians, 23, 172-173
politics, 21, 69, 129, 147, 157-158, 162, 199
poor, 14, 30, 36, 40-45, 47, 53-55, 59, 67-68, 71, 77, 80, 82, 85, 88, 90, 96, 171, 181, 189
population, 14, 19, 22, 40, 52, 55, 58-59, 73-74, 77-78, 80, 84, 99, 120, 161, 171, 178, 182, 188
position, 24, 39, 46, 81, 110, 112, 118, 127, 145, 151, 156, 189, 191
positive, 14, 27, 67, 77, 104, 110, 112, 160, 175, 181-182, 193, 195
possibilities, 44, 68, 99, 113, 136, 141, 145, 147
post-apartheid, 27-28, 145
postmodern, 174, 194, 198, 204, 207
poverty, 14, 16-17, 20, 22, 31-32, 36, 39-41, 44-48, 52, 55, 69-72, 82, 94, 99-100, 147-148, 161, 166-168, 171, 177, 188, 200
power, 22, 36, 61, 69, 98, 120, 122, 145, 153-154, 156, 159-160, 162, 165, 169, 171-173, 182, 184, 202, 206
powerful, 122, 167, 171, 199
practical, 29, 38, 40-41, 58, 100, 102, 118-119, 133, 136, 140-141, 147, 150, 168, 175, 180, 184-185, 190
practice, 17, 19, 48, 82, 87-88, 94, 101-102, 108-109, 111, 116-118, 130-131, 133, 140-142, 152-154, 157-158, 161, 167, 173, 181, 184, 190
praxis, 175
pressure, 55, 77-78, 83, 89-90, 97, 157
prevent, 77, 88, 167, 179
primary, 56, 58, 79, 109, 111-113, 118, 169, 172, 177, 182, 189
private, 31, 96, 116, 131, 153, 179, 181
proactive, 109, 168
probability, 98
problem, 18, 20-21, 36, 39-41, 44-47, 64, 73, 77-79, 85-86, 108-109, 140-141, 153, 160-161, 164, 176-177, 180, 188-194, 200-202, 204-205
problematic, 140, 153, 201
problem-solving, 41, 164, 191
process, 15, 20, 31, 33, 36, 40-41, 43, 47-48, 74, 82-84, 88, 95, 101, 103, 107, 110, 115, 118, 142, 144-146, 148-154, 156-157, 159-161, 164-166, 172, 178, 183, 193-194, 196, 199-200
processes, 30-31, 110, 116, 133, 140, 142, 144-147, 151-154, 173, 196
produce, 14, 28, 74, 76-77, 79, 81, 83, 88-90, 105, 150, 159
profession, 196
professional, 104, 119, 122, 170, 190

Index

profit, 30, 37, 42, 44-45, 47, 94-95, 98, 140, 161, 167
profound, 120, 198
program, 30, 176
programme, 14, 46, 70, 103, 140, 142, 148-149, 151, 154, 175, 200
progress, 16, 31, 36, 40, 52, 72, 85, 104, 162, 166, 182, 184, 195, 202
promise, 198, 205-206
promise-command, 206
prosecution, 29
protection, 67, 72, 109
public administration, 25, 28
public, 23, 25, 28, 33, 52, 55, 85, 94-96, 98, 101, 116, 120, 123-124, 131, 133, 149, 173-175, 179, 181, 188, 191, 197
purpose, 42, 87, 96, 109, 114, 189, 193, 201, 204

Q
qualities, 47-48
quality education, 19
quite, 32, 104, 113, 122-125, 143, 200

R
race, 125, 157, 170
racist, 172
rape, 179
rational, 20, 192-195, 197-201, 203
realities, 115, 148, 182
reason, 31, 56, 62, 64, 94, 114, 158, 171, 177, 179, 190, 194, 200, 202, 204
reciprocal, 48, 95, 101
recognition, 136, 158, 188
recovery, 15-17, 130
recruitment, 177
reflection, 15, 25, 30, 117-118, 124, 145, 150, 167-168, 178, 184
reformed, 121, 129, 147, 149-150, 154
refugees, 26
regenerative agriculture, 74, 79-82, 89
relation, 38, 133, 139-140, 142, 144-146, 148, 150, 152, 154, 156
relational, 131, 140, 142, 144-145, 147, 152, 154
relationality, 140, 142, 144
relations, 26-27, 98, 107, 122, 128-129, 131-132, 145, 147, 164, 189
relationship, 38, 40, 47, 74, 82, 107, 114-115, 129, 140, 143, 146-147, 149-151, 154, 159, 166, 196, 199, 201
relevance, 14, 32, 149, 197
religion, 13, 19, 30, 35, 41, 46-47, 51, 73, 120, 133-134, 155-156, 163, 167, 187, 197, 199
renewal, 43, 45, 130, 169, 195, 206
representation, 104

requirements, 20, 74, 80-81, 83, 86, 89, 152, 160, 205
research, 13, 19, 30, 37, 43-44, 73, 77-78, 82, 84, 87-88, 90-91, 94, 97-98, 100-101, 107, 111-113, 115, 119-122, 124, 126-127, 134, 136, 139, 141, 143, 148, 150, 152, 155-157, 159, 168, 175-176, 191-192, 197, 201
residential coal use, 51-54, 56, 58, 60, 62, 64, 66, 68-72
resolution, 21, 184, 188
resolve, 172
resource, 77-78, 86, 88, 97-98, 153, 183, 198
resources, 14, 18, 38, 42-43, 48, 69-70, 74, 76-80, 83-86, 89-90, 94, 96, 106, 110, 115-116, 166
respect, 41, 47, 74, 89, 184, 189, 191
respond, 31, 76, 160
responsibilities, 95-96, 189, 196-197
responsibility, 41, 45, 48, 104, 155, 173, 189, 194, 196, 202
responsible, 22, 104, 115, 179, 194, 196-197, 203
restoration, 146, 169
restore, 94, 175
result, 14, 16-18, 22, 29, 39, 66-67, 77, 80, 82, 84, 88, 156, 158, 160-161, 164, 173, 184, 194
results, 14, 28, 56, 58, 108-109, 111-113, 122, 141, 176
return on investment, 107
reveal, 128, 145
revelation, 128-129
revolution, 16, 69, 127, 195
rights, 19, 22, 27, 166, 168
rigid, 47
risk, 19, 31, 78, 84-85, 87-88, 98, 108, 161, 163, 177
risks, 78, 85, 87-88, 115
robust, 117
role, 15-18, 20, 22, 30, 33-34, 36-37, 41, 44, 54, 56, 67, 76, 78, 81, 83, 89, 95, 97-102, 104, 106-107, 110-113, 115, 119-120, 128, 133-134, 148-150, 155, 157-160, 165-166, 168-169, 175-176, 178, 181, 184, 189-191, 193, 199
root, 19, 103, 111, 141
rules, 36, 44, 80

S
sacrament, 127-129
sacred place, 119-134, 136
sacredness, 120-129, 131, 133-134, 136
safety, 87, 159, 161
save, 41
scale, 20, 38-40, 42, 44-45, 54, 67, 74, 76-77, 79-84, 86-90, 94-97, 125, 146, 148, 154, 174, 197, 199

232

school, 16, 19, 24, 32, 40, 47, 105, 126, 145, 169, 171, 176-177, 179-180, 188, 191
science, 33, 36, 51, 69, 136, 156, 159, 162-166, 189-192, 197, 199, 206
scope, 32, 103, 120, 157, 165, 196, 199
self, 24-25, 27-28, 43-44, 48, 60, 77, 81-82, 88, 94-95, 128-129, 143, 145, 164, 170-173, 175, 196
self-esteem, 170
senior citizens, 171, 173
senior, 30, 113, 171, 173, 183
sense, 15, 24, 29, 38, 74, 89, 130, 133, 144-145, 154, 162, 164, 170, 175, 188, 193, 195-196, 199, 202
separate, 37-38, 46, 62, 81, 103, 120, 122, 142-143, 149, 190, 196, 199-200
separation, 36, 147, 173
services, 16, 19, 26, 28, 55, 71, 82, 86, 90, 94, 96, 99, 105, 107, 148, 161, 175, 180
sex, 177, 179
shameful, 39
shortcomings, 113, 169
significant, 22, 26, 30, 38, 52, 56-57, 71, 88, 93, 108, 111, 117, 151, 153, 157, 198
site, 174
skills, 36, 95, 97-98, 105, 107, 115, 152, 157-158, 161-162, 165, 178, 188
social business, 44-47
social change, 145, 147
social interaction, 125, 131, 133
social justice, 75-76
social sciences, 143-144
social, 17-18, 28-29, 33, 38-39, 44-48, 53-54, 68, 71-72, 74-76, 82, 88, 93-98, 100-101, 104, 107, 111, 113-116, 120, 125, 131, 133, 135, 140, 142-147, 151, 157-161, 164-165, 168, 172-173, 176, 183, 185, 187-190, 198-199
societies, 27-28, 37-42, 46-47, 94, 158, 169, 172, 183
society, 14, 18, 29, 35-48, 66, 69, 90, 94, 96, 127, 143, 151, 155, 157-158, 167-170, 172-180, 182-184, 187-190, 195-203
socio-economic, 27, 32, 77, 82, 113, 139, 157, 177
solidarity, 22, 173, 176, 181
son, 204-206
soul, 32, 121, 130, 136
sources, 52, 68-71, 75, 78-79, 100, 105, 113
South Africa, 13, 25-29, 35, 51-58, 60-62, 64, 66, 68-70, 72-73, 78, 80, 82-85, 87, 91, 93-95, 98-100, 108, 112, 139, 145, 148-149, 154-156, 158-159, 163, 166-167, 170-174, 179-181, 187
Southern African Development Community, 15

space, 16, 52, 54, 56, 60, 63, 65, 67-69, 71, 74, 79, 81-82, 89, 95, 108, 117, 120, 122-123, 128, 132-133, 145-147, 166, 180
speaking, 193, 195, 205
specifications, 165
spirit, 120, 131, 136, 204
spirituality, 135, 156
stability, 46, 164, 179, 198
staff, 26, 102-103, 110, 112-113, 152-153, 177-178, 180, 183
stage, 20, 53, 117, 121, 143, 149
stages, 53, 118, 122, 196
stakeholders, 31, 41-43, 107, 115, 117, 172, 176, 181
standard, 20, 56, 107
state, 18, 21-22, 24-28, 35, 54, 56-60, 70, 85, 93, 99-102, 104, 112, 148, 188, 190, 197
statement, 24-25, 31, 143, 157, 188
statistics, 55-57, 69, 179
status, 28, 54, 95, 108, 135
STEAM, 159-160
stigma, 71
storied place, 121, 131, 133
stories, 36, 94, 116-117, 121-122, 124-125, 132-134, 136, 169-170, 204
story, 36, 38-39, 42, 95, 117, 122, 131-134, 171, 198, 204, 206
strangers, 120
strategy, 22, 25, 43, 89, 116, 161, 203
strength, 33, 121, 181
stress, 76, 129, 173
structure, 35, 40, 45, 47, 98-99, 103, 105, 113, 127-128, 136, 183, 198
struggle, 28, 36, 40, 67, 174, 189, 191
Sub-Saharan Africa, 20, 81
success, 27, 77, 94, 97, 107, 109, 111, 117, 151, 177, 181
suffering, 82, 133, 168, 180-181
sustainability, 17-18, 20, 41, 74-76, 78, 89, 95, 122, 136, 140, 165-166, 187-188, 190, 192, 194, 196, 198, 200, 202, 204, 206
sustainable development, 17, 20, 33, 37, 96, 196-197
sustainable economic growth, 17
sustainable, 17, 20, 33-34, 37, 41-42, 73-76, 78-82, 84-86, 88-90, 94, 96, 120, 140-142, 144, 146-147, 152-154, 167, 181, 196-197
system, 26, 28-29, 33, 36, 39-40, 46, 69, 76-78, 80-81, 83, 88-90, 127, 134, 151, 156, 172, 177, 179, 188-190, 192, 194, 196-198, 200

T
talent, 161
targets, 43

Index

task, 31, 112, 131, 152, 157, 161, 165, 182-183, 196, 207
teach, 39, 59, 82, 157, 165-166, 177, 179
teaching, 44, 111-113, 115, 155-157, 168, 196
team, 21, 31, 141, 159, 163, 167, 175-184
technique, 199
techniques, 18, 89
technology, 18, 33, 35-42, 44, 46, 48, 74, 127, 136, 140, 149, 152, 156-166, 189-190, 195-203, 206
temple, 129
terms, 22, 36, 45, 68, 74, 79, 81-84, 86-90, 94, 98, 103, 108-109, 114, 122, 144, 146, 149-150, 163, 190, 198-199, 201
textbooks, 161
the problem of evil, 189-190, 201, 204-205
theology of place, 128, 130
theology, 13, 35, 51, 73, 119, 121-122, 128-131, 136, 140, 147-148, 150, 155, 167, 175, 187, 189, 197
think, 14, 21, 38, 62, 64, 119, 123, 129, 133, 165, 183, 195
time, 13-14, 22, 27-30, 32, 36, 38, 40, 44, 52, 56, 63-64, 67, 69, 78, 85, 89, 96-97, 99-101, 109-110, 113-117, 123-124, 128, 132, 134, 143, 145, 147, 149-152, 155, 159-160, 162-164, 171, 177, 179-180, 188, 191, 197, 204, 206-207
tolerance, 18
tool, 107, 149, 169, 196
tools, 36, 109, 158, 195, 198, 203
total, 30, 46, 54, 57-59, 61-62, 83, 170, 173
trading, 152
tradition, 31, 128-129, 133, 145, 156, 193-194, 198, 202
traditionally, 25, 151, 157
traditions, 18, 33, 46, 82, 140, 156, 162, 166, 205
trained, 152
training, 58, 98, 102-105, 107, 110, 115, 147, 150, 152, 168, 185, 190
traits, 68
transactions, 104
trans-disciplinary, 139-142, 144, 146, 148-150, 152, 154, 176
transfer, 19, 33, 155, 175, 201
transform, 134, 146, 164, 183
transformation, 16, 41, 104, 127, 149, 152, 167-170, 172-176, 178, 180-184, 196
translated, 188
transparency, 95
transportation, 84
trauma, 178
travel, 118, 129
treat, 45, 171
treatment, 26, 84-85

trend, 46, 56-57, 80
trial, 87, 200, 205-206
triple, 42
trust, 18, 43, 45, 95, 97, 99-100, 107, 114-115, 117, 173, 184, 204
truth, 159

U

ubuntu, 27
unacceptable, 85
uncertainty, 96, 98, 198
uncomfortable, 23, 124
uncover, 146
understanding, 20, 23-24, 33, 42-45, 48, 53, 56, 67-69, 75, 95, 97, 111, 115, 136, 140, 142, 145-146, 157, 159-160, 165-166, 169, 175, 178-179, 188-189, 194-195, 197, 199, 201-203, 206
unemployment, 22, 176, 178
unethical, 173
unity, 22, 136, 149, 206
universal, 29, 36, 143, 145, 163, 205
unknown, 88
unless, 63, 199, 207
unpredictable, 198
urban, 15, 54-55, 70, 72, 77, 81-83, 88-90, 94, 99, 116, 119-123, 126, 133, 136, 154, 161, 173-174
urbanism, 120
urgent, 85, 148, 180
utilisation, 79, 104, 116, 152-153

V

valid, 39, 47, 157
valuable, 24, 41, 62, 107, 146
value, 18, 32, 37-38, 41, 56, 61-62, 65, 68, 71, 81, 84, 96-98, 117, 126, 129, 141, 146, 148, 165, 173, 181-182, 188
variable, 61, 70
venture, 101, 103, 107-108, 110
view, 14, 23-24, 29, 37-43, 46-47, 75, 94, 109, 112, 123, 126, 129-130, 132, 135, 144, 146, 153, 156-158, 162-163, 166, 190, 192-193, 195, 201-203
viewed, 111, 128, 136, 152, 154
views, 20, 22-26, 42, 115, 120, 146, 150, 153, 157-158, 195, 200
village, 29, 54, 149-150, 169, 180
violence, 22, 28, 165, 171, 176, 183-185, 204
vision, 30, 34, 44, 99, 101, 113-115, 117, 129, 165-166, 173, 190, 194-195, 197, 200-201
vital, 25-26, 43, 101, 120, 124
vulnerability, 188, 193
vulnerable, 53, 171

W

wars, 144, 203
water, 18, 26, 56, 60, 63, 66, 68-69, 71, 73-74, 76, 78-80, 82, 84-91, 125, 157, 161, 175
weak, 42, 47, 55, 141
weaknesses, 103, 113
welcoming, 113
welfare, 169, 190
well-being, 68, 76, 114, 180
wicked problems, 187-190, 192, 195, 198, 200, 202-203, 206-207
win, 29
wisdom, 107, 161, 172-173, 175, 179, 183-184, 198
witness, 128, 154
women, 19, 31, 53, 62-64, 152, 171, 173-174, 179, 184
working, 20, 23, 28, 30, 36, 46, 63-64, 81-82, 90, 97, 101, 119, 124, 148, 159, 171, 174, 179, 182, 188
workplace, 161
worldview, 122
worth, 88, 111, 130, 168, 175
written, 25, 120-121, 146, 201

X

xenophobia, 171

www.ingramcontent.com/pod-product-compliance
Lightning Source LLC
Chambersburg PA
CBHW081348230426
43667CB00017B/2764